Market Encounters

NEW AFRICAN HISTORIES

SERIES EDITORS: JEAN ALLMAN, ALLEN ISAACMAN, AND DEREK R. PETERSON

David William Cohen and E. S. Atieno Odhiambo, *The Risks of Knowledge*

Belinda Bozzoli, *Theatres of Struggle and the End of Apartheid*

Gary Kynoch, *We Are Fighting the World*

Stephanie Newell, *The Forger's Tale*

Jacob A. Tropp, *Natures of Colonial Change*

Jan Bender Shetler, *Imagining Serengeti*

Cheikh Anta Babou, *Fighting the Greater Jihad*

Marc Epprecht, *Heterosexual Africa?*

Marissa J. Moorman, *Intonations*

Karen E. Flint, *Healing Traditions*

Derek R. Peterson and Giacomo Macola, editors, *Recasting the Past*

Moses E. Ochonu, *Colonial Meltdown*

Emily S. Burrill, Richard L. Roberts, and Elizabeth Thornberry, editors, *Domestic Violence and the Law in Colonial and Postcolonial Africa*

Daniel R. Magaziner, *The Law and the Prophets*

Emily Lynn Osborn, *Our New Husbands Are Here*

Robert Trent Vinson, *The Americans Are Coming!*

James R. Brennan, *Taifa*

Benjamin N. Lawrance and Richard L. Roberts, editors, *Trafficking in Slavery's Wake*

David M. Gordon, *Invisible Agents*

Allen F. Isaacman and Barbara S. Isaacman, *Dams, Displacement, and the Delusion of Development*

Stephanie Newell, *The Power to Name*

Gibril R. Cole, *The Krio of West Africa*

Matthew M. Heaton, *Black Skin, White Coats*

Meredith Terretta, *Nation of Outlaws, State of Violence*

Paolo Israel, *In Step with the Times*

Michelle R. Moyd, *Violent Intermediaries*

Abosede A. George, *Making Modern Girls*

Alicia C. Decker, *In Idi Amin's Shadow*

Rachel Jean-Baptiste, *Conjugal Rights*

Shobana Shankar, *Who Shall Enter Paradise?*

Emily S. Burrill, *States of Marriage*

Todd Cleveland, *Diamonds in the Rough*

Carina E. Ray, *Crossing the Color Line*

Sarah Van Beurden, *Authentically African*

Giacomo Macola, *The Gun in Central Africa*

Lynn Schler, *Nation on Board*

Julie MacArthur, *Cartography and the Political Imagination*

Abou B. Bamba, *African Miracle, African Mirage*

Daniel Magaziner, *The Art of Life in South Africa*

Paul Ocobock, *An Uncertain Age*

Keren Weitzberg, *We Do Not Have Borders*

Nuno Domingos, *Football and Colonialism*

Jeffrey S. Ahlman, *Living with Nkrumahism*

Bianca Murillo, *Market Encounters*

Laura Fair, *Reel Pleasures*

Thomas F. McDow, *Buying Time*

Jon Soske, *Internal Frontiers*

Market Encounters

Consumer Cultures in Twentieth-Century Ghana

Bianca Murillo

OHIO UNIVERSITY PRESS ⁓ ATHENS

Ohio University Press, Athens, Ohio 45701
ohioswallow.com
© 2017 by Ohio University Press
All rights reserved

To obtain permission to quote, reprint, or otherwise reproduce or distribute material from Ohio University Press publications, please contact our rights and permissions department at (740) 593-1154 or (740) 593-4536 (fax).

Printed in the United States of America
Ohio University Press books are printed on acid-free paper ♾™

27 26 25 24 23 22 21 20 19 18 17   5 4 3 2 1

A version of chapter three is based on Bianca Murillo, "'The Modern Shopping Experience': Kingsway Department Store and Consumer Politics in Ghana," *Africa: Journal of the International African Institute* 82, no. 3 (2012): 368–92, © 2012 by Cambridge University Press. Reprinted with permission from Cambridge University Press.

COVER IMAGE. Miss Ghana, Monica Amekoafia, visits Kingsway Department Store, Accra, April 1957. Reproduced with kind permission of Unilever from the original at the Unilever Archives, UAC/2/10/B1/8/1/15.

Library of Congress Cataloging-in-Publication Data

Names: Murillo, Bianca, author.
Title: Market encounters : consumer cultures in twentieth-century Ghana / Bianca Murillo.
Other titles: New African histories series.
Description: Athens, Ohio : Ohio University Press, 2017. | Series: New African histories | Includes bibliographical references and index.
Identifiers: LCCN 2017027990| ISBN 9780821422885 (hc : alk. paper) | ISBN 9780821422892 (pb : alk. paper) | ISBN 9780821446133 (pdf)
Subjects: LCSH: Consumption (Economics)—Ghana—History—20th century. | Consumption (Economics)—Political aspects—Ghana. | Consumers—Ghana—History—20th century. | Ghana—Commerce—History—20th century.
Classification: LCC HC1060.Z9 C64 2017 | DDC 381.309667—dc23
LC record available at https://lccn.loc.gov/2017027990

To Teresa Rubie

Contents

Illustrations

FIGURES

TABLE

Acknowledgments

I AM FOREVER INDEBTED to the mentors, colleagues, students, friends, and family who have supported me in the process of writing this book. At the University of California–Santa Barbara I had the honor of working with an inspiring group of mentors. I am deeply indebted to Stephan Miescher, who initially sparked my interest in Ghana's history as a young undergraduate and has continued to offer endless support, deep insight, and intellectual guidance through the years. His passion and commitment to teaching, writing, and researching in the field of African history has served as a model and constant source of motivation. Erika Rappaport advocated for the importance of my research from its earliest stages. Her inventions have been deeply formative, as have the rigor and creativity she brings to historical writing. Eileen Boris pushed me to look beyond the obvious in studying race and gender and helped sharpen my feminist approach; her scholarship and political commitments to mentoring students are a model for me. I have also benefited from the scholarship and teaching of Catherine Cole and Sylvester Ogbechie. UCSB graduate courses with Adrienne Edgar, Sharon Farmer, Lisa Jacobson, Joan Judge, Cecilia Méndez, Leila Rupp, and at University of California–Los Angeles with Andrew Apter further influenced this work.

In Ghana my research would not have been possible without the support and generosity of many people. I am grateful to Emily Asiedu, "Auntie," for opening her home to me year after year and for introducing me to the family of a legendary United Africa Company credit customer. At the University of Ghana, professors Takyiwaa Manuh and Dzodzi Tsikata offered research advice and arranged venues where I could present my work. I owe an enormous thanks to the interviewees who generously shared their time and knowledge with me; among them, Nana Anwasi Agyemang, Kwesi Akumenya Cato, Edward Akurang Dankwa, Sadiku Musah, and Deborah Quartey deserve special mention. I am also grateful to Vicki Wireko-Andoh from Unilever Ghana for her help; to Benjamin Buadu Codjoe and Kobina A. Dodoo for their invaluable research assistance and good company; to my Twi teachers, Yaw Douglas Ansomani and Charles Owu-Ewie, for their patience; to Hannah Serwah Bonsu, Stella "Beauty" Mensah, and Hajara Sanni for their friendship; and to Alicia, Abdul, Mama Boats, Ohemaa, and Yaa for sharing their youthful spirits.

Over the years I have also been privileged to work with brilliant Africanist colleagues who have offered critical insights, asked challenging questions, and provided invaluable advice on my research, both in formal conference proceedings and in the informal exchanges that drive much of what we do as researchers and writers. For helping to make this a much better book, I thank Gareth Austin, Jeffrey Ahlman, Charles Ambler, Karin Barber, Sara Berry, Peter Bloom, Lynne Brydon, Mhoze Chikowero, Stephanie Decker, Laura Fair, Amadou Fofana, Harcourt Fuller, Jennifer Hart, Jennifer Hasty, Anne Hugon, Lisa Lindsay, Tom McCaskie, Ghislaine Lydon, Stephanie Newell, Paul Nugent, Nate Plageman, Ato Quyason, Carina Ray, Kate Skinner, Lynn Thomas, Dmitri van den Bersalaar, Sarah Watkins, and Alice Wiemers. I offer thanks also for the support and feedback received from participants at conferences and workshops organized by the UC African Studies Multi-Campus Research Group in Accra and Dakar; the Berkshire Conferences on the History of Women; the Capitalismo desde el Sur/ Capitalism from Below conference at the Tepoztlán Institute for Transnational History of the Americas, and several sessions at the annual meeting of the African Studies Association. Purnima Bose and Kundai Chirindo also deserve thanks for their comments on later chapter drafts.

The research for this book would not have been possible without the generous assistance of numerous librarians and archivists. I am grateful for the staff at the Public Records and Archives Administration Department (PRAAD) in Accra, Cape Coast, and Sunyani; the Institute of Statistical, Social, and Economic Research at the University of Ghana, the National Archives in London; the Guildhall Library in London; the Bodleian Library at Oxford University; the Unilever Historical Archive in Port Sunlight, England; and the Basel Mission Archives in Basel. In particular, I wish to thank Cletus Azangweo, Judith Botchway, and Bright Botwe, who facilitated my research at PRAAD. The entire staff at PRAAD-Sunyani deserves a special thank you for making my daily work in their small reading room so pleasurable. My gratitude also goes to Guy Thomas, whose knowledge of the Union Trading Company collection at the Basel Mission Archives was invaluable. Finally, I am enormously grateful to Diane Backhouse and her successor Helen Unsworth for helping me "leave no stone unturned." By tracking down rare photographs, digging through unmarked boxes, and pointing out last minute details, both went above and beyond as archivists.

My research came to life as a book during my assistant professorship in the History Department at Willamette University. I am grateful to department colleagues Wendy Peterson Boring, Seth Cotlar, Leslie Dunlap, Bill Duvall, Ellen Eisenberg, Jennifer Jopp, and Bill Smaldone for providing me with the autonomy, encouragement, and support to focus on my manuscript and hone my skills as a teacher-scholar. Department chair Cecily MacCaffrey deserves special mention as a friend, colleague, and committed advocate of my work.

This book was also inspired by a number of students have energized me in the classroom and beyond. A special thank you to Noor Amr, Hannah Leslie, Christina Luedtke, Lindsay Russell, Désirée Werlen, Kelley Villa, who all served as research and editing assistants. In 2016, I joined the History Department at California State University–Dominguez Hills (CSUDH). I am lucky for the opportunity to work alongside another group of colleagues that uphold a strong teacher-scholar ethic. Becoming a member of a diverse campus community that is politically committed, in theory and practice, to serving its students has been a privilege. At CSUDH, Alvin Okoreeh also deserves thanks for editing support in the final stages.

I must also thank a number of institutions that generously provided the funding required for such a project. Research and travel to Ghana, Switzerland, and the United Kingdom was supported by a University of California Regents Fellowship and a Fulbright-Hays Doctoral Research Grant, as well as generous funds and research leaves awarded by the College of Liberal Arts at Willamette University. I am also grateful for publication subvention support from CSUDH's College of Arts and Humanities. I would especially like to acknowledge the Woodrow Wilson Junior Faculty Career Enhancement Fellowship Program; the research funds and one-year research leave it granted me was fundamental to bringing my manuscript to completion. Most important, its built-in mentorship program allowed me to work closely with Jean Allman, whose book *"I Will Not Eat Stone": A Woman's History of Colonial Asante* transformed the way I thought about history as a young undergraduate and has remained in heavy rotation on my course syllabi. Jean's work as a scholar and her commitment to African Studies through institutional leadership, program building, and mentoring junior scholars continues to inspire me.

I am also indebted to many people who have offered good company and opened their homes to me during the research and writing of this book: in Abetifi and Santa Barbara, Lane Clark and Stephan Miescher; in Accra, Emily

Asiedu; in Liverpool, Dmitri van den Bersalaar and Stephanie Decker; in London, Walter and Barbara Prime, and Jean Smith; and in Suhum, Elizabeth Konadu Yiadom, "Nana." I would like to acknowledge colleagues who have become close friends for looking after me in their cities and proving to be some of the best traveling companions: Serena Dankwa, Gabriel Klager, Sophie Mew, Tim Mechlinski, Thomas Yarrow, Duncan Yoon, and Leandra Zarnow.

My gratitude also goes to the staff and series editors at Ohio University Press: Jean Allman, Allen Isaacman, and Derek Peterson, and to Gillian Berchowitz for believing in my research from the very beginning and guiding me through the process. This book has benefited tremendously from our conversations and their sharp editorial notes, as well as the feedback provided by two anonymous readers. Thank you also to David Lobenstine for editing assistance; your advice to "make these pages sing" guided me through each chapter revision.

I also owe an especially large intellectual and personal debt to Justin Bengry, Ellen Caldwell, Jonneke Koomen, Uri McMillian, Brooke Mascagni, and Roy Pérez for sharing so much of their brilliant minds and big hearts. For years our caffeinated writing dates, late-night phone chats, I5 carpool rides, shared meals; happy hours, shopping breaks, weekend excursions, and guaranteed laughs kept me grounded. I thank also my closest childhood friends, who are like sisters to me and who, often times without knowing it, helped me write this book; for so much love, thank you Megan Adams and Lauren Pfeiffer. And to my goddaughter Lucy Jane Williams, our special bond brings me joy.

Finally, I am grateful to my family for their unconditional love and support. I am especially thankful for growing up alongside so many smart, creative, and bold women: my grandmothers Elizabeth Mae Rubie and Vilma Susanna Saballos Nino Murillo; my aunts, the seven Rubie sisters, Carla, Diane, Jackie, Janice, Kathy, Liz, and Margaret; and my cousins Monica and Natalie Cuevas, who have been a constant source of friendship and empowerment. My father Alfonso Murillo and my younger brother Lucas have also encouraged and believed in me. Above all, I thank my mother, Teresa Rubie, for giving her everything to invest in me and my dreams. This book is dedicated to her.

Abbreviations

AWAM	Association of West African Merchants
BMA	Basel Mission Archives
BRG	Brong-Ahafo Region
CFAO	Compagnie Française de l'Afrique Occidentale
CPP	Convention People's Party
EAS	Export Advertising Service
FP	Frederick Pedler Papers
GBO	G. B. Ollivant
GNTC	Ghana National Trading Corporation
NAUK	National Archives of the United Kingdom
NLC	National Liberation Council
NRC	National Redemption Council
PNDC	Provisional National Defense Council
PRAAD-A	Public Records and Archives Administration Department, Accra
PRAAD-S	Public Records and Archives Administration Department, Sunyani
RHL	Rhodes House Library
SAT	Swiss African Trading Company
SCOA	Société Commerciale de l'Ouest African
SMC	Supreme Military Council
UAC	United Africa Company
UARM	Unilever Archives and Records Management
UGL	Unilever Ghana Limited Archive
UTC	Union Trading Company

Introduction

Consuming Histories and Creating Economies

In the afternoon on Saturday, February 28, 1948, over a thousand African veterans gathered in the center of Accra, the capital of present-day Ghana (then called the Gold Coast). The men assembled on the Old Polo Grounds, opposite Parliament House, and headed toward the governor's residence.[1] Their goal was to demand compensation from the British colonial government for their service during the Second World War, and they intended to present their list of grievances to the governor in person. Having fought in the British Army alongside Allied forces in Burma, Ceylon, and India, many of these soldiers returned home and found themselves destitute. According to the Ex-Serviceman's Union, the colonial government had made promises—of paid employment, disability pensions, business grants, and affordable housing—that were never fulfilled.[2] Singing old war songs and marching in unison, the ex-servicemen, accompanied by more than two thousand supporters, were stopped en route by a group of armed police and instructed to turn back.

The official commission of inquiry that was appointed in the following weeks to investigate the events reported that the confrontation quickly became aggressive. The crowd, determined to pass, hurled stones and insults at officers. A few minutes later, just after 3:00 p.m., the head of police ordered his men to open fire in order to "control the mob." Three demonstrators were shot dead and several others were wounded. The angry crowd retaliated. Yet they did not attack the governor's residence, just a few blocks away, nor other centers of government power against which the men had been protesting; instead they burned and looted offices, warehouses, and wholesale and retail stores owned by Europeans and other foreigners.[3]

What became known as the Accra Riots have long been familiar to historians of Ghana. That day in February 1948 features consistently in nationalist narratives as a watershed moment that pushed the country on the path toward independence from Britain, which would come less than a decade later in 1957. But few have closely analyzed what it meant for a very different (though inextricably linked) path that the country was on—toward becoming an emerging nation of African consumers.[4] Although sympathy for the veterans no doubt rallied supporters that Saturday afternoon, much of the crowd also consisted of those fed up with the restrictive economy that had been imposed under Britain's rule. For decades the colonial government had enabled large foreign trading firms, mostly European, to control the West African import-export market. Allowed to operate with little government regulation, large firms dominated the commercial scene, controlling commodity prices, credit terms, and channels of distribution. During the war, essential imported commodities like rice, sugar, milk, kerosene, and cotton piece goods were in short supply, and the resulting spike in prices fueled resentment against these large firms, who by that point controlled more than two-thirds of all goods that were imported and sold in the colony.[5] Various groups including African nationalists, businessmen, retailers, cocoa farmers, and consumers accused foreign firms, especially those belonging to the Association of West African Merchants (AWAM), of artificially inflating prices, conspiring with the colonial government, monopolizing trade, and cheating customers.[6] Though some of these accusations were overblown, many were on target. Firms associated with AWAM *had* engaged in price fixing and engineered market sharing agreements that cut Africans out of commercial trade and restricted consumer aspirations.

The Accra Riots were thus about a broad and growing sense of economic injustice and financial frustration as much as they were about the soldiers themselves. The government-appointed commission that investigated the underlying causes of the protest reported that the administration's failure to seriously address rising prices and allegations against AWAM firms paved the way for "the resentment which manifested itself in the looting and useless destruction which took place in Accra and elsewhere."[7] After all, this was not the first time Gold Coasters had protested the practices of foreign firms. Cartel-like behavior and price fixing were among the primary causes of the Gold Coast cocoa hold-ups organized by farmers, brokers, and chiefs in 1920, 1930–31, and 1937–38.[8] Similarly, in 1947, Nii Kwabena Bonne II, an Accra chief and businessman, created the Anti-Inflation Committee and sent an ultimatum to the city's chamber of commerce demanding that firms lower profit margins and reduce retail prices. Several local chiefs supported the campaign and established Anti-Inflation Committees in their own districts. Underestimating the seriousness of these grievances, foreign firms brushed these demands aside. As a result, in January 1948 a month-long boycott of imported goods ensued.[9]

February 28, 1948, was not just the day ex-servicemen marched in protest; it was also the day several firms were to finally announce price cuts in an attempt to end the boycott.[10] As the commission of inquiry under the chairmanship of Aiken Watson pointed out, a number of "spectators and sympathizers" that afternoon had actively participated in the boycott during the previous month.[11] The marginal reductions announced by firms, however, were not enough. As the veterans were gathering at the Old Polo Grounds, organized looting and violence broke out in towns throughout the Colony and Ashanti regions, and intensified later that day as news of the shootings in Accra spread.[12] The destruction ensued for several days. In response, on March 5, 1948, Governor Charles Noble Arden-Clarke declared a state of emergency. Special constables, including the European employees of a number of trading firms, were sworn in and provided with rifles and other equipment to police towns. The colonial government also brought in military forces from the Northern Territories and Nigeria to support the effort.[13] In the end, losses from damage to property and looting were considerable, with costs estimated to be over one million pounds.[14] Another loss was less obvious but more portentous: within days of the events, AWAM member firms also agreed that the association should be dissolved, a decision that forced companies to re-evaluate their business activities and finally address long-standing public criticism.[15]

The Accra Riots, and the simultaneous boycott, hint at the importance of consumer politics to decolonization but, just as important, they help us situate these and many other postwar dramas as part of a longer and larger struggle within Ghanaian society over access to commodities and consumer markets. Contrary to what nationalist narratives would have us believe, not all Gold Coasters joined the 1947 boycott, and events that followed were less black and white than they are often portrayed as being. For instance, Nii Bonne recalled that certain Kwawus, especially those in Korforidua, still bought from those boycotted firms "on the sly,"[16] and a Union Trading Company (UTC) agent reported to his superiors that the women in Winneba "abused the menfolk" for obeying orders given by the chief and the police to not participate in the looting.[17] Further, while African-owned businesses were supposedly spared, African sales managers and storekeepers employed by foreign firms received physical intimidation and death threats from looters at their homes and shops.[18] Some of these threats turned fatal. In Sekondi, a group of men armed with bows and arrows attacked a United Africa Company (UAC) store and killed a watchman there.[19] In a letter to the general manager of the UAC it was also reported that loyal African staff were denounced as "stooges" and their names posted on signs all over towns.[20]

High prices were not the only source of contention among angry consumers. Equally infuriating were the firms' practices, carried out by both European and African staff, including behind-the-counter sales, conditional sales, refusal of sales, and favoritism given to employees' relatives, wives, and girlfriends. Consumers complained that these actions contributed to artificial shortages. More important, they argued that such practices led to unfair distribution or sales based on a person's ability to tap into personal networks.

This frustration was not new. In 1943, the colonial government had set up a commission of inquiry to investigate wartime shortages. Led by W. E. Conway, who was then the comptroller of customs, the commission conducted informal interviews with representatives of all the major firms, collected and examined evidence, and invited members of the public to submit complaints and suggestions in writing. It also held thirteen public hearings and listened to fifty-seven witness accounts. As one Accra customer testified, "During peacetime, I could go to any store and buy commodities such as tobacco, cigarettes, kerosene, candles, sugar, drinks, and drugs. But now it is impossible. . . . Whilst I cannot obtain these things in stores I could, provided I pay black market prices, obtain them from petty and private traders." He later described purchasing kerosene from a woman's private residence in Adabraka and declared to the commission, "I have been forced to buy on the black market."[21]

Another Accra witness recounted how firms' agents and shopkeepers regularly reserved goods for their "market women friends" and influential people in town, such as "certain lawyers and pressmen," to gain their favor.[22] This practice, he explained, led to refusal of sales from storekeepers even when goods were available. He recounted, "I once went to a store in Accra. I saw four cases of beer behind the counter and two on the counter. I presumed they had been sold, and I asked the European in charge for two cases. He told me he had no beer. I asked him, 'Why is it that there are four cases of beer behind the counter and yet you say there is none for sale?' He said I should not trouble him."[23] What angered consumers was not only that employees of trading firms and their "favorites" reaped high profits by increasing the price of commodities in short supply, but that their activities also determined who had the right to buy.

While the commission recommended that colony-wide fixed prices or price controls on scarce goods, although difficult to enforce, could alleviate high costs, it considered unfair allocations and distribution by firms through "parasitic middlemen"—those petty and private traders described by witnesses—a larger problem. At the same time, however, it recognized that petty traders or "keepers of small stores, market traders, and hawkers" were absolutely essential to consumer markets: "The petty trader plays a very important part in the distribution of goods to the actual consumer . . . he sells in units within the spending power of the poorest members of the community and reaches the smallest villages in the bush."[24] While the resale of goods through middlemen by foreign firms had been an integral part of the West African economy since the inception of overseas trade, wartime shortages exposed the complexities of this system and made clear that consumption was not only an economic transaction guided by the laws of supply and demand but also one that was deeply embedded in the social.

As the complaints about "certain Kwahus," men in Winneba, and "market women friends" reveal, the clash between European trading firms and African consumers, driven by what some scholars have identified as a growing sense of economic nationalism, was only part of the story. Such a narrow focus also fails to explain how similar conflicts over the market persisted in the decades following political independence. To better understand the complexities of Ghana's economic landscape both before and after independence, we must go back and consider a variety of other encounters and exchanges responsible for its creation. Both fierce opposition and unlikely alliances—forged between people as different as European managers and African market women, nationalist politicians and foreign investors, and military soldiers and chiefs—together shaped how goods made their way off shelves and into consumers' hands. Yet these personal and often unexpectedly intimate social relations have largely been forgotten in accounts of Ghana's economic past.

To uncover how people actively engaged consumer markets requires that we first move beyond the standard explanations of how African economies work. Here I refer particularly to the "European exploitation versus African resistance" binary that has shaded much of what we know about African economic and business history, especially regarding the twentieth century.[25] Although narratives of resistance against extractive and violent colonial regimes—everything from worker's strikes to hold-ups to boycotts—have been essential to uncovering African agency, this bifurcated view has actually narrowed our understanding of how imperialism and capitalism intertwine and how they play out in people's lives. More importantly, it has obscured the fundamental contests and sophisticated cultural repertories that underlie consumer culture in Ghana. While battles against colonial and neocolonial domination undoubtedly shaped the trajectories of consumer markets, so too did ongoing controversies over the meaning of wealth and proper accumulation, the role of the state and political authority, and the formation of gendered and racial ideologies.[26] I also argue that though the firms themselves, alongside government business policies and practices, are typically seen as inevitable or governed by sound economic logic, they have a contested social history that needs to be examined.

Market Encounters is an attempt to explore the multitude of relationships that shaped Ghana's economic reality and structured capitalist exchange throughout the twentieth century. Anthropologist Brenda Chalfin, writing about the power of the state in contemporary Ghana, argues that "before we can understand how it is subverted and undermined" we need to consider how it is "manufactured, institutionalized, and recursively inscribed."[27] Shouldn't we interrogate the economic in similar ways? My answer is yes. It is far too easy to consider the sometimes dry and impersonal specifics of economic data as wholly distinct from the highly charged and deeply personal experiences of which everyday life is composed. This division, all too common among scholars, blinds us from considering the relentless interweaving of both. Our blindness is particularly acute when it comes to economics. The discipline rests on claims of scientific objectivity, but like much of the substance of human life, it relies on a series of tropes, metaphors, and storytelling devices. Central to the story I tell here are what literary scholar Erika Beckman calls "capital fictions"—the process in which ideology and imagination are fashioned into commonsensical truths that allow capitalism to function.[28] Our story, then, is an effort to fuse economics and business history with social and cultural history. Such a method attempts to uncover how economic power is "manufactured, institutionalized, and recursively inscribed" while interrogating the fictions from which that power emerges. By weaving together two seemingly distinct sources—corporate archives and oral histories—I hope to offer a more textured sense of how people navigated the complex social terrains that made the buying and selling of goods in modern Ghana possible.

LOCATING THE "AFRICAN CONSUMER" AND CHALLENGING CONSUMPTION STUDIES

Before delving into any history of consumption, we must contend with a more basic question: Who, exactly, was the "consumer"? Early scholarship on consumer culture, starting in the 1970s, tended to paint the consumer in one of two ways, as either a "passive creature created by cultural industries and advertising" or as an "'active' or 'citizen consumer'—a creative, confident, and rational being articulating personal identity."[29] These tropes have dominated the field of consumption studies and the ways we have come to know the consumer, though they have not gone unchallenged. Over the past ten years, historians have argued that the category *consumer* needs to be interrogated rather than assumed.[30] Most notably, Frank Trentmann argues that "while all human societies have been engaged in consumption and have purchased, exchanged, gifted, or used objects and services, it has only been in specific contexts in the nineteenth and twentieth centuries that some (not all) practices of consumption have been connected to a sense of being a 'consumer,' as an identity, audience, or analytical category."[31] Simply put, *consumer* is far from a timeless or inevitable category. The consumer did not magically appear from a world of goods, rather, the consumer was created in particular historical moments and in dynamic relations with other actors and agencies. *Market Encounters* carefully engages scholarship in consumption studies—both its older simplicities and its newer complexities—to understand the development of consumer markets in West Africa. In doing so I am not suggesting that we superimpose a Western model of consumption on African societies; rather, I contend that by directly engaging this literature, historians of Africa can offer fresh insights and develop new areas of inquiry that expand consumption studies altogether.

Yet identifying the consumer is not just the distant task of scholars looking back on the historical record. In Ghana's case, as we will see, firms and colonial and postcolonial governments have been equally determined to figure out who they are selling to. Therefore, any history of consumer culture in Ghana must account for "locating the consumer" as an intellectual project initiated by the work of historians and consumer studies scholars, as well as a political project framed by the interests of capitalist firms and the different regimes that seized state power. In other words, the question of who the consumer was in Ghana is both a historiographical one and a historical one that emerges in different periods of the twentieth century.

In Ghana, *consumer* was a blurry and unstable category, but not exactly in the ways that scholars of consumption might expect. As with other former

West African colonies, a large physical distance existed between African consumers and manufacturers abroad. The British colonial government was far more interested in resource extraction than in creating and supporting local industries.[32] As historian Adu Boahen aptly puts it, essential to the political economy of colonialism was the "total neglect of industrialization and manufacturing and the refusal to process locally produced raw materials." As a result, the majority of commodities had to be imported, from large items like building materials and cars, to popular food products like meats, vegetables, jams, milk, tomatoes, and sardines, to staples like rice, flour, sugar, and salt. The British government empowered a handful of foreign firms to control the flow of goods into and out of the colony. Those firms in turn relied heavily on local, often preexisting, trade networks to distribute the commodities. In this way a firm's success depended on its ability to maintain relationships with thousands of African men and women who sold on the firm's behalf, and who facilitated the movement of imported goods from the two major port cities, Accra and Takoradi, to small towns scattered throughout the interior.[33] From a financial standpoint, this system allowed firms to keep their overhead costs low, saving them from having to invest money in building and maintaining physical retail structures. From a social standpoint, this system meant that Ghana's economy was forged to a remarkable degree by a disparate blend of thousands of individuals. This web of distribution and sales, a group of what I call *commercial intermediaries*, encompassed a range of different people.[34] It included those hired as shopkeepers, assistants, and clerks who received monthly salaries and worked at company-owned wholesale and retail stores as well as those entrusted as credit customers—people who bought goods from firms at wholesale prices, collected commission on sales, and sold mostly in areas where company-owned stores were nonexistent.

The reliance on intermediaries created a division between the firms and the actual consumers they (eventually) sold to, and was further complicated by the widespread practice of reselling. The breaking down of goods into smaller units for resale incorporated an even larger network of people into the pipeline of distribution and sales; this makes identifying the consumer even more difficult. The sale of matches is one of many examples. Several firms bought cases of matches from factories abroad, and imported them by boat to Accra. At the port, a firms' receiving agent would divide the shipment, which typically contained hundreds of cases, and send some to both Accra and upcountry wholesale stores. A wholesale storekeeper would then break down cases into "zincs," each containing about six metal containers. Those "zincs" would then be further broken up into packages and either distributed or sold, package by package, to retail shops owned by the firm or directly to credit customers. Each package contained ten to twelve boxes of matches, and retail storekeepers and credit customers often sold one box at a time to petty traders or consumers. Yet the point of sale did not stop there, as that same box, which contained seventy to eighty matchsticks, could then be divided by traders or the "consumer" into smaller and more affordable units of ten sticks for resale based on individual need.[35]

The business of reselling thus made divisions among the categories of wholesaler, retailer, and consumer highly ambiguous. In a 1950 company publication, the UAC admitted that "apart from high class retail stores in large towns, it is difficult if not impossible to know which of the buyers are ultimately consumers . . . [this] applies not only to divisible merchandise such as matches in bulk, but also to indivisible items, such as bicycles."[36] Even this confession was an understatement. A former African employee of Kingsway Department Stores also described difficulties in identifying "real consumers,"[37] and store policies that prohibited the sale of large quantities to suspected resellers further illustrate the dilemma. But trouble locating the consumer was not strictly the concern of firms and their employees; colonial governments also tried to make distinctions between people who bought for personal use and those who intended to engage in resale. A whole assortment of names cropped up around efforts to pinpoint this difference. "The ultimate consumer," "the end-use consumer," and the "the bona-fide customer" were used in both corporate and government documents in attempts to make this distinction. At this point, we need to consider a question: If firms were still collecting profits and keeping overhead costs low, why would they care about identifying the "ultimate" or "end-use" consumer? One reason was that the system of reselling made collecting statistics on sales and creating standardized policies extremely difficult; it also made firms' compliance with postwar government-imposed price controls and quotas an arduous, and often expensive, task.

However, the other, more profound reason, was about power. This system of commodity distribution could be quite profitable, but it had a lasting consequence: it created a large gap in what the firms actually knew about local consumer demand and desire. On the West African coast, trends changed rapidly, especially in the sale of textiles or wax prints. As an agent of the UTC stationed in Akuse warned, "any European staff taking a leave lasting more than two months" would have to completely relearn consumer tastes.[38] Gaps in market knowledge led to huge profit losses. As a former UTC manager reflecting on his forty-year career wrote in 1961, "Nobody took pains to do market research . . . the stores were filled with products that were many times useless."[39] Full shelves of rotting supplies, the overstocking of unpopular brands, and unsold items sitting in warehouses for years: all these realities were a constant source of frustration among firms. As we all know from every trip to the grocery store, changes in packaging and a product's overall aesthetic can also affect sales.[40] Bottles of Brilliantine hair product would only sell if wrapped in paper; sugar sold in cardboard boxes was preferred to that sold in paper bags; sleeping mats had to have red instead of blue trim, and only blue and green cars should be ordered, as red cars were "very unpopular." Even details like an item's smell had to be considered; on a stocktaking visit to various stores, one UAC employee asked, "Can we not obtain tablet soap similar to White Windsor with Eucalyptus scent?"[41] What Africans perceived as poor packaging, the wrong color, or an unpleasant smell were as consequential to an item's saleability as they were baffling to the firms' management a world away in London or Basel.

As in most aspects of colonialism, stereotypes framed by racialized assumptions about the colonized abounded; firms often classified African consumer behavior as conservative, selective, and overly brand conscious. One reason cited for this selectiveness was that African consumers had particular difficulties in obtaining redress for defective merchandise from overseas producers.[42] Another reason was the low income of farmers and wage earners, who had to shop carefully because of limited funds. What is less apparent in these observations is that when firms described "the African consumer" they were mainly referring to the demands of their storekeepers and credit customers who were responsible for resale. This gap between firms and ordinary consumers put European managers in a difficult predicament: invaluable market knowledge could only be gained through the feedback of African intermediaries, and this dependency was fragile—it had to be cultivated, maintained, and renewed. Of course, commercial intermediaries reflected the preferences of those they sold to; they, too, wanted to make a profit, but this was not always the case. Intermediaries thus wielded power in determining which goods gained popularity in the market and had a huge impact on shaping and translating consumer demand.

Let us now turn to the role of advertising in locating the consumer. As one of the primary means through which historians have studied how consumers were imagined and created, advertising often had different objectives in Ghana. The practice of using advertisements, and the principles of marketing, developed in their current form around the 1920s in the United States and other Western markets, were neither as established nor as meaningful in West Africa.[43] Even after the Second World War, advertising geared toward African audiences was considered "in its infancy," according to one UAC merchandise director.[44] A large percentage of early print advertising in Ghana was focused on promoting the reputation of certain firms rather than endorsing specific products. Many ads were produced to convince African businessmen and retailers to buy stock from firms (rather than from other sources like mail-order catalogs) and thus carried a different message. The hope was to deter African retailers from importing on their own. Of course, print advertisements geared toward elite and middle-class African shoppers existed. Early Gold Coast newspapers were full of ads for brands like Ideal milk, Ovaltine, Wright biscuits, Tin-apa pilchards, and Waterman pens, but the images in the ads featured mostly Europeans.[45] Posters and signboards hanging in stores and high–traffic areas like railway stations were also part of urban landscapes.[46] In most cases, however, print advertisements reflected the competition among various trading firms attempting to attract potential retailers to sell on their behalf; the need to cultivate and stimulate consumer demand for a particular product seemed secondary. Furthermore, in times of commodity rationing and scarcity, product-directed advertising became obsolete.

During the period of decolonization and in the years following Ghanaian independence, firms appropriated advertising for another purpose—namely, they used advertisements as a tool to build up goodwill toward a company and publicize corporate policies. The goal was to link the firm to ideas of reciprocity and quality rather than to promote a particular product. UAC campaigns and advertisements announcing their role in "Africanization," or policies focused on promoting Africans to managerial positions that were formerly reserved for Europeans, were some key examples.[47] While firms paid lip service to courting the African consumer, advertising and marketing were not the primary ways they did so. Prior to the 1950s, efforts were limited mainly to questioning African staff about what products they preferred and used. The first large-scale market research project, titled Project Joseph, was not undertaken until 1954. Paid for by the UAC and conducted by the Export Advertising Service to test West African reactions to different forms of press advertising, the project was primarily geared toward helping the firm improve its public image in response to anticolonial activism. As a result, whatever market research was gained was not specific enough to actually change a product's design or production, nor was it apparently intended for that purpose. Furthermore, tests were conducted on six hundred of the UAC's own staff from the Gambia, the Gold Coast, Nigeria, and Sierra Leone. While recognizing that the firm must have considered its own African staff members as archetypal middle-class shoppers who warranted research, its strategy also showed a continued reliance on information from intermediaries. Thus, drawing on market research and advertising to uncover the underlying assumptions and changing values of consumers, as a number of other studies on consumerism have done, carries certain limitations when applied to the Ghanaian context.

The "ultimate consumer" did not become any easier to single out after independence in 1957. As foreign firms retreated due to nationalist pressures and a number of policies put in place to curb their power, state-owned corporations like the Ghana National Trading Corporation (GNTC) were established and replaced many of the firms' long-standing functions. By 1961 the GNTC, under President Kwame Nkrumah and his Convention People's Party (CPP), took over a number of wholesale and retail outlets across the country as well as credit customer accounts. Though it was intended to protect the consumer, state ownership did not introduce any major changes in how people accessed and purchased goods, and the GNTC reproduced some of the same problems identified by ordinary Ghanaians during the colonial period. In the years following independence, similar accusations of favoritism and the creation of artificial shortages emerged. Like many African nationalist leaders, Nkrumah hoped to reduce dependency on foreign firms through investment in local manufacturing and by implementing import substitution strategies via state-owned enterprises.[48] But industrial development did not catch up with the demand for goods. Additionally, the world market price of cocoa (the country's primary source of foreign exchange) plummeted; the years 1964–66 were especially bad. Commodity shortages swept through the country, and irregular issuing of import licenses and the funneling of state funds for personal use by select CPP members and high-ranking government ministers further reduced the number of goods available on the market.

By the mid-1960s, it was not uncommon to see hundreds of people lining up for long hours outside retail stores. Shoppers regularly lined the street in front of Ghana House, the GNTC's Accra department store, well before opening hours in hopes of buying the most basic items. While the GNTC claimed that lines were necessary to weed out reselling and ensure that each person received his or her fair share of milk, rice, and sugar, customers developed a whole range of sly tactics to evade government control. As an official commission of inquiry into trade malpractices reported, these lines "should not fool anyone into thinking that the distributor firms are issuing goods to consumers." Instances of customers rejoining the line two or three times after each sale, and of customers hiring four or five other people to stand in on their behalf, were common.[49] Thus, the imposition of lines as a method for firms to ensure fair distribution by identifying and selling to the "real" consumer was largely unsuccessful.

While the CPP government claimed that tighter control over distribution through the GNTC was a method of protecting consumers from unfair trading practices, such strategies frustrated customers even more. It became a common practice for stores to stagger their business hours to coincide with the off-duty hours of workers and to regulate the release of goods at specific times. Debates about identifying the genuine consumer persisted and were manifested in the state-controlled media, pitting consumers and retailers against one another. Above all, the consumer was depicted as a victim of self-serving traders who ransacked store shelves, hiked up prices, and hoarded essential commodities for profit. Inflation and shortages were framed as a by-product of greedy retailers who monopolized goods rather than the result of state mismanagement. Efforts to distinguish the genuine consumer from a person who intended to purchase goods for resale were reminiscent of attempts undertaken by European firms during the colonial period. Echoing reports like the 1943 Conway Commission, the GNTC accused market women in particular of undermining Ghana's economic stability. Stories of crowds of women stampeding GNTC stores, abusing staff, and intimidating "respectable" shoppers were featured in the national news.[50] Described in a newspaper article as "human vultures," market women's practices were positioned as the antithesis of modern economic development. Indeed, these criticisms also revealed a larger ongoing social concern—specifically, the threat posed by women's financial autonomy.

General discontent with the economy provided part of the momentum for the 1966 military and police coup that overthrew President Nkrumah. As commodity shortages persisted in the 1970s, Ghana's second military government—the National Redemption Council, under Ignatius Kutu Acheampong—empowered the army and police to ensure fair distribution and price controls by force. Soldiers patrolled retail centers and commercial main streets, and violence was inflicted on retailers as well as consumers thought to be selling and buying beyond permissible daily usage, or what the government called "normal requirements." During what is now remembered by older Ghanaians as "Acheampong's time," stores and marketplaces throughout Ghana became sites of fear and intimidation. The military arrested hundreds of people accused of *kalabule*, a term that came to define a number of unlawful selling and consumption practices including hoarding, profiteering, smuggling, and selling on the black market. Soldiers also seized goods from private homes in military exercises like Operation Bring Out. In some regions, like Brong-Ahafo, military barracks became retail sites as soldiers took control of selling confiscated items to people they deemed "real" consumers. The category *consumer* thus continued to bedevil, even amid the supposed idealism of postrevolution rule; now one was deemed an authentic consumer through military discretion, a judgment backed by the threat of physical punishment, jail time, and exorbitant fines for those who failed to fit the image.

I begin with this brief genealogy of the consumer to encourage a rethinking of consumer studies from an African-centered perspective. The focus on consumer choice, demand, and desire, which has been the usual terrain of studying consumer culture, has limitations when applied to Ghana's history.[51] First, the organization and regulation of distribution channels were often as important to accessing commodities and shaping the consumer's experience as was the amount of money in that consumer's pocket. I therefore argue that histories of commodity distribution, typically the domain of economists and development policy planners, are not separate from consumer culture and have an economic and social history that demand examination. Second, to study consumerism in Ghana also requires that we take seriously an economic past characterized by boom and bust cycles and a general lack of stability. Such an economic reality created dramatic shifts from periods in which people enjoyed relative abundance to periods in which people suffered debilitating scarcity. So stark were some years that people remember month-long shortages that were interrupted only by an occasional flooding of a commodity that lasted for mere hours and then disappeared once more. The popular saying "plenty money, no goods" that was frequently evoked to describe the market (particularly from the late 1960s through the mid-1980s) further illuminates the need to account for these conditions. Here, my intentions are aligned with the work of consumer historian Sherene Seikaly, who has argued that "managing scarcity" in British-ruled Palestine was crucial to a longer process of "creating needs and desires."[52] This is not to say that people did not make sophisticated shopping choices when goods were available. Rather, the impetus is to have us move from interrogating the consumer as an identity (both individual and collective) to exploring the historical processes that brought that identity to fruition.

While this book seeks to locate the consumer as part of larger developments in Ghana's economic past, it is by no means an origins story. We will not find here a tale about the "birth of the consumer" in Ghana. In this sense, my research diverges from early consumer histories that traced the emergence of consumer culture during industrial revolutions in Britain and the United States or focused on a specific historical event like the American Revolution or World War II.[53] As we have seen, the British colonial economy produced a system in which the identity of the consumer, as a subject of corporate policy and state regulation, was never clear. I interpret this elusiveness as an opportunity for a critical engagement into the operation of power rather than as an obstacle or gap in the historical record. As Jean and John Comaroff, following Antonio Gramsci and Stuart Hall, remind us, "At any particular moment, in any marked event, a meaning or a social arrangement may appear free floating, underdetermined, ambiguous. But it is often the very attempt to harness that indeterminacy, the seemingly unfixed signifier, that animates both the exercise of power and the resistance to which it may give rise. Such arguments and struggles though are seldom equal."[54] Specifically, this vagueness allows us to examine how the consumer was implicated in various projects that went beyond what might typically be defined as market or economic exchange.

As we shall see, for much of the twentieth century in Ghana *consumer* was used as both an aspirational category and a value term. Both private and, later, state-owned firms deployed the notion of the consumer in flexible ways to serve their interests and legitimize their authority. Ordinary Ghanaians similarly evoked the category to advocate for greater control over the political and economic life of their country, as well as for more accountability from leadership. Consequently, different versions of the consumer surfaced at specific historical moments. However, these versions were never universal, consistent, or equally acknowledged. By questioning the assumed identity of the consumer we can gain a deeper understanding of what was at stake for different people who participated in the market, and what knowledge, justification, and cultural values framed their encounters.

REWRITING AFRICAN CONSUMER CULTURE AND RETHINKING ECONOMIC HISTORY

While the formation and organization of colonial capitalism made the African consumer an ambiguous figure, perceptions of the continent—popular and academic alike—also color what we know about African consumer history. Typically we think of consumerism in Africa as either a recent phenomenon or a result of Western cultural hegemony. Media images of Asante chiefs using the latest iPhone model or Congolese youth donning Gucci and Christian Dior fashions are used as representations to both celebrate "third world advancement" and signify the dangers of globalization and capitalist culture. These images are sometimes intended to shock and surprise Western audiences, who tend to still see the continent as different, distant, and underdeveloped. In many ways, academic literature also perpetuates some of these tired tropes. For example, in global studies of consumption the development of African consumerism is often positioned as part of a linear progression that slowly creeps across the globe or as a "last stop" in a process that originated in Europe or North America.[55] Additionally, histories of global commerce persistently portray African men and women as either producers of raw materials or as industrial laborers catering to the demands of Western markets and consumers.

Certainly this is not the case, as a number of scholars in the field of African history have shown. We know that West Africans participated in precolonial commercial networks and have traded long distance with Europeans since the fifteenth century, beginning with the Portuguese. In fact, the economic history of Ghana is extremely rich. Studies of African merchant communities and histories of prominent coastal trading families that predated colonial rule have been at the center of several foundational works.[56] Despite Ghana's significant economic past, Africans as consumers have not been the primary focus in the literature. Given that the trafficking in slaves (figured as "Atlantic commodities" by slave traders) and the violence that permeated it dominated commercial life on the Gold Coast,[57] early economic scholarship concentrated mainly on the organization and impact of transatlantic slave trade economies. This lack of attention to the consumer was also shaped by theories of underdevelopment that dominated African economic scholarship in the 1970s. Walter Rodney's influential study *How Europe Underdeveloped Africa* marked a crucial shift in African economic history from a Eurocentric to an African- and Caribbean-centered perspective, bringing to the forefront the term capitalist imperialism—the idea that imperialism was, and should be understood, as an economic phenomenon. Here Rodney directly took on a generation of European (and North American) economic historians like D. K. Fieldhouse, who argued against the severity of colonialism on the basis that it was "not that profitable" for Europeans. In attempting to counter these claims by tracing the roots of underdevelopment through centuries of institutions that exploited African labor and resources, however, Rodney's work did not consider the role of Africans as consumers or active participants in a larger Atlantic economy of goods. The only mention of consumerism in his book was in combating the work of colonial apologists who used African consumerism as some sort of evidence that the European slave trade "was undoubtedly a *moral evil,* but it was *economically good* for Africa."[58] In many ways, African consumer histories have been trapped within this uncertain space, between bourgeois and radical Marxist debates that have persisted in various forms for decades.[59]

Within these confines, however, we can find glimpses of the goods being exchanged as well as the manners in which imports were first used. Challenging popular myths that Africa was a dumping ground for "assorted rubbish"—that early trade goods consisted of cheap liquor, useless trinkets, and defective firearms—historians of material culture have cataloged detailed lists of various commodities registered and sold along the coast. For instance, even before the eighteenth century, Dutch traders stored 218 types of merchandise in Elmina Castle. Indian textiles, European linen, felt hats, Venetian beads, smoking pipes, mirrors, and paper, along with fancier goods like multicolored umbrellas, silver-headed canes, velvet-upholstered armchairs, and Turkish carpets were among the items listed on customs records, trading post inventories, and orders placed by African merchants.[60] Such evidence, however small, testifies to the engagement of Africans as consumers within the Atlantic economy. The variety of goods listed further demonstrates desires beyond those stereotypical staples of the slave trade, like guns and liquor—two commodities that are often blamed for perpetuating further violence and destruction on the West African coast.

Scholarship since the late 1960s on the ending of the slave trade and the shift to "legitimate" commerce introduced new areas of economic and historical study.[61] Even so, the consumer still figures as only a marginal character in a larger story that tends to focus on two types of activities: the business of large colonial trading firms and changes in agricultural production. In the first type, historians focused on the rise of merchant capital and the relationship between European firms and the emerging colonial state. Some of this literature falls into the category of corporate or company history and was written by firms' European employees. Frederick Pedler, a former colonial officer and the deputy chairman of the UAC from 1965 to 1968, wrote *The Lion and the Unicorn in Africa*, one of the first published histories of the UAC and the various British and Dutch firms that came to form it. Other studies were interested in evaluating the extent of collusion between merchant firms and the colonial administration. D. K. Fieldhouse made a distinction between the interests of colonialists and capitalists, while historians like Adu Boahen, Rhonda Howard, and certainly Walter Rodney saw their interests as basically one and the same. Another body of literature within this first type, written over the last two decades by business historians, explores the implications of Gold Coast nationalist politics and decolonization on European firms. Stephanie Decker and Sarah Stockwell, for instance, have traced the strategies used by British business to legitimize their continued presence amid nationalist agitation and protest in the years following the Second World War.[62]

The second type of economic scholarship centers on the activities surrounding agricultural production—specifically, the development of the Gold Coast cocoa industry. Scholarship by Jean Allman and Victoria

Tashjian, Gareth Austin, Polly Hill, Gwendolyn Mikell, and Ivor Wilks has been foundational in shaping the contours of this literature.[63] By 1911 cocoa had become the colony's largest export and main source of income. To illustrate, estimates from cocoa sales in Asante rose from £63,000 in 1909 to £700,000 in 1915.[64] Unlike eastern and southern Africa, there was never a large European or white settler population in the Gold Coast, so profits from cash crop farming remained, for the most part, in African hands.[65] Many cocoa-buying points, especially in the growing areas, had attached wholesale and retail stores where farmers were encouraged to spend their cash. Firms' produce buyers therefore acted as storekeepers and took responsibility for both sides of the business: the buying of the cocoa crop for export and the selling of imports to consumers. Among some cocoa farmers, the two activities were synonymous; in his memoir about his childhood in Asante, Thomas E. Kyei equates traveling with his father to cocoa buying stations with opportunities to view and buy items from abroad or goods from "the country of white men."[66] While the increase in consumer imports grew alongside the cocoa business, the production side of the cocoa industry has always overshadowed the consumption side in most of these histories.

Through a third type of scholarship framed by the concerns of early labor historians and feminist scholars that focused on women's contributions, we are able to catch a small glimpse into the lives of consumers. We know from Gold Coast labor historians like Jeff Crisp, Raymond Dumett, and Richard Jefferies that access to consumer goods spurred industrial workers to strike for higher wages in the gold mines and on the railways as early as 1918.[67] Furthermore, we learn how women came to dominate retail trade as men shifted their energies toward cocoa profits and wage employment. Studies by Gloria Addae, Gracia Clark, and Claire Robertson also reveal how Ghanaian women devised intricate strategies though market trading, temporary liaisons with European and African men (privileged in the colonial order), and economic solidarity with each other to obtain goods, from basic foodstuffs to kitchen utensils and cosmetics.[68] As Clark eloquently puts it in her study on market women in Kumasi, "Whether this balancing act resembles harmonious orchestration or frantic juggling, in the experience of a trader it holds the key to daily survival and successful accumulation."[69] Rather than positioning these struggles as reactions or responses to changing economic structures, I wish to explore them as fundamental to shaping how colonial capitalism was constituted in the first place. Through the lens of consumption rather than production, the present volume seeks to revisit this early economic literature and emphasize these "balancing acts" as embedded in the very fabric of African consumer histories.

Over the past ten years scholars of Africa have become increasingly interested in African consumer practices and the social logics of demand. Much of this literature, however, is dominated by research on specific commodities. Major works on African consumerism, including Timothy Burke's 1996 groundbreaking study *Lifebuoy Men, Lux Women*, concentrate on the circulation and use of particular goods like cosmetics, cloth, and alcohol.[70] Burke shows how African consumers rearticulated the meanings of foreign manufactured items like soap, cosmetics, and other toiletries prescribed by European companies, missionaries, and white settlers; he argues that African consumption practices became central to battles over economic power, white supremacy, and African respectability. Some whites viewed the consumption and adoption of their products by Africans as a sign of the pliability of the continent and a justification for their "civilizing mission." Other white settlers perceived African consumption of certain items as a complete disregard for public codes of deference. As one anxious white settler expressed, "Our civilization is in the shop windows and if we don't guide them carefully, they will come and get it." Burke's study reveals how deep-seated settler racism not only shaped Africans' access *to* goods but also their perceptions *of* goods.

Reaching back into the nineteenth century, Jeremy Prestholdt demonstrates how East African consumer desire influenced global patterns of trade and stimulated the industrialization of cities like Bombay, India, and Salem, Massachusetts. The cultural process of *domestication*, or what he defines as the remaking of foreign goods into something familiar and usable, is at the core of Prestholdt's analysis. Among Zanzabaris, for instance, the consumption of imported clocks, mirrors, and umbrellas was rearticulated to reflect ongoing debates about modernity, personhood, and status. While Prestholdt builds on Burke's work, he argues that East African consumers used commodities to not only address the particularities of culture in the Indian Ocean region but also project new senses of self to the larger global world. By excavating these "forgotten histories of mutuality and global interdependence," Prestholdt challenges long-standing assumptions about Africa's relation to other parts of the world—namely, he refutes the idea that African consumerism has been largely shaped by the interests of others.[71]

While he categorizes his study on alcohol as a social history, I consider Emmanuel Akyeampong's *Drink, Power, and Social Change* to be the first full-length consumer history of Ghana.[72] Tracing alcohol's role as a ritual object, a marker of personal identity, and an economic commodity, Akyeampong uses it to historicize the circulation and legitimization of power and authority. Focusing on Asante worldviews, he illustrates how access to alcohol informed intergenerational and gender conflicts in precolonial Ghana and shaped the formation of urban social life in the early colonial period. Akyeampong's investigation into temperance agitation and the history of liquor legislation, which included tariffs on imported liquor and licensing fees for liquor outlets, is particularly insightful. As these tariffs and fees accounted for as much as 40 percent of total government revenues in the period immediately preceding World War I, debates over liquor prohibition became an important factor in the extension of colonial hegemony and key to solidifying indirect rule—the British policy of ruling through "traditional" chiefs and local authorities implemented throughout West Africa.

Taking the many insights of this diverse scholarship, we will here depart from the persistent focus on the social meaning of *things* and instead foreground the centrality of *people*—and, in particular, the human relationships that have created, constituted, and counteracted the participation of African consumers within the world of goods.[73] Rendering visible these various encounters demands a rethinking of the very starting point for our inquiry—namely, the term *consumer culture.* Our decades-old concept of consumer culture has been generated predominately from research on mass consumption in Britain and the United States, and the resulting studies have primarily addressed the cultural meanings behind consumer choice and the construction of desire.[74] These meanings are, of course, relevant to our study of Ghana, but our inquiry must move in many other directions, as well. Therefore, rather than focus on consumer culture, I use the term *consumer politics* instead. This shift in terms will, I hope, allow us to expand upon the definition of consumer culture and to emphasize the fact that consumer markets are the products of shifting power relations and competing interests. For instance, while elements like advertising, branding, salesmanship, and market research have shaped consumer markets in Ghana, just as they have done in Britain, the United States, and other places around the world, the restrictive nature of the colonial and postcolonial economies made other issues—including the regulation of retail stores and marketplaces, international supply networks and import licensing, and price controls and government contracts—equally significant.

Just as important, in relation to the specifics of our terms, is that I wish to redefine the way we currently use *consumer politics*, a term that has a much shorter academic history than *consumer culture* and a relatively slim historiography dating mainly from the last ten years. Additionally it has typically been linked to large-scale consumer revolutions, or at least consumer-led movements.[75] But far beyond the obvious instances of boycotts and protests, I see struggles over big market forces as happening all the time, within ordinary face-to-face interactions that took place in wholesale and supply offices, across retail and credit counters, at trade fairs and promotional events, and on department store selling floors. As Tony Ballantyne and Antoinette Burton have argued, "Nuanced analyses of a range of cultural spaces—from the classroom to the hospital, the asylum to the family album, the nursery to the archive—have made it possible to understand how and why imperial power operated through the colonization of spatialized domains brought into the purview of the colonial state and its reformist agendas."[76] Commercial spaces are no different, though they may seem at first glance to be static or predictable. They, too, are always changing and animated by "the collusions and collisions" of bodies, power, and regimes—not unlike the spaces that Ballantyne and Burton describe. I therefore apply this spatial analytic to market encounters of all kinds in order to piece together the mixture of beliefs, emotions, and desires that dictated consumer exchange and persisted beyond the "end of empire." Therefore, I define *consumer politics* as the everyday contests over access to goods and channels of distribution (retailing and wholesaling) as well as the regulation of consumer practices and consumer spaces by both the state and other systems of social authority and power.

To write about consumer histories in Ghana is also to write about the operation of global capitalism more broadly. My research shares the intentions of modern African business history and critical anthropological work, which has documented African businesspeople as everything from transporters to cattle suppliers, financiers to street vendors, and has shown them actively shaping local, regional, and international political economies. This research has uncovered transnational business networks from Freetown to Fouta Djallon, from Brazzaville to Paris, and in multiple routes across the Sahara that have long shaped the methods and modes of commercial exchange within and beyond the African continent.[77] My analysis of similar linkages is further informed by feminist and critical race scholarship, two areas of study that have been essential to understanding the construction, circulation, and maintenance of power and inequality in Ghana. By applying these rigorous frameworks to the ways in which colonial and postcolonial consumer markets are constituted, I hope to offer new ways to think first about how gender and race are embedded in the policies and the practices of "doing business" and, second, about how the circulation of transnational capital is both a gendered and racialized experience.[78] As Anna Tsing reminds us, "Rather than assume we know exactly what global capitalism is, even before it arrives, we need to find out how it operates in friction."[79] I argue that the history of consumer politics in modern Ghana provides one entry point for undertaking such a challenge.

CULLING THE CORPORATE ARCHIVE AND ANIMATING THE MARKET

My hope through this book is to offer a more interconnected vision of African consumer worlds. My aim in documenting the various social relationships that shaped the history of consumption is to not only show markets as contested spaces but also to encompass the range of experiences (excitement, hope, and determination, as well as fear, panic, and disillusion) that animated individual encounters with the market. To do so I draw on a wide range of sources, collected in Switzerland, the United Kingdom, the United States, and throughout Ghana from a wide swath of both daily life and official business: government reports and correspondence, newspapers and magazines, economic and household surveys, advertising copy and images, private papers and memoirs. While each of these sources introduces its own set of problems and challenges, together they enable the book's larger goal of putting disparate sources into conversation in order to offer a more holistic understanding of consumer politics. Nowhere is this disparate feeling, and both the problems and challenges that accompany it, more evident than with my two most important types of sources: corporate archives and oral histories.

Economic and business historians regularly rely on corporate sources to reconstruct economic pasts; I believe that corporate archives have untapped potential for reconstructing social and cultural history.[80] Such history, particularly for this time and place, usually relies on the records kept by governments and religious missions—and as a result, these histories tend to focus on how people's lives intersected with such institutions as schools, courts, and hospitals. Yet these sources often lack a sense of how Africans engaged with private industry and business; therefore, the resulting histories too often ignore African relationships with the market beyond top-down legislation. In contrast, my use of staff correspondence, managers' circulars, and district reports provide crucial details about the role that Africans—not to mention Europeans, Indians, and Lebanese—played in the rocky terrain of West African commerce.

The contents of these corporate sources are surprisingly rich. Firms like the UAC and UTC had much to gain or lose with regard to their West African businesses, and they kept impressive records on all aspects of Ghana's import-export trade that span both the colonial and postcolonial periods. Furthermore, some European managers wrote extensively about the lives of individual African employees on issues that extended beyond what would be considered a typical business, including family and inheritance, religion and the supernatural, and entertainment and leisure activities. One European manager even took it upon himself to produce a type of amateur ethnography on his African coworkers—unbeknownst to them.[81] Other groups were included in these reports as well; the business of Indian and Syrian merchants (whose numbers had increasingly grown after the First World War) and the recruitment of Greeks as salesmen served as additional topics of inquiry.[82]

There is one aspect of these corporate archives that is, not surprisingly, lacking. Aside from a few responses to managers' inquiries and the UAC's in-house staff magazines—the *Gold Coast UAC News* and the *Unicorn*—I found very little material authored by Africans. Because most company records were written by and for European employees, I was constantly aware of the power of the corporate archive to both document and also silence African experiences. As a result, I approached the corporate archive not as a depository of facts but as a space to investigate the negotiation of power.[83] A critical reading of corporate sources demanded both the unpacking of contradictions and inconsistencies in firms' policy versus practice and an interpretation of what these moments of dissonance revealed about the development of consumer markets in Ghana more broadly. I read hundreds of districts reports, nearly all of them dry and obligatory, but when I viewed them not merely as catalogs of dutifully noted events but as active sites of contestation, I turned my focus from *what* was reported to *how* it was written. Such an analysis also demanded situating corporate sources within a broader context. To do so I drew on a number of African-authored newspapers and magazines (especially editorials), letters from readers, opinion and advice columns, and business publications like *Business Weekly* and the *Ghana Trade Journal.*

The accumulation of all this material, written both by and for Africans, is abundant and rich, but it was not sufficient. Thus, at the heart of this work are oral interviews I conducted with a wide range of men and women throughout Ghana, including former managers, wholesale and retail storekeepers, and credit customers and consumers.[84] Talking with these people proved invaluable to understanding shifts in consumer practices and generated new questions about the boundaries and limitations of consumer capitalism.[85] I use oral history not as a tool to "identify or extract overlying falsities to get an underlying truth" but as a method to comprehend how "Africans saw their lives, their worlds, their histories" and how they "*felt* about—or understood and represented" their experiences.[86] Simply put, I did not use oral sources to supplement or fill in missing gaps from the corporate record. Instead I attempted to create a dialogue between corporate and oral sources to uncover the intricacies of colonial capitalism. Uncovering the ways in which such an economic system structured a variety of institutional and intimate relationships, as well as affective experiences, was central to this process.

Most interviews took place inside private homes, as well as in public spaces like stores and offices, and were informal and conversational. The average age of interviewees was sixty-eight, with the youngest being fifty-five and the eldest around ninety-five. I first located interviewees through the public relations office at Unilever Ghana in Tema. I was aware that this was not a representative sample, and assumed that Unilever would link me to those who held high-level positions and would speak favorably of their experiences. While in some instances this was the case, in others I found that interviewees spoke rather freely about blatant racism and poor treatment. Through these interactions I also learned that many interviewees had been employed in various positions throughout the course of their working lives. For instance, those who had started as storekeepers or clerks in the 1940s and 1950s had become managers by the end of their careers, and this allowed them to speak from multiple perspectives on a wide range of topics and various aspects of the business. Most of these interviewees, however, were predominantly men who had received some sort of postsecondary education in Ghana or abroad.

To gain access to a larger, more diverse group of interviewees, I cast my net wider. I shared my research with practically everyone I met, including neighbors, friends, colleagues, and strangers, asking if people knew of men or women who had worked as storekeepers, credit customers, or employees of foreign firms. This method proved extremely successful—particularly in smaller towns, where I was usually connected with someone who either agreed to be interviewed or put me in contact with others. Another technique was locating interviewees through the tried-and-true snowball sampling method: after each interview, I asked interviewees if they would introduce me to others in their social network. Both of these strategies expanded the scope of the project to include not only employees of the UTC and the GNTC but also a range of people who worked with firms but were not formally employed by them.[87] These methods also led me to a number of women, including one of Accra's most infamous credit customers. Finally, I gained a deeper understanding of how people conducted business in spite of the various restrictions that limited their autonomy and under conditions that at moments made it risky to sell even a tin of milk.

Although historians have used interviews with former African staff to reconstruct corporate histories, few have investigated how local employees navigated the various colonial and postcolonial social worlds of which they were a part.[88] While I did ask structured questions about firms' practices (selling, storekeeping, advertising, relating to customers) to begin and guide conversations, I also asked more open-ended questions about interviewees' backgrounds, education, families, and day-to-day lives. These questions varied from interview to interview based on individuals' willingness to share and their interest in a given topic. With those who were particularly enthusiastic, I conducted follow-up interviews. I also shared materials from the corporate archive with interviewees; copies of the *Unicorn*, old advertising campaigns, and photographs of stores and shoppers sparked vivid memories and led us to new topics and unintended conversations about changing tastes and desires, cautionary tales about certain products, and the pleasures and dangers of consuming.

The result is a history of African consumer politics, but also—and notably—an exploration of the social relations, practices, beliefs, and sentiments responsible for that history. While *Market Encounters* is organized chronologically, the structure is not linear. Instead, it reads as a series of case studies; sometimes these overlap, sometimes they stand alone. Each chapter emerges from a specific historical moment and space to capture the varied interactions and encounters that animated Ghana's commercial landscape. District wholesale offices, shops and market stalls, urban department stores, international trade fairs, and military barracks provide the backdrops for these histories. Anxious European managers, energetic storekeepers, glamorous saleswomen, frustrated consumers, and opportunistic soldiers serve as some of the book's central characters.

I begin by placing the expansion of consumer markets at the center of the social, cultural, and political transformations that not only shaped the colonial period but also Ghana's relationship to the global economy. I uncover transnational business networks as key sites where knowledge about Africa, African markets, and the nature of global exchange were produced by foreign trading firms to establish commercial superiority. The growth of foreign capital after the First World War required fabricating a parallel narrative about African businesspeople as untrustworthy and immoral and the African market as a space of commercial chaos and danger. Chapter 1, which focuses specifically on the relationships between foreign firms and their African employees and consumers, reveals the colonial state as not just a political and military apparatus but a commercial one that produced a specific set of social relations for its own benefit. Yet those efforts were fraught and often illusory. The superior market knowledge of Africans, the contradictions between a firm's policy and its practice, and the dilemmas of on-the-ground interactions all demonstrated the limits of colonial capitalism, as did

African counternarratives about capitalist expansion and the potential dangers of consuming, which persistently disrupted efforts by the UAC and UTC to fully control and dictate market terms.

This fundamental struggle of foreign firms—between the desire to maintain commercial authority and their reliance on African knowledge about the market—defined commercial life in the first of half of the twentieth century. However, tensions escalated during World War II; shortages and the inability of firms to implement government-imposed quotas and price controls revealed the extent of this dependency. Set in the 1940s and 1950s, chapter 2 takes a closer look at the specific strategies employed by African shopkeepers and credit customers in shaping corporate policies and the international circuits through which firms operated. My analysis of the UAC's credit customer business, in particular, asks us to consider how preexisting ideas about racial and gender inferiority affected market relations and how these constructs were produced within the ongoing structuring of global capitalism. Through the corporate language of professionalization, we see how the market expertise of African women was refigured as deceptive and outdated, and thus how these women were placed at a distance from and at odds with modern economic development.

The book's remaining chapters address the late 1950s through the 1970s—the decades that spanned the movement toward independence, self-rule under Kwame Nkrumah and the CPP, and control of the government by two different military regimes. The debates surrounding the planning, construction, and operation of Kingsway, one of Ghana's largest and most famous department stores, are the backbone of chapter 3. Embedded in the politics of decolonization, this centerpiece of Accra's shopping district demonstrated a new relationship with foreign capital and symbolized Nkrumah's hopes for legitimizing Ghana as a newly independent nation. Owned and operated by the UAC, Kingsway was part of a larger public relations strategy prompted by decolonization. Fueled by demands from Nkrumah and Accra residents, the building of Kingsway revealed a temporary inversion of a past colonial relationship. Yet the project of postcolonial nation building and the fulfillment of consumer aspirations were often at odds. Beneath the store's sleek exterior, modern technologies, and promises of convenience and efficiency festered generational conflict and inequalities of class and gender. Young salaried saleswomen became objects of desire and disgust, while young, educated managers found it difficult to assert their authority over older employees who refused to see a fancy education as trumping age and experience.

Chapters 4 and 5 focus on the militarization of the market—namely, the efforts undertaken by military regimes to control the consumer market and define the boundaries of consumption. After the 1966 coup, the National Liberation Council (NLC) used ideologies of consumerism to attract foreign investors and the support of local businessmen who had been neglected under Nkrumah's socialist agenda. Chapter 4 analyzes Ghana's first International Trade Fair as part of a larger NLC refashioning project that celebrated the country's transition to a free market capitalist economy. Through the fair, the NLC also reintroduced older ideas about wealth and accumulation considered vital for the country's economic, political, and moral reconstruction. The NLC accused Nkrumah and the CPP of dismantling the authority of chiefs, elders, and parents and corrupting the morals of youth—especially young women. The fair thus established a new, more disciplined form of consumerism that proscribed certain limitations and restrictions in the name of national reform. Ghana's second coup in 1972 and the violence undertaken to instill market discipline serve as the backdrop of chapter 5. Under dire economic conditions and commodity shortages, the National Redemption Council led by Acheampong seized power and aimed to legitimize their rule through a policy of state-guaranteed economic stabilization. Strict regulations (reminiscent of colonial market controls) required military and police involvement in all facets of the market. Via oral histories of this market scarcity, we reconstruct the experiences of those targeted by volunteer price inspectors and government-appointed antihoarding squads. I show how the criminalization of those buying and selling outside state-regulated guidelines shaped people's relationship with goods and the ways in which they perceived themselves as consumers.

In sum, the book's exploration of consumer politics in modern Ghana complicates the old "European exploitation versus African resistance" binary and disrupts representations of Africans as merely laborers or producers for consumers elsewhere. The analytical shift from consumer culture to consumer politics also allows us to account for how issues like gender and racial inequalities are implicated in—and act as driving forces behind—commercial and business networks that span the globe. By emphasizing the centrality of people and human relationships to Ghana's economic past, *Market Encounters* introduces a radical rethinking of consumption studies from an African-centered perspective. Such a vantage point enhances our understanding of colonial capitalism in all of its intricacies, legacies, and contradictions.

1 ⇜ A Door "Wide Open"

Imagining Gold Coast Markets

IN APRIL 1915, the *African Mail*, a weekly British trade publication, featured an editorial titled "Africa to the Fore." Emphasizing the British public's increasing knowledge about the continent, the article declared that "there has never been a period in the history of West Africa when she has been so much in the public eye. The 'man in the street' [is] rapidly becoming familiar with place names which a few months ago were undreamt of." While the author of the editorial, Edmund D. Morel, was of course referring to World War I and events like the invasion of Germany's West African colonies, which had made headlines around the globe, the piece was concerned with much more than the success of the Allied troops. Specifically addressing British "men of business," Morel wrote, "The war is providing new opportunities, but are we taking them? Hardware, machinery, cycles, apparel, perfumery, drugs and medicines, disinfectants, agricultural implements, foodstuffs, motors, constructional buildings, all of these things find a ready and constantly expanding sale . . . the manufacturers of this country should be preparing their campaign . . . but the attack must be made now." His conclusion was simple: "the door of Africa is lying wide open."[1] Morel's use of "to attack" as a way to discuss economic expansion is particularly telling evidence of the imbrication of commerce and militarism.

This chapter situates Morel's call to commercial action within the larger realm of the West African import-export trade after the First World War and, in particular, the increasing power of large European firms to shape that trade. We know that, from the late nineteenth century onward, firms forged relationships with colonial governments throughout Africa to monopolize markets and in the process seized power once shared with African businesspeople. But what we have not explored is how these efforts to consolidate and organize trade actually played out on the ground.[2] Imperial thinking about the fundamental inferiority of nonwhite subjects influenced how firms imagined and encountered the Gold Coast market, but those ideas were also shaped by day-to-day business interactions with firms' African staff and customers themselves. This argument has far-reaching implications for rethinking the expansion of consumer capitalism in Ghana. We will see that the banal places of business—company offices, wholesale stores, and retail shops—became spaces where ideas about race, cultural difference, and development were constructed, reinforced, and institutionalized through corporate policy. By drawing on inspection reports, monthly circulars, and correspondence between firms' headquarters in Europe, main offices in the Gold Coast, and district branches throughout the colony, I demonstrate that "doing business" was itself a process where fictions about the untapped African market and the inability of Africans to control its potential were created by foreign firms to justify their financial and cultural intrusions.[3]

Yet this process of imagining was never unidirectional. The power of these European firms, just like the colonial governments they supported, is obvious to us; it is easy to see African staff and consumers as merely on the receiving end of this power. And indeed, most of what we know about African consumer history is about how firms, manufacturers, and advertisers envisioned African markets and imposed their own commercial agendas. Here we will consider imagining as a reciprocal rather than a one-sided process; through oral histories, I will show how African staff and consumers constructed their own counterfictions about firms that emerged from local beliefs, including those about the circulation of wealth and proper accumulation. For instance, the United Africa Company was often associated with bad magic and witchcraft; such beliefs reflected popular anxieties about the power of foreign capital, but also the reality that Africans after World War I increasingly lost control over market terms. These rich criticisms of the practices and policies of foreign firms further demonstrate that African men and women were, and are, far from passive recipients of global economic change. Links made between firms and witchcraft, typically expressed through humorous tropes and cautionary tales, were acute analyses of the tendencies of capital to push excessive growth and foster fetishism in consumers. The resilience of these stories, which still circulate in historical memory, reveal the importance of theorizing about the global economy "from the south" to disrupt the common sense assumptions that underlie fictive visions of how capitalism works.

I will first analyze the expansion of consumer markets in the Gold Coast at the turn of the nineteenth century and then consider how everyday commercial interactions between firms' directors and district agents and African staff and customers shaped this process. While this chapter focuses mainly on the activities of the United Africa Company and Union Trading Company before the Second World War, I will also draw on personal memoirs, commercial guides, and photographs and recollections by the staff from other firms such as G. B. Ollivant and John Holt & Company. My focus on the experiences of European management and staff is not to overshadow the contributions of African businesspeople, who will become central to our story in chapter 2, but to explore the role of this professional managerial class of men in shaping and mediating capitalist relations in the colonies. These foreign firms established power, at least in part, by fabricating ideas about Africa and Africans as inherently untrustworthy and immoral.[4] Discrepancies between policy and practice within firms, as well as African staff members' own narratives about capitalist expansion, worked to counter these misconceptions, however. As historian Frederick Cooper has argued, "the story of European firms in West Africa is neither a saga of triumph of superior organization nor a tale of every-growing monsters sweeping the innocent before them."[5] The tension between the available language used by European managers to describe and define Africa and the quotidian operations of the merchandise business that proved their conceptions otherwise offers a more nuanced picture of how colonial capitalism operated. Above all, the relationship between European management and African staff and consumers reveals imperialism as not only a political and military apparatus but also as a commercial one both created and contested by the daily—and inseparable—interactions of culture and commerce.

SETTING THE COMMERCIAL SCENE

Until about the 1880s, Africa's commercial trade with Europeans was confined to a few coastal enclaves, and the import-export business was conducted in cooperation with African merchants. While much of this trade had been administered through state-chartered firms like the Royal African Company (established in 1672), the eighteenth century saw the rise of individual private traders—the British, Dutch, French, German, Portuguese, and occasionally Americans.[6] Most of these private traders were active in the transatlantic slave trade. Among other works, Margaret Priestley's history on the elite coastal trading family, the Brews, provides details about the formation of these early West African merchant societies. For the purposes of this study it is important to note that foreign merchants, like Irish slave trader Richard Brew, often lived on the coast for extended periods of time and were subject to intense bargaining with wealthy African merchants and middlemen who owned businesses as large as some of the European companies. Some of these foreign merchants also married African women according to local custom; the range of benefits gained from such unions were pivotal to European men's commercial success prior to the second half of the nineteenth century.[7] For the most part, however, the European trading community was restricted and small; this allowed the African elite merchant class, also known as "merchant princes," to hold strong bargaining positions and to play European rivals against one another.[8]

The abolition and suppression of the transatlantic slave trade at the turn of the nineteenth century began to reshape the terms of business between European and African merchants. Referred to by historians as a shift to "legitimate" commerce (in order to distinguish it from the illegal trade in slaves), this era saw the replacement of the trade in human beings with the trade in raw materials such as palm oil, groundnuts, rubber, timber, and minerals.[9] Propelled in part by the spread of industrial capitalism and the need to supply new factories in Europe, the import-export trade among British, French, German, Swiss, and occasionally US firms in West Africa grew increasingly competitive.[10] The circulation of standardized currencies, the absence of tariff barriers, and the mass production of consumables further contributed to this surge. The pace of trade also sped up with the invention of the steamship. As A. G. Hopkins points out, "in the middle of the century sailing ships took about thirty-five days to reach West Africa, but by 1900 the steamer had reduced this time by half."[11]

Such developments made it easier for both African and European newcomers to enter the commercial scene. As a result, a number of small private firms popped up along the coast. In contrast to the merchants before them, these people had little to no previous connection to West Africa. The Manchester firms John Walkden and Pickering & Berthound, as well as the Liverpool brothers who formed John Holt & Company, were some key examples (fig. 1.1). Likewise, shifting trading conditions introduced a new group of African businessmen. Distinct from wealthy African merchant princes who dictated the terms of overseas trade and agreements with foreigners, this new group mainly consisted of people who acted "either as independent wholesalers and retailers, or as agents selling goods on commission for manufacturing firms in Europe."[12] This was a transition from

FIGURE 1.1. Exterior of provision store, Sekondi, ca. 1910. Reproduced with kind permission of Unilever from the original at the Unilever Archives, UAC/1/11/9/12/31.

previous decades in which African merchants operated mostly independent businesses outside the purview of European firms and supervisors.

Thus, when British colonial officials arrived and officially claimed Accra as the capital of their crown colony in 1874, they carried forward an economic process that was already under way. In 1902 the creation of the Gold Coast colony was completed when the British annexed Asante and the Northern Territories and brought both regions under their jurisdiction. Most foreign firms continued to conduct business as usual with little interference from the colonial state. Major changes to the commercial landscape were the size, structure, and geographical location of firms' operations; companies that had been situated on the coast for decades started to establish wholesale and retail stores inland. According to historian Kwame Arhin, in 1897 "trade in goods of European manufacture was microscopic" within northern Asante and the Northern Territories, but this trade expanded significantly after colonialism. Within "five years of the establishment of colonial rule," demand soared for items including silk handkerchiefs, cheap cloth, assorted perfumes, combs, knives, tin spoons, hairpins, buttons, pomade, and mirrors.[13] The imposition of colonial caravan tolls in 1898 to control trans-Saharan commerce and a general policing of trade routes in the two regions also contributed to this shift. We know that in the precolonial era trade with other West African countries had been particularly important. What was left of these networks with the imposition of colonialism was mainly trade with other British West African colonies.[14]

The expansion of firms into the interior was further aided by improvements in transportation and communication networks. To facilitate the extraction and export of raw materials such as cocoa, gold, and rubber, the Colonial Office began improving transportation, mostly through railway construction. Completed by 1902, new railway routes from Sekondi to Tarkwa to Kumasi were equipped with a telegraph system, a technology that improved internal communication within firms.[15] The increasing number of all-weather roads was, however, the result of African rather than British achievement. These road networks made it easier for merchants to travel hundreds of miles from the coast to sell all types of goods, and to sell them more cheaply, to towns deep in the interior.[16] (Before this time, porters balanced goods on their heads and carried them for several miles on foot—a journey that often took several days.) The new mobility shortened distances between population centers, areas of production, and ports. Imports of motor vehicles for commercial use, mostly Ford cars and light American trucks, rose from twenty-one in 1912 to 133 by 1913.[17] New roads and railways determined the location and construction of new stores. Firms' employees, as well as African chiefs, often cited "good roads" in appeals to firms for opening stores in their towns.[18]

New thinking in Britain about colonial markets also refocused manufacturers' and exporters' attention on Africa. British imperialists had long dreamed of their colonies as a vital market for British goods. Men like Cecil Rhodes and Joseph Chamberlin invoked the image of "new markets" abroad to "woo support for their imperial ambitions" among the British working class. Access to new markets, they assured the voting public, "would secure the future of British capitalism and thus British jobs."[19] Yet, it was not until after World War I that imperialist fantasies would begin to materialize. As historian Richard Rathbone argues, Africa before 1914 "was for the most part a dream for the greedy speculator."[20] The devastation of the war and the economic stagnation that followed it introduced a new sense of urgency; imperial markets became essential to Britain's recovery. This sentiment was echoed in British commercial publications, reinforced at public events like the British Empire Exhibition of 1924–25, and bolstered by individual businessmen who claimed that the African market was "one of the world's hopes for the future."[21] Strengthening economic links between Britain and its colonial possessions became central to parliamentary discussions and was reflected in a series of tariff reforms throughout the interwar period. These initiatives allowed exports from the colonies free entry into Britain, whereas those outside the empire had to pay duties and set limits on the amount of goods imported into British West Africa from other countries. The rhetoric of imperial preference further increased awareness of the colonies as economically vital to the metropole. In 1926 the colonial secretary established the Empire Marketing Board as a means of promoting intra-empire trade and, through public marketing campaigns, convincing British consumers to buy commodities from the colonies.[22] Interwar development efforts initiated by the Colonial Office further encouraged financial links between Britain and its imperial possessions. The Colonial Development Act of 1929, for instance, incentivized British capital investment throughout the empire.[23]

It is from this interwar context that large foreign firms—which are central to the present study's analysis—would emerge. In contrast to state-chartered companies and private firms, formed by one man or a partnership, twentieth-century firms were large limited liability companies established through the taking over of other firms. Among economic historians the years between 1880 and 1930 are known as the era of acquisitions. As smaller firms were swept up through mergers and takeovers, commercial power was concentrated in the hands of a few large firms. While some older firms, including John Holt & Company, outlasted this process, most did not. Independent African businessmen suffered most, however; African import-export businesses did not completely disappear, but many struggled to compete with the emergence of these large conglomerates. Operating with less capital, African-owned firms were more vulnerable to rapid changes in market fluctuations and could not match the capabilities of larger firms to import goods in large quantities at once. Combined with colonial policy that favored European business, these changes increasingly pushed African merchants "out to the margins in the system they had helped to create." Specifically, they were "denied access to credit, price-fixing agreements, shipping rebates, and others sorts of concessions which Europeans enjoyed."[24] Additionally, there was fierce competition with Lebanese and Syrian businessmen, whose numbers grew steadily after the war. The Gold Coast government categorized Lebanese and Syrians as a single group, and commercial records often used the terms interchangeably. Thus, in West Africa, the terms *Syrian* and *Lebanese* encompassed both groups as well as other Eastern Mediterranean migrants.[25] Commercial competition was further fueled by European firms that preferred to do business with these—slightly less foreign seeming—Lebanese businessmen over Africans. While historians have demonstrated how shrewd business strategies aided the success of Lebanese trading families, proximity to whiteness was also an important factor in their growing success as a new group of commercial middlemen operating between firms and African retailers and customers.[26]

By 1930, three large firms prevailed: the United Africa Company (UAC), the Union Trading Company (UTC), and the Compagnie Française de l'Afrique Occidentale (CFAO).[27] In the Gold Coast, the main business activities of these commercial giants included the purchase, packaging, and export of raw materials (mainly cocoa) from producers and the importation, distribution, and sales of manufactured goods to consumers. All of these firms also operated shipping lines and owned large fleets of vehicles for delivery. Given that most manufacturers in Britain, Europe, and the United States did not build factories or open offices of their own, the services provided by large firms—shipping, distribution, sales, and promotion—were essential to reaching African markets. The commercial networks of these large firms were vast, comparable in size and importance to the administrative system operated by the colonial government, and as such a firm's district agent in a single area often held more influence than the colonial district officer in charge. Timothy Burke refers to large firms like the UAC as "new modern monopoly firms" and argues that they became central to the operation and structure of colonial capitalism.[28]

Out of the three major firms that came to dominate the West African commercial scene, the UAC was the largest and most powerful. Known as the West African trading arm of the Anglo-Dutch multinational Unilever, the UAC was established in 1929 through a series of mergers and the acquisition of a number of other firms, some of which had dated back to the seventeenth century. Among the most important were the Royal Niger Company and the African & Eastern Trade Corporation, the latter an amalgamation of a number of firms (F. & A. Swanzy, Miller Brothers, and the African Association). Through the process of amalgamation, the UAC would inherit more than twelve thousand retail stores, fifty-eight wholesale stores, and thousands of credit customer accounts.[29] By the mid-1930s the UAC also purchased G. B. Ollivant (GBO) and the Swiss African Trading Company (SAT), yet these firms were allowed to retain their original company names, trademarks, and network of stores. By 1940 it also acquired the CFAO (a major competitor in French West Africa) and the German firm of G. Gottschalck. African customers often perceived of GBO and the SAT as separate from the UAC.[30] While the UAC had business interests in Morocco, in almost every country along the West African coast from Senegal to Angola, in the east and south from Kenya, Uganda, and Tanzania to Zambia and Zimbabwe, the bulk of its assets remained in Nigeria and the

Gold Coast. Although its parent company Unilever was formed in part by Dutch investment, the UAC's headquarters remained in London; its directors, as well as most of its management and staff in the Gold Coast, were British.[31]

In the Gold Coast the UAC's major competitor was the UTC. While the structure of the UTC's merchandise business was similar to that of the UAC, the history of its formation as a "Christian enterprise" was quite different. First registered in Basel in 1859 under its German name Missions-Handlungs-Gesellschaft Basel, the Basel Mission Trading Company (BMTC) was originally part of the Basel Mission Society (BMS)—a pietistic organization from Switzerland with strong ties to southern Germany. By 1900 the BMS recorded over eleven mission stations throughout the Gold Coast with about seventeen thousand members. Profits from the BMTC were intended to finance the activities of the mission society, and BMTC stores were to provide missionaries with a regular supply of goods from Europe. From its inception, the BMTC was used by the BMS as an "instrument in transmitting their ethic and practices of work to their converts."[32] Through the teaching of "fair trading practices," missionaries believed that qualities like self-discipline, hard work, and thriftiness could be cultivated. During the First World War, the British government regarded the company as "enemy property" and confiscated the BMTC due to the company's high number of German personnel; the government deported the BMTC's European staff. After a long legal battle, however, the company was awarded £250,000 and was allowed to reenter the Gold Coast in 1928 under its new name—the Union Trading Company.[33] While the UTC legally decoupled itself from the BMS after the war, the firm still expected its staff members to uphold and regularly practice Christian values through their work. The correlation between Christianity and commerce was central to the UTC's operations in the Gold Coast and, as others have shown, integral to the way in which consumer capitalism developed in other African colonies.[34]

PLACES OF BUSINESS AND PROFILES

Before examining places of business and the people who embodied them, let us first consider how channels of commodity distribution in the Gold Coast were structured.[35] Here I focus mainly on the merchandise side of business or the activities involved in the purchase and resale of manufactured goods rather than the produce side or the activities involved in cocoa buying and export. All imported goods—everything from farm equipment and toiletries to leather boots and automobiles—arrived via steamship at one of several ports spread along the coast. After its completion in 1928, the deepwater port at Takoradi would facilitate most of this traffic. Merchandise was received on-site by a firm's agent, and a small army of African port workers divided it up and loaded it into trucks that transported it to district branches run by district agents or managers (the two titles were often used interchangeably). Each district branch acted as the main wholesale store for a region. Branches were typically located in highly populated coastal cities or in towns situated near busy transportation links. For the UAC these originally included branches in the cities of Aboso, Accra, Bekwai, Cape Coast, Koforidua, Konongo, Kumasi, Nkawkaw, Nsawam, Obuasi, Saltpond, Sekondi, Suhum, and Tarkwa.[36] At each district branch goods were further divided and were sent either to company-owned retail stores or sold to company credit customers. District branches responsible for overseeing larger regions, like the one at Kumasi, also had to supply various sub-branches. Both company credit customers and retail storekeepers then sold to three constituencies: independent storekeepers, petty traders, and individual consumers (meaning anyone who bought an item for personal consumption rather than to resell it). The petty traders and independent storekeepers, in turn, sold their goods to the same constituency of "end-use" consumers.[37]

While branches located in coastal towns typically experienced a steady flow of customers, the pace of business at inland branches was dominated by the cocoa-growing season. Because the main cocoa harvest marketed from mid-October to mid-February, sales of goods peaked between October and December; the number of staff members thus fluctuated depending on a branch's location and the time of year. In a detailed account of daily tasks and staff relations in a "typical cocoa town," a European agent employed by John Holt & Company listed a total of nine permanent or salaried staff, as well as a number of other nonsalaried workers. Salaried staff positions included a bookkeeper, a main shop clerk, a wholesale shopkeeper, a cashier, a debt note clerk, an assistant debt note clerk, a statistics clerk, a truck driver, and a typist. The agent also included two salaried laborers who assisted staff with various tasks and errands and unloaded and unpacked crates of merchandise when they arrived. These laborers were also responsible for checking for breakage and theft and rounding up additional workers when big shipments came in. Nonsalaried staff included other people like the wholesale keeper's apprentice (who was often a relative) and the truck driver's partner. Based on other reports, salaried staff could also include a day and night watchman and a few salesmen attached to the branch; these sales positions were often filled temporarily by existing African clerks, during the slow selling months, or by others, like young men from Greece, recruited specifically for this purpose. The main tasks of salesmen included attracting new credit customers, converting those who worked for competitors, and promoting the use and sale of new products.

All district branches, and thus all district agents, were under the administration of a general manager in the firm's main office, typically located in Accra.[38] The general manager was responsible for overseeing operations throughout the entire colony and directly answered to a firms' board of directors, who were based at its headquarters abroad. A district agent was charged with overseeing all wholesale activities, managing the company-owned retail stores, stocktaking, and debt collection. In almost all cases district agent and other supervisory positions were held by European men; it was not until the 1930s that these managerial types of jobs were opened to a selected few Africans, and even then transition was slow and varied from firm to firm.[39] Both Europeans and Africans filled staff or clerk positions, but this depended on a branch's location. The UAC used *clerk* as an umbrella term that could include a bookkeeper, a cashier, a typist, and anyone in charge of debit notes and credit accounts. Monthly salaries were varied based on a pay grade or a company's compensation system based on a worker's experience, performance evaluations, and length of service. Company-owned retail stores also followed a hierarchy based on race. One European storekeeper and a few African assistants usually ran the stores in larger towns, while firms entrusted African storekeepers to oversee entire stores in smaller towns, though—unlike European staff members—most African staff members, including clerks, had to be secured by a bond. The UTC, for instance, issued contracts that required Africans holding positions "where there was a possibility of theft and fraud" to pay a cash deposit as a form of security or insurance. Even though they did not receive salaries, company credit customers were also required to provide a deposit before being issued a company passbook, a paper book used to record transactions on a deposit account. The terms of these agreements varied considerably, and as I will show in chapter 2, both company storekeepers and credit customers actively evaded oversight by European agents.

The primary sites of contact between European staff and African staff and customers were district branches (wholesale stores) and company-owned retail stores. Upon entering a typical early twentieth-century wholesale or retail store, contemporary observers would immediately be struck by the organization, the variety of goods on display, and the heavy wooden counter that separated the customer from the storekeeper and his assistants (fig. 1.2). With few exceptions, most goods were kept behind the counter and sold for set prices that could not be negotiated. Almost any and every type of commodity could be bought in these stores. Felt hats, metal pots and buckets, biscuits, oil lamps, a variety of liquor and tinned provisions, cloth, canvas shoes and leather boots, trunks, and umbrellas were stacked high on shelves behind the storekeeper. Bicycles, buckets, and lanterns hung from hooks attached to beams or railings that crisscrossed the ceiling. More expensive items including watches, sewing machines, drugs, perfumes, and silk headscarves were displayed in locked glass cases. How a storekeeper displayed an item was often more important than the item itself; glass protected an item from dust and dirt, but also added to the overall prestige of a commodity and the store that sold it.[40] In his urgent request for a "huge vitrine," for instance, a UTC agent at Akuse reported to the head office that items like "shirts, pajamas and trousers are only bought when they are properly displayed"—that is, behind glass.[41] Except for a cash register or the storekeeper's credit account book, store counters were to be kept bare. To create even more of a barrier between buyer and seller, some firms installed tall metal gates that sat on top of sales counters. These partitions were used to prevent theft, but also to create a certain type of commercial order that made distinctions between the role of the storekeeper and that of the customer.

FIGURE 1.2. Interior of provision store, Accra, May 1907. Reproduced with kind permission of Unilever from the original at the Unilever Archives, UAC/1/11/9/10/17.

Most district branches, and some larger retail stores, were also places of residence: the first floor consisted of the warehouse, store, and offices, and the second floor was typically reserved for living quarters. While the district agent and senior staff could occupy a private corner of the building or live off-site in a bungalow (usually in the European part of town), junior staff shared accommodations. More than just places of business, district branches were often where European staff slept, ate, and socialized, though all the domestic labor, including cooking, cleaning, and grounds keeping, was done by African staff. In some cases a sole European staff member was assigned to an "outstation"—a sub-branch or store located outside the major towns and cities; miles away from the coast, he often lived alone.

One of the major differences between this group of European men who filled agent and staff positions and managed the operations of district branches and stores, versus those who came before them, was the amount of time spent in the Gold Coast. In striking contrast to the past generations of European men who stayed for long periods of time—some who even settled permanently in coastal towns, married African women, and raised children—this newer group worked on short, renewable, two-year contracts.[42] It was commonly held that two years was the minimum time required for "a man to get used to his job."[43] Indeed, some men did stay on twenty to thirty uninterrupted years, without periodic leaves to Europe, and they built long careers, but by the early twentieth century these Old Coasters, as they were known, would grow to be the exception. Besides senior management, who presumably served multiple contracts working their way up to such positions, most European staff were unmarried men in their early twenties. UAC directors preferred men around the age of twenty-two and while they allowed youth "who appeared to have a matured physique and mentality at an earlier age," they refused to hire men over the age of twenty-six.[44] Initially, firms did not generally allow staff to bring their wives or families from Europe, but with special permission, European wives of staff often worked alongside their husbands. Some even gained "manageress" titles and kept stores in their husbands' absence or independently. This, was not common practice however, as most men sent to the Gold Coast were young and single.

By the time this new generation of men entered the commercial scene, images of Africa as wild, dangerous, and primitive were well established. The first internationally circulated commercial guide, the *Red Book of West Africa* (1920), echoed nineteenth-century pseudoscientific racist tropes that upheld ideals of white supremacy and were used to justify European imperial expansion. Belief in the "white man's burden," the idea that it was the moral duty of white men to civilize and rule black and brown people, was also upheld in European commercial circles. Since the nineteenth century, European thinkers and economists positioned the consumption of goods as a key attribute of a "civilized" society. Lack of this desire in Africa, Asia, and Latin America, they argued, was a sign of these societies as primitive and backward.[45] Employees of predecessor firms, like F. & A. Swanzy, for instance, were celebrated in Europe as "white pioneers" who "laid the foundations of civilization" through commerce. According to the *Red Book*, it was commercial men—not explorers, travelers, or missionaries—who had tamed "one of the most appalling territories in the world," described in detail as the "headquarters of the slave trade, where death in innumerable ways menaced the white man, and fierce tribes exemplified the lowest forms of savagery and horror indescribable."[46] Such images not only bolstered imperial expansion but positioned the existence of European enterprise and its control over African markets as self-evident. This was the discourse imparted to European commercial men arriving in Africa to work for large firms, and many of these men adopted imperial rhetoric to describe and make sense of their experiences.[47] But as we shall see, profit making in the Gold Coast merchandise business required other types of myths and stories.

CONSTRUCTING A COMMERCIAL BATTLEFIELD

In his impressive 832-page history of merchant capital in West Africa, historian D. K. Fieldhouse characterizes the West African economy, prior to 1939, as a "commercial jungle." Because it was geared to the international commodity market, which was highly speculative, Fieldhouse argues that "its domestic market fluctuated far more erratically than that of industrialized countries."[48] The initial absence of trade barriers also led to market crowding and intense competition among British, French, German, Swiss, and occasionally US companies. His description of West Africa as a wild and dangerous place, economically speaking, further captures the era of acquisitions and company mergers after the First World War. According to Fieldhouse, economic conditions in West Africa resembled Thomas Hobbes's definition of the state of nature: "the life of most firms proved to be solitary, poor, nasty, brutish, and short."[49] It is unclear if Fieldhouse's analysis of the West African market as a "jungle" comes from his own perceptions or was gleaned from his research in corporate archives, mainly those of the UAC; regardless, the imperialist connotations of his language are striking.

Among European directors, agents, and staff of foreign firms, the Gold Coast market was relentlessly represented as a place of uncertainty, opposition, and conflict. At their extreme, the firms' records and correspondence compared doing business in Africa to going to war, not unlike the *African Mail* editorial that opened this chapter. Especially during times of heightened competition, firms' employees likened the African market to a battlefield, a place to attack and conquer; directors and general managers equated their European staff with troops in combat.[50] War rhetoric was used to encourage district agents to fight like soldiers on the firm's behalf and thus inspire a sense of duty and allegiance to the firm.[51] Less clear is where this war imagery situated Africans; sometimes they seem to be considered subjects—far from equal, but hopefully loyal—in a larger fight between competing firms, and at other times they are implied as potential enemies or as prizes to be "won."[52]

Battlefield and market comparisons further constructed the Gold Coast itself as a place of danger, fear, and disease. Descriptions of physical exhaustion and poor health are constant in correspondence between district branches and headquarters. In a 1923 letter, an agent at Saltpond went as far as to describe the Gold Coast as the "land of death" and European employees as its "victims."[53] While malaria, yellow fever, and other illnesses did affect a number of staff in the years before the regular use of quinine (around 1906), the idea that doing business in West Africa was dangerous, and could literally kill, was constructed and reinforced through letters from younger staff long after.[54] For instance, the UTC published death tolls among its staff in official company histories meant for European readership.[55] The image of Africa as the "White Man's Grave," which referred to the high mortality rates of early white missionaries and colonists, was evoked frequently to explain poor business conditions and to request a leave back to Europe.[56] As other scholars have demonstrated, narratives that dramatized the physical vulnerability of Europeans in the colonies were not limited to Africa. A similar phenomenon in nostalgic narratives about the British-ruled Raj also constructed India as a place of death.[57] While it is difficult to measure the extent to which fears about life in the tropics affected firms' staff physically and mentally, the fact that employees wrote about such concerns with regularity in their letters home suggests they either believed sincerely in such dangers or had a stake in continuing this vision of the land around them.[58]

If West Africa was figured as a place of potential death and the market as a place of combat, how did these representations influence day-to-day business relations? Within European business circles there was widespread suspicion of Africans in general, and these attitudes manifested themselves in firms' policies. Strict credit terms, for example, were premised on the idea that Africans were inherently dishonest; in its 1909 instruction manual the BMTC advised its agents that credit to Africans was to be given sparingly, citing "the Negro's unreliable character and his natural bent for the untruth and fraud." According to the manual, agents were to exercise caution in all business dealings with Africans; "bad characteristics" including carelessness, deceit, incompetence, and immorality were named as prime examples.[59] Not much had changed in these attitudes thirty years later. In a 1936 report to one of the UAC's managing directors, D. D. Pitcher advised agents to more carefully control and manage the issuing of credit. The accumulation of large debts was due in part to lack of self-restraint and ease of temptation. Rather than account for poor economic conditions or call into question the firms rigid credit terms, Pitcher blamed the accumulation of large debts on "the African" who "so invariably cannot resist."[60] These accusations, produced three decades apart, reveal the persistence of such beliefs among firms—particularly in crafting guidelines for their European staff.

This general mistrust of Africans was echoed by branch agents, especially in letters to their superiors concerning the hiring and supervising of African staff. In response to queries about his inability to find an African storekeeper, one UTC agent from Akuse complained that identifying good Africans in his district required time and patience because most were "not honest."[61] He therefore explained the need to scrupulously evaluate the character, outlook, background, and family of potential candidates. By deploying familiar tropes about Africans as fundamentally suspect, the Akuse agent was able to avoid accountability, if only temporarily, for what may have been his own ineptitude in recruiting and retaining local staff. The agent's fear of being terminated was a legitimate concern; other firms, like GBO, considered similar instances as grounds for dismissal. For example, in a series of letters concerning a European agent at Tarkwa, his superiors concluded that the agent's failure to "bring African storekeepers into line" called for his replacement by "a much stronger type of man."[62] The cumulative effect of all of these laments, instructions, and insinuations was to pathologize the behavior of Africans. As with endless other instances of colonial thinking, these Europeans rarely seemed to acknowledge that they were making vast generalizations about an entire country's people, often on the basis of a few brief encounters.[63]

Such attitudes further shaped the practice of shopkeeping. Product display and surveillance policies were of particular concern. While the UTC reminded its European storekeepers in a 1939 instruction manual to "never forget that the black trader, the modest worker or the small bushman in front of the counter are all his customers bringing in earnings/income," the firm also emphasized the need to maintain "strict control" of the staff and of African customers inside a store. The manual is worth quoting at length:

> The European shopkeeper is not allowed to leave the shop without calling another European as a replacement . . . blind corners in the shop have to be eliminated because black employees or customers could get into mischief. We need to pay attention that there are no goods piled up that would impede the view over the store. The supervision of the black staff is [also] very important. This strict control is necessary because of these people's tendency towards unjust good. . . . It is important never to turn against the counter and to always watch closely so that no goods disappear whilst helping customers.[64]

Even though firms later noted that most theft was by customers, not employees, and occurred at the sales counter, it was not uncommon for European agents and storekeepers to search African employees' pockets at the end of each day. In some instances, African staff were required to walk by supervisors with "reversed pockets" after every shift before heading home. African clerks and shop assistants were also forbidden from handling a customer's money and from handing over the items purchased. Such guidelines suggested that tills or cash registers were to be operated by Europeans only. African staff that acted otherwise were subject to fines or dismissal. Thus, the organization of company-owned stores was premised on the understanding that African staff and shoppers were inherently suspect, and the daily work of transactions with shoppers and relations with staff was saturated in racial mistrust. With such constant reminders that European staff must proceed with caution, shopkeeping entailed more than just selling goods; firms also constructed it as a defensive position.

Relations with African women, both professional and personal, were also a topic of official policy, and the most vivid demonstration of firms' attempts to enforce racial separation between their white staff and local communities. As a former UTC employee hired in the 1960s, Arthur Wettstein explains that the distance between African and European employees was actively promoted by the UTC's "policy of prudence." He remembers, "It was not without purpose that prior to departure from the Head Office in Basel a voluminous document on do's and don'ts was handed to every candidate, which among other prominent rules contained a prohibition of intense contact with African women on threat of dismissal."[65] Such efforts to restrict intimate relations between Europeans and Africans, particularly African women, confirms that company employees were not adhering to the rules.[66] As former SAT manager Hans Rudolf Roth recalled, many of his coworkers in Kumasi had African girlfriends, including his supervisor who lived in town with his Swiss wife.

While the "intense contact" rule did not prevent sexual relationships, it did deter many European employees from legally marrying their African girlfriends and from fulfilling obligations to children from these relationships.[67] Efforts to enforce rules on staffs' private and sexual lives reveal the measures firms undertook to police racial boundaries in the name of commerce. Such top-down policies suggest that company leaders believed interracial unions—even when their relationships were publicly recognized and legitimated through marriage—could threaten a staff members' loyalty, could tarnish a firm's reputation, and were bad for business overall.

Another important aspect of company policy, and another effort to maintain divisions, was the expectation that European employees were there to set an example for Africans. For instance, Wettstein remembers, "We often heard that 'we are a Christian enterprise' and were obviously expected to act accordingly in private and business life."[68] Based on notions that African men and women lacked the capacity to conduct business without European guidance, the UTC claimed that, without its leadership, business would "end in chaos."[69] Modeling proper behavior could mean everything from upholding company policies to demonstrating cleanliness and proper sartorial practices.[70] A 1931 circular to all UTC district agents justified the importance of these tasks as necessary to "encourage further reflection, and initiative and that also teaches independence."[71] For the UTC, upholding Christian values, hard work, self-discipline, and frugality through moral education defined commercial relations with Africans long after its formal ties with the BMS were severed. As Stephan Miescher has shown, Basel missionaries expected converts to live according to the *Gemeindeordnung*, a set of rules that intervened in every aspect of daily life including gender relations, living arrangements, and time management and "made conscious efforts to reshape African personhood."[72] Although less overtly religious, the UAC also considered itself a model for proper selling, through a responsibility for upholding retail standards and teaching Africans the correct way to do business. Corporate policy continued to position commerce as a civilizing force and the market as a space that held transformative power. It is no accident that African men and women would grow increasingly suspicious of its operation and effects.

Not all Africans were considered equally dishonest or untrustworthy. Correspondence with headquarters back in Europe reveals an ongoing quest by agents for good and truthful staff—particularly shopkeepers. In the process, firms created ethnic hierarchies based on what groups proved easiest to manage. According to the UTC, the Kwawu were considered the most dependable.[73] Originally itinerant traders from a region about one hundred miles from the coast (on Asante's eastern border), the Kwawu had by the 1920s settled in prosperous cocoa towns and also based themselves, often temporarily, in commercial cities along the coast.[74] In a 1927 general report the UTC agent at Saltpond described good storekeepers in the Fante districts, located along the coast, as "rare as gold!"[75] Three years later, another agent in Saltpond offered his own reasoning to explain the storekeeper shortage. He claimed that Fantes did not understand proper store management or the importance of cleanliness. "These people are very stubborn," he argued, "which is not the case with the Kwahus or Asante."[76] In an earlier, private letter an agent in Kumasi reported just the opposite, however, asserting that the Asante made bad storekeepers because they were "obsessed with money and profit" and his preference was for "Fante people."[77] Through the hiring process, agents evoked and reinforced ethnic stereotypes, somewhat arbitrarily, to describe and categorize African ability. Church membership was also used to categorize potential hires, and agents made sharp distinctions between Africans belonging to the various missionary societies. Certainly the UTC preferred to hire Christian converts associated with the Basel Mission, but agents also considered those who were part of the Wesleyan Church acceptable and indeed much preferred over Catholics.[78]

UAC employees' relations with Greek staff were also a point of contention. In 1933, the company began recruiting employees from poor areas of Greece to fill what they described as the "intermediate positions between Europeans and African staff" similar to those of Lebanese businessmen.[79] Jobs for Greeks, however, were specially classified as "salaried salesmen" positions. While Greeks were never labeled as untrustworthy or dishonest, as African staff were, company directors argued that "differences in background, racial characteristics, and temperament" made them a problem for senior management.[80] Such differences were used to explain difficulties with Greek staff and to instruct agents on how best to manage them. That Greek staff were considered lower class, and not white, contributed to what company directors described as their "excitable and sensitive" character.[81] Conflicts with management may have instead stemmed from frustration and anger felt by Greek staff who saw themselves as equal to and just as capable as their British employers or who sought distance from any association with those Lebanese and Africans who also held "intermediate positions."

It should be noted that the character of non-Africans, including other Europeans, was also a topic of concern among company executives and management. Responding to a 1928 letter of inquiry into an incident that occurred at his previous post, a UTC agent at Nkawkaw blamed problems associated with his twenty-nine-year-old Swiss wife's smoking, drinking, and late nights out on her interactions with British women whom he defined as "bad friends." He explained to the regional office that "in general British women are not the right friends for our women."[82] The statement suggests that his wife's nightly antics, details that were never fully disclosed, may have been considered grounds for termination. He begged, "I swear that the things that happened at Saltpond will not happen here. . . . You can trust me, I will live an orderly family life based on Christian norms with my wife." According to the agent, the "British ladies" in question had disrupted his Swiss wife's moral compass. The agent's inability to manage his wife's behavior must have been amusing to the African staff, but most of all it called into question his capacity to manage a district branch and his role as an authority figure. Certainly the head office was concerned with upholding the firm's reputation, but the poor behavior of the agent's wife had larger implications. It troubled notions about white superiority and the sanctity of white womanhood—ideas on which the UTC's business, and colonial race relations more broadly, rested.

As is recorded in correspondence between headquarters in Europe, main offices, and district branches, "doing business" not only drew on preexisting attitudes about Africa and Africans but was itself an act of knowledge production. European agents and staff in the Gold Coast constructed racial hierarchies and cultural differences between themselves and African staff and customers through their daily work. Yet they also had to contend with corporate policies handed down by headquarters. These directives, printed in staff manuals and instructional guides, were just as much about the imaginings and fears projected by senior management back in Europe. Moreover, as Ann Stoler reminds us, racist ideology and a preoccupation with white prestige were not only statements about Africans but also directives aimed at "dissenting European underlings" whose behavior had the potential to threaten the image of white superiority.[83] Categories based on race, class, and ethnicity were never clear cut, and the persistence of company policies to enforce them suggests that staff may have found prescribed boundaries either too burdensome or too difficult to uphold. After all, success in the merchandise business often meant deferring to African knowledge about the market, a reality that often made top-down company directives pointless—or simply not profitable. This was one of the major reasons for the lack of consistency between and among district branches and the inability of firms to fully control the market terms.

RECONCILING POLICY AND PRACTICE

Discrepancies between policy and practice repeatedly reveal the difficulties in policing boundaries—especially those prescribed by superiors who were hundreds of miles away—as well as contradictions in the racial logic that cast Africans as inferior and in need of guidance. For some European employees, their supervisors' expectations to be morally superior and more knowledgeable about business proved difficult to uphold and created isolation—and, consequently, additional stress. In letters to their superiors, agents often described everyday life at district branches in the 1920s and 1930s as lonely, depressing, and friendless.[84] One UTC agent wrote, "Nkoko [*sic*] is a completely different region than Saltpond. With the exception of one Swiss I did not cultivate any friends and it will remain this way in the future." While the letter describes differences between doing business in Nkawkaw versus Saltpond, the agent's inability to find friends in both towns was consistent. Meaningful friendships and relationships were defined by those made with other Europeans, not Africans. This social distance, which contributed to agents' loneliness and isolation, was shaped by prior assumptions about racial difference and a company culture that promoted and attempted to enforce such attitudes.

Yet the organization of district branches and retail stores demanded that Europeans and Africans—staff and customers alike—work in intimate quarters. Wholesale and retail stores were often quite small, and always crowded (fig. 1.3). Typically, the area behind the counter had to accommodate all the goods for sale as well as the storekeeper and his assistants. Depending on where the store was located, around four to eight people could be working behind the counter at once, fetching items, operating the register, recording purchases in account books, and attending to customers. European and African staff also traveled together on stocktaking and debt collection trips at least every two months.[85] These trips lasted anywhere from one to three days and often required overnight stays. A former SAT employee described visiting a total of thirty stores in one month, the farthest being 150 miles away from the district branch. This unavoidable closeness of employees is a primary reason why early handbooks prescribing the dos and don'ts of acceptable behavior were so detailed. The interactions that happened every day offered abundant instances where "common sense rubrics of racial differentiation failed to work" and also made clear how dependent European management was on African staff.[86] While some European agents attempted to strictly abide by company policies—sometimes at the expense of their mental health, as illustrated by the Saltpond agent above—others abandoned rules

FIGURE 1.3. Interior of provision store, Sekondi, ca. 1912. Reproduced with kind permission of Unilever from the original at the Unilever Archives, UAC11/11/9/12/44.

altogether. A look at day-to-day encounters reveals this variation and shows how other factors like individual personalities and bonds forged between staff members could shape business operations in unpredictable and unintended ways.

Standardization of corporate policy in order to maximize profits was a goal for all firms operating on the coast. Creating consistency across district branches and retail stores was especially important during the era of acquisitions, when firms like the UAC grew in size and expanded their operations. Standardizing selling practices was the primary method firms used to centralize their business in hopes of cutting costs and increasing efficiency. But many corporate policies, such as those relating to passbooks, debt collection, and relations with African staff, proved to be far too rigid to implement on the ground. As a 1943 colonial commission of inquiry would report, most district branches had been operating as "self-contained units for decades," with each "estimating its own requirements, and placing its own orders, and enforcing policy haphazardly."[87] Another problem was the system of commodity distribution. While firms tried to ensure that all district branches were given equal amounts of goods and sold to customers at comparable prices, this was not always the case. In other words, what happened once goods arrived at branches often depended on the personal relationships among agents, their African staff (including clerks, salesmen, and storekeepers), and credit customers. Storekeepers often reserved choice goods for favored customers, agents reduced set prices to attract more sales, and African staff supplied credit customers with goods beyond the value of their credit limits and then split the profits. A 1930 report on internal organization by the UTC's general manager further confirmed that the autonomy of district offices was not only a UAC problem. "Everybody acts according to his own opinion and head," he argued. "We need to have stronger organization."[88]

Poor coordination across a company's various branches and internal competition within firms also made it difficult to implement and standardize policy. For instance, responding to instructions from the UTC's general manager to terminate passbooks in the flour and sugar trade, the agent in Nkawkaw angrily wrote, "I have already stopped all the passbooks without exception . . . whatever is decided though needs to be carried out everywhere the same . . . we *need* a clear uniform system."[89] Some agents may have also intentionally ignored the policy. After all, the elimination of passbooks—a system that had rested on maintaining good relations with African retailers and was facilitated by credit—was commercial self-sabotage. A refusal to follow orders suggests that on occasion agents considered loyalty to customers in their district (supplying them with necessary goods on credit) as more important than complying with company rules or creating a united front with their European colleagues. Further exposing the extent of such disorganization and the lack of systematic consistency, another UTC agent at Kumasi notified head offices of mutual price undercutting and competition among stores within the UTC and not just with outside competitors.[90] Similar offenses were recorded elsewhere by the UAC. After his 1929 inspection of more than thirty stores located in and around Kumasi, D. D. Pitcher reported, "In their anxiety to obtain maximum turnover, the Agents are inclined to allow internal competition to creep in."[91] Agents employed by the same firms, as well as those subject to the same agreed-upon selling prices, frequently sold at lower rates, willfully violating minimum price agreements to attract more sales.

The experiences of individual agents also contributed to a lack of consistency. District agents living near and working closely with African staff and customers did not always agree with the main office in Accra, the head office abroad, or even with each other on best policy. On the topic of the UTC's inability to find "good African storekeepers," some agents believed that factors like low pay and "miserable conditions" also came into play.[92] One agent blamed constant turnover not on African unreliability but on the better wages offered by the other companies. UTC storekeepers often quit to work for other firms like GBO, Holt, and the UAC, all of which were known to pay higher wages.[93] Another agent revealed that "good Africans" preferred a clerk position over that of storekeeper, which was considered a risky job.[94] While agents may not have outwardly disputed the racial ideologies that categorized African storekeepers as suspicious, the fact that they provided alternative reasoning for the difficulty of identifying a stable African workforce challenged blanket assumptions that all Africans should not be trusted. It also shows how attitudes toward African staff differed among agents. Thus operations at district branches varied depending on the agent in charge and his ability to comply.

The unpublished memoir of long-term UTC employee Christian Spoerri, who began his career in 1915, further demonstrates these inconsistencies and the tensions between corporate policy and everyday practices: "None of us white people in the wholesale was more informed than Martin Sowah, our head wholesale clerk. He was an all-around product expert and I was learning a lot from him. At this point I have to emphasize that I was never embarrassed to learn from an African."[95] It is unclear whether Spoerri ever expressed this attitude while officially employed by the UTC or whether he recognized his reliance on Sowah only in retrospect. In this instance, however, we see how Spoerri's trust in Sowah's expertise illustrates a possibility—namely, that the assumed power relationship between European agents and their African staff could be temporarily inverted. It is important to note that Spoerri's superiors distinguished him from other agents, describing his "abrupt and strong" attitude in a private letter, a distinction that suggests that his views were atypical.[96] Spoerri's statement that he was never embarrassed to learn from Africans suggests that other agents definitely were.

Other examples of European dependence on African staff emerged within written recommendations to retain particular African staff members. Sometimes these types of letters came from an agent's supervisors, who often knew more about a branch's operations than did a newly arrived agent. In a 1938 letter, a European agent at Hohoe was warned against his plans to fire the branch's African clerk; his superiors explained, "It is very useful to have at least one native at the trading post. . . . A native knows the procedures, knows everything about the debtors, and if he is a good accountant, like Honue whom you can trust . . . then he can definitely overlook some of his flaws. . . . We think Honue is such a man and thus caution you against dismissing him lightly."[97] They concluded by defending Honue's intelligence and prudence against the young agent's accusations of Honue's inadequacy. The agent was also instructed that Honue be allowed to operate the till, a job that was typically forbidden for African staff.

Even so, the recording of these instances was not common; my review of hundreds of pages of correspondence between directors, general managers, and agents resulted in only a dozen such examples.[98] For the most part, the names of African staff mainly appear in the form of complaints; most frequent were charges of fraud, embezzlement, price gouging, missing goods, and faking numbers in account books. The names of those who had been fired and blacklisted from firms and those who had racked up outrageous amounts of debt were also included.

We can see here how vacillations in attitudes among European agents affected how corporate policy was implemented and the extent to which it was enforced. Conflicting views about African staff existed, and they were surely affected by factors like an agent's personal temperament, selling experience, sense of self-importance, emotional maturity, and years of service to the firm. The same agent could complain about a certain African staff member one day and praise another the very next. There were also cases of firing and rehiring the same African staff member over the course of a few months. Such was the relationship between the UTC Cape Coast agent and his storekeeper Appiah Elmina. It is unclear whether the agent felt he had made a mistake or was ordered to rehire Elmina, but his superiors accepted his rehire request, noting that "we are glad you looked for him and gave him back his employment."[99]

The recognition of African initiative by individual Europeans should not be confused with an absence of racist thinking overall; notions about Africans as unreliable and suspicious were rampant, especially during moments of heightened competition between firms. While not always overt, these ideas about white superiority emerged in subtle ways. For instance, in hopes of striking a chord with his superiors and forcing them to reconsider their pricing policy, one "European underling" appealed to an us-versus-them worldview to contest directives from above. First he accused the UAC of trying to destroy all other companies by stealing customers and cutting prices; he was equally upset that African retailers profited from competitive conditions. Even more alarming, he exclaimed, was that "they make fun of the naïve European."[100] While loss of profit is cited as an issue, the agent was also upset because increased market competition had jeopardized his position as "the European," which bestowed him with authority in his district based on whiteness. Although concerned with losing sales, the agent was just as upset that he had become the butt of African jokes. In explaining how he was made to look foolish and incompetent by African staff and customers, he hoped to gain sympathy from his European superiors.

While European management and employees' perceptions of Africa as wild and dangerous and Africans as fundamentally inferior shaped the development and structure of consumer markets, African imaginings of European firms also contributed to the terms of exchange. The ways in which firms, their practices, and their products were integrated into local cosmologies offer important insight into the key concerns and anxieties about the expansion of foreign capital and consumerism. Here I focus solely on the UAC, the largest firm on the Gold Coast and the second largest employer of African labor after the colonial government. Whereas European managers and staff perceived African markets as battlefields, African staff and customers perceived the firm's efforts at expansion as invasive and potentially dangerous.

Many popular perceptions of the UAC circulated as humor. Former UAC manager William Atta Krofah, who began as a typist in 1956, remembers that company employees had long joked that the letters *U-A-C* stood for "Until Africa Collapses." He recalls, "[It] means that you can see UAC everywhere in Africa; their presence was so interwoven . . . that they will not disengage themselves until Africa no longer exists. . . . They were everywhere, so you may have a main sales depot, let's say in Swedru, but the credit customer would be somewhere in the hamlet . . . they had a UAC [sign]board there so you would see UAC in every little village through trading."[101] Although "Until Africa Collapses" may have struck some company employees as funny, for others—especially smaller independent retailers who competed for consumers—the UAC's omnipresence was no laughing matter. Achille Mbembe's argument that words used for fun or mockery are "active statements about the human condition" holds true in the case of the UAC;[102] "Until Africa Collapses" reflected not only anxieties about the UAC's commercial power but also its ability to impose itself on everyday life in "every little village." Krofah's statement hints at a capitalism that was ubiquitous across the landscape, and in turn it articulates a perception—that capitalism had an insatiable appetite. This critique was not limited to the UAC's activities in Ghana. Kwesi Akumenya Cato, who joined the firm as one of the first African manager trainees in 1943, remembers that the UAC was "firmly entrenched" in all of Africa, "not only Ghana [but] Nigeria, even Congo Brazzaville."[103] Depictions of the UAC's stronghold over the continent, combined with its refusal to "disengage," suggest that its practices were both aggressive and invasive.[104]

Another well-known idiom compared the power of the UAC to the vitality of Ghana itself. As Jutus Nii Kpako Allotey, a former Unilever employee, explains, "UAC is Ghana, Ghana is UAC . . . we grew up to know that slogan. All because, from the word go, UAC is patronized in all aspects of life in Ghana . . . so without UAC no Ghana, and without Ghana no UAC."[105] Saying "UAC is Ghana" establishes a dependent relationship—Ghana's very existence rested on the UAC's continued presence—and thus implies that the interests of the state were identical to those of the firm. Indeed, this was the exact correlation that Gold Coast nationalists and those participating in the 1948 boycotts made to condemn the relationship between foreign firms and the colonial state. But an alternative reading that focuses on the "Ghana is UAC" part of the idiom also suggests awareness among Ghanaians that the firm's existence also depended on them. Such a proposition was true; the UAC could not have survived in Ghana without its local staff and loyal customers. Even so, this mutual dependency was rarely on equal terms.

Discussions among African staff further reflected the popular belief that the UAC possessed some sort of supernatural or otherworldly power. According to both Krofah and another former employee, Sadiku Musah, several people equated UAC activities with witchcraft.[106] "UAC was literally likened to be a witch," Krofah recalls. "You know, everything that happened under the sun, UAC was involved in it. And it could only be witchcraft that could do that. So you refer to some bad omen that this was UAC inspired . . . meaning that it was UAC witchcraft that has caused it."[107] For believers, witchcraft represented an omnipresence of spiritual forces that individuals could garner for either good or evil. That the UAC was characterized as a witch who could control the course of events, and that the firm's presence was considered a bad omen or a sign of something terrible to come, provides a larger critique (and prediction) about the UAC's practices and the infiltration of foreign capital more broadly. The firm itself was imbued with transformative power, and its activities were potentially destructive if left unchecked. The extensive literature on witchcraft and modernity in African studies views witchcraft accusations as a manifestation of social uncertainties and expressions of fear and vulnerability.[108] Given the firm's historical association with witchcraft, at the time of Ghana's independence Kwame Nkrumah would refer to the UAC and its parent company Unilever as "the devil we know."[109] While justifying to the Ghanaian public his decision to continue business with the UAC rather than with newer, less familiar, firms, Nkrumah must have also been inspired by this notion of the firm as a powerful witch.

Public accusations of witchcraft, or of the use of juju, bad magic, or bad medicine, were also a way to criticize what felt like improper accumulation and use of wealth. Social norms held the rich responsible for the "maintenance and continuity of society." Hoarding money and amassing large amounts of individual wealth was (and is today) treated with suspicion in Ghana. From gift-giving to funding community projects, social norms required that the rich legitimize their wealth by redistributing it. The idea that the UAC failed to fulfill these obligations is further illustrated in another popular name given to the firm. Edward Akurang Dankwa, the son of a UAC storekeeper who operated three stores in and around Agona Swedru, remembers that his father called the UAC the "United Adufudee Pa Company."[110] *Adufudee pa* is a term used to refer to a person who wants things very cheaply or to someone who is stingy. African staff and customers sometimes likened the UAC to a "cheapskate" or a "freeloader" who tried to avoid paying its fair share of costs or expenses.[111] This accusation could apply in various contexts; among storekeepers the UAC's miserly ways might be attributed to its terms of hiring or its refusal to support the additional costs associated with storekeeping. Funds for transportation, and beer and liquor licenses, as well as extra money to pay a watchman or extra assistants, were some areas up for dispute.[112] More broadly, the firm as *adufudee* hinted at another widespread critique about how the UAC used its profits—specifically, that the firm took its profits back to Europe rather than reinvesting in the local economy. The company's ability to accumulate huge profits without redistribution was a major factor in shaping its negative reputation.

In addition to reflecting moral anxieties about the circulation of wealth, witchcraft accusations were a means to reassert older patriarchal forms of authority.[113] For instance, people living in larger coastal cities used the abbreviation UAC as a nickname for prostitutes, particularly older ones known for amassing large amounts of independent wealth.[114] As Emmanuel Akyeampong argues, throughout the 1930s and 1940s the connections between accumulation, consumption, and witchcraft came to a head in debates about urban prostitution. Of most concern was the fact that these women accumulated wealth solely for themselves, outside the prescribed boundaries of marriage and kinship, and it was a wealth that could be spent on conspicuous consumption. The association also demonstrates that the UAC was also considered as acting outside proper boundaries—accumulating wealth in a way that did not support the foundational structures of society. What's more, the comparison suggests that capitalism itself could be defined as antisocial behavior, dangerously elevating individual desires over the collective good and leading to isolation and disconnection.

Since popular perceptions linked UAC business activities to witchcraft, it is no surprise that African consumers would also describe the UAC's merchandise as being tainted with juju. When asked by the UAC why she preferred British goods, Frances Sam, the daughter of a prominent UAC credit customer replied, "there has grown in me, as if by fetish, an inexplainable [*sic*] bias against any goods that are not British, . . . At the age of 24 years now . . . I have imbibed my mother's 'Juju' so much that I prefer British goods to any other."[115] The young woman explained her attraction to imported commodities as akin to being possessed by some otherworldly force. Certainly her attraction to British-made goods over "any other" was due in part to the UAC's dominance in the local economy and its promotion of British-made products. But we also see here a connection to Karl Marx's concept of commodity fetishism—that is, the idea that in capitalist societies people begin to treat commodities as if value existed in the objects themselves rather than in the amount of real labor expended to produce them. Marx argues that such a condition conceals and displaces the actual state of relations between people and in the process alienates producers from their labor.[116] But Sam's recognition of this power, of commodities as fetishes, signifies her awareness that goods are imbued with meanings that do not necessarily reflect their actual use. While she goes on to describe the durability, cheapness, and beauty of British goods, Sam is no dupe; through describing her "bias," she is also naming the very conditions that allow capitalism to operate. She describes her own mother, a longtime UAC credit customer, as having juju powers based on her association with the company.[117] Thus, UAC goods, as well as the company itself, were seen to have had the power to persuade consumers and empty pocketbooks.

As we can see, shifts in the market were not accepted unwittingly or considered completely inevitable. Gold Coast retailers were also suspicious of UAC marketing techniques and saw them as potentially dangerous. Both Nana Oworae and Nana Opare Ameyaw, former UAC store assistants hired in the mid-1950s, viewed UAC selling strategies as deceptive. Both considered the UAC's practice of giving away tokens that could later be exchanged for larger, more expensive prizes as a successful but manipulative advertising tool. Strong disapproval arises when remembering special promotions for items like cigarettes and beer at their store in Berekum. Ameyaw recalls that the UAC "put coins into the tins of cigarettes, so as a man, when you came back from the farm you found ways of buying this tin of cigarette just so you could get these tokens. . . . After a while they took away the tokens and by then people had already become habitual smokers . . . Also, beer was another [thing] that people didn't really like. It was said to be fever inducing. So again they did canvassing with it: if you bought one, two more were added to it for you."[118] Both men believed that UAC promotion strategies influenced consumer choices and introduced lifestyle changes that led to larger cultural shifts in the consumption of harmful products. They also noted that these developments had an adverse effect on African consumers, creating dependency on cigarettes and unhealthy addictions. This predatory marketing offered a cautionary tale: companies like the UAC had the power to seduce consumers into purchasing and using goods, so Ghanaians should be careful not to overindulge or give in to material temptations.[119]

Ranging from jokes to serious allegations, articulations of the UAC reflected popular anxieties about the power of foreign capital and the effects of consumption on everyday life. While Gold Coasters may have poked fun at the company to alleviate the stresses brought on by such a powerful commercial force, such critiques also provided a very serious commentary about modern capitalist relations. Narratives that cast the UAC as an invader, a witch, a freeloader, or a greedy prostitute, as well as understandings of shopping and the purchase of imported goods as a form of possession, also reveal uneasiness about what capitalism does. Here I share the hesitation on the part of Timothy Burke in accepting Marx's analysis in *Capital* wholeheartedly. As Burke notes, Marx's analysis "has engendered an interpretive tradition that sees fetishism as a process, by which 'false needs' are made and 'real' relations concealed by the conscious agency of the ruling class."[120] Although referring specifically to how objects gain meaning, I think Burke's insight can also be applied to the expansion of consumer cultures more broadly. In a colonial context, "real relations" were never fully concealed. Former employees and customers had a sophisticated understanding of the UAC's capacity to manipulate the market and of capitalism as a force that could transform people, places, and beliefs. Of course, the system of capitalism manufactured new social relations and desires but, like the UAC, it had to contend with history or prior meanings about the accumulation of wealth, redistribution, and sociability. These values worked to accommodate, change, and restrict how consumer capitalism functioned.

While it is difficult to measure the extent to which these perceptions (held by everyday consumers and UAC employees alike) directly affected the firm's day-to-day policies, corporate records do express the company's concern about negative public opinion. By 1948, for instance, the UAC's *Pep Talk for New Arrivals* included line-by-line responses for European staff to use if confronted with criticisms from Africans or European staff from other firms.[121] In fact, senior management expected its staff to defend the firm, arguing that fighting "stupid lies and scandal" was "part of [the] job." These anxieties came to a head in the 1950s as the UAC launched a series of goodwill campaigns and funded a number of community building projects throughout the Gold Coast in order to defuse the resentment and tensions evidenced by these oral histories.[122] The Second World War and the period of decolonization changed the terms of the game. As chapter 2 will demonstrate, state intervention and increasing African discontent forced the UAC, and foreign firms in general, to legitimatize their continued presence in the colony.

Firms' early experiences with African staff and consumers shaped the contours of capitalist development on the Gold Coast and were key to guiding the trajectories of both domestic and international consumer markets. Economic and business historians have analyzed the relations between companies and African staff, but research has focused primarily on the period of decolonization, on policies of Africanization in the 1950s, and on the experiences of senior management.[123] Distribution systems and business policies were shaped by long-standing assumptions about race, ability, and development. For firms, racialization—the process by which meanings were ascribed to racial difference—was necessary; that process made business possible. Furthermore, on-the-ground experiences at district branches reveal the boundaries and limitations of such attitudes, poking holes in the logic that cast European firms and staff as commercially superior to their African counterparts.

Discrepancies between policy and practice, as well as the stories of former employees, also reveal the difficulties of upholding racial hierarchies, not to mention the extent to which companies and certain staff members were willing to go in order to police them. Memoirs and correspondence make it clear that European firms depended on African initiative, a reality challenging imperial ideologies that positioned Africans as needing European guidance. Recognizing Africans' superior market knowledge, however, did not erase racist thinking or the notion of white supremacy on which it rested. One major bulwark that perpetuated racist thinking was that large foreign firms still had a tremendous amount of power in representing the African market to the rest of the world. European agents and staff on the ground knew otherwise, and some even openly admitted to learning from and following the directives of their African staff. Yet the inability of Africans to properly participate in modern market developments (due to their "natural bent for the untruth and fraud") was the image that companies painted for audiences at home and around the world. The outbreak of World War II would exacerbate many of these existing tensions, and it would also introduce new pressures resulting from wartime rationing, government restrictions, and increased competition.

Despite these fictions, Africans were not passive recipients of capitalist expansion. The existence of counternarratives reminds us of the far murkier reality on the ground. The extent to which African voices, opinions, and knowledge directly affected corporate policies is impossible to measure, though ideologies about the proper ways that wealth should accumulate and circulate did shape the way that consumer capitalism unfolded throughout the Gold Coast. Cautionary tales about witchcraft and addiction served to protect local communities from the potential dangers of consuming and to remind shoppers that new systems of value were not necessarily superior. We often think of global capitalism as a vast homogenizing force, one that is utterly impersonal and acts on all of us equally. But the juxtaposition of corporate records and oral histories in this chapter shows how capitalism is actually a product of lived experience, shaped by social and cultural concerns that sometimes override and challenge market logic.

2 ∽ "We Cannot Afford to Be Fooled"

African Intermediaries on Shifting Commercial Terrain

> *As a whole the business does not give the satisfaction one should wish, yet we have to be satisfied with our conditions which compare so favourable with those in Europe and elsewhere. . . . In the midst of plenty, far away from the war zone, we still keep rather fit, although the influence of the tropical climate and continuous struggle with the special character of the Africans makes us often weary and nervous.*
>
> —J. Lenggenhager, senior agent, Union Trading Company, October 3, 1941

WHILE THE SECOND WORLD WAR introduced a new set of business challenges, it also heightened tensions between firms and their local intermediaries. As captured in J. Lenggenhager's 1941 letter, work and life for the agent was a "continuous struggle."[1] Yet this was not simply a report about general wartime conditions in the city of Cape Coast. Since most of his duties involved managing the day-to-day operations of the district branch or wholesale, nearly all of Lenggenhager's interactions with "the Africans" were with those men and women who worked for or did business with the Union Trading Company. The Cape Coast agent's description of exhaustion and nervousness reflected his encounters with a large group of commercial intermediaries, including African clerks, company storekeepers, and credit customers on whom he depended for product distribution and feedback about customers in his district. His attitudes must therefore be understood within the context of these relationships and the competing agendas that framed them.

Lenggenhager's position, like that of most European agents or district managers, was a precarious one. His business success depended not only on a combination of humility, flexibility, and administering top-down directives but also rested on his ability to cultivate and maintain close connections to a broad network of "reliable" African intermediaries. While all firms acknowledged intermediaries as necessary to the merchandise side of business, government-imposed price controls and quotas that began during World War II, and an increasingly competitive market that followed immediately after the war, created new pressures and stricter terms on which these relationships had to be negotiated. For foreign firms, trading in the 1940s became a fragile balancing act between complying with new laws and policies handed down by the colonial administration and managing relations with thousands of African intermediaries throughout the colony.

Yet African men and women who worked for and with firms had their own agendas. While these intermediaries obviously helped firms profit, many used their positions to forward their own political and economic interests and secure their own futures. Storekeepers undercut the company by sharing commissions and bonuses with customers; credit customers created alliances that forced firms to reduce prices; and savvy employees used market information as leverage to obtain loans and special privileges. The forty-year career of Isaac A. Ogoe, a United Africa Company (UAC) storekeeper turned manager, and the disagreements among his superiors about retaining him, illustrates the extent to which intermediaries were able to simultaneously bolster and undermine a company. Ogoe used his knowledge of local politics and his connections with prominent merchants, chiefs, and other local authorities to make demands on the UAC and secure material benefits for himself and his immediate and extended family.

Similarly, the activities of credit customers—the UAC's almost all-women sales force—demonstrate how some intermediaries established themselves independently from the firm in ways that altered, and sometimes inverted, the presumed power of colonial capitalism. Many of the credit customers (six thousand strong by 1950) became successful entrepreneurs, building up their own clientele of smaller distributors and using profits to invest in other types of business, including cocoa farming and construction. Credit customers' superior market knowledge and sales skills were a constant source of anxiety and suspicion among European agents and staff, particularly when they affected profit margins, but also because of gendered and racialized notions that figured African women as sneaky and deceptive. During the war the credit customer system, which had for at least eighty years allowed firms to tap into local distribution networks, became a liability. Firms defended themselves against government accusations of unfair selling by arguing that the behavior of intermediaries, especially credit customers and "petty traders," prevented them from fully obtaining accurate statistics about sales and from enforcing new government quotas and price controls.

This chapter examines the shifting role of African intermediaries in shaping the international circuits though which firms operated. It contextualizes these changes within broader transformations in merchandising and distribution during and after the Second World War and focuses mainly on the UAC, which by the mid-1930s had dominated the Gold Coast commercial scene. It argues that firms constantly juggled two opposing realities: the fact that their success relied on trusting the abilities of and learning from Africans, and the belief that their commercial superiority rested on dictating and regulating their actions. This struggle was exacerbated by their encounters with the savvy business tactics of credit customers. The nervousness expressed in Lenggenhager's 1941 letter is a product of these racial and gendered tensions, part of a growing chorus of anxiety and frustration—seen from the comments of agents to the top-down policies from the firms' head offices—that would in the years after the war lead to the phasing out of salaried company storekeepers and the passbook system altogether.

SITUATING INTERMEDIARIES

Known by such academic terms as *cross-cultural brokers*, *middle figures*, and *indigenous go-betweens*, African intermediaries are a broad group of people who, since the beginning of colonial period, have navigated between the linguistic and cultural boundaries that separated Europeans from African communities.[2] While historians have demonstrated the importance of intermediaries in the precolonial period, others have argued that the nature of formal European colonial rule, the expanding power of foreign capitalist enterprise, and the growing cash economy decreased intermediaries' ability to negotiate their terms of engagement.[3] Yet as Moses Ochonu has documented, within the context of indirect rule some African groups continued to transcend their colonial mandates and leverage power for their own purposes outside the roles that British colonizers imagined for them.[4] Most historical research on African intermediaries, however, has focused on either those employed by the colonial state or those associated with other colonial institutions such as churches, schools, and hospitals.[5] By shifting attention away from the colonial government and onto the activities of private commercial firms, this chapter offers a new perspective on a group of intermediaries that wielded a considerable amount of authority in shaping the colonial economy and the demands associated with capitalist exchange.

Refusing the simplistic "collaboration versus resistance" model, Kenneth Onwuka Dike has demonstrated how the activities of nineteenth-century African commercial intermediaries operated on a continuum, ranging from those who successfully used their positions to advance their own interests to those who simply worked for others.[6] While recognizing this broad spectrum, the current scholarship on intermediaries typically falls into two different yet overlapping categories. The first type of study concentrates on material gains and how mediating positions were used to enhance personal wealth, political power, and status. In the early twentieth century, for example, African interpreters, tax collectors, chiefs, and clerks were central to enabling communication and providing information as well as transmitting and interpreting colonial policies. Control over translation placed them at the center of exchanges of information, allowing some to rise to positions of considerable authority.[7] Studies in this category show that while some intermediaries used their influence and acquired skills to get rich, sometimes by demanding bribes, others used their positions to make demands on their colonial employers for certain benefits and privileges. For example, African civil servants and industrial wage laborers manipulated the rhetoric used by European employers and mobilized to demand better working conditions, salaries, and family allowances.[8]

The second type of study focuses more on the social worlds of African intermediaries and the construction of identities. This literature illustrates how groups of intermediaries constructed their own synthesis of different cultural practices, borrowing from precolonial, colonial, European, and other models. Stephan Miescher reveals this synthesis at work with mission-trained teachers in colonial Ghana, and argues that while mission societies dominated formal education, using schools to shape boys into a certain kind of Christian man, African teachers selectively combined those Presbyterian values with their own cultural ideals.[9] The expectations and obligations associated with marriage, fatherhood, and being an elder were among those under negotiation. Carolyn Brown finds that Nigerian coal miners navigated between a "masculine work culture" characterized by skill, physical strength, solidarity with friends, and an Igbo worldview that valued individual pride, social standing, and community improvement to construct their own models of development and "modernity."[10] In all cases, the enactment of different ideals was determined by place and by how one was positioned within larger structures of power—social, institutional, and spiritual.

With few exceptions, most research on African intermediaries concentrates on men and male labor. This focus is not surprising, as the colonial government employed mostly men to fill salaried and wage labor positions ranging from secretaries, clerks, and interpreters to household servants, cooks, and guards. While girls and women were no less active in making the colonial world, their ties to the colonial state were less direct, and European officials tended to view them as dependents of men—as wives, mothers, and daughters rather than as workers themselves.[11] It was only in the last decades of colonialism, starting in the 1930s, that a small number of African women, from mostly elite and privileged backgrounds, began to enter colonial institutions as nurses, midwives, and teachers.[12] Yet their expansion into those institutions, while notable, was only the more obvious edge of a larger phenomenon; African women played an increasingly dominant mediating role in the commercial sphere. As the cash economy expanded in the first half of the twentieth century, so too did women's control of the marketing, distribution, and retailing of goods.[13] Along with African men as storekeepers, African women as credit customers would become central to shaping the distribution and retailing networks through which large foreign firms like the UAC operated.

BEYOND STOREKEEPING

Following the hiring practices of the colonial state, firms trained and hired African men almost exclusively to fill clerk and storekeeper positions.[14] While the terms of storekeeping were never consistent, it was not uncommon in prewar years for African storekeepers to receive a monthly salary and commissions of up to 5 percent on selected goods. Storekeepers were also eligible for paid holidays, medical care, and extra allowances to hire store assistants and watchmen.[15] Additionally, the UAC was also known to offer educational scholarships to children of longtime employees.[16]

The role of company storekeepers extended far beyond that of just selling goods. After spending four months in the Gold Coast in 1936, collecting information for the UAC on local trade, D. D. Pitcher noted that "the African Retail Storekeeper . . . holds much the same position in the Merchandise trade as does the large Broker in the Cocoa trade."[17] Like the large cocoa broker who mediated between cocoa-buying firms and farmers and provided short-term credit, small loans, and crop advances to secure a steady supply of cocoa beans for export each season, the African storekeeper supplied firms with customers by offering credit—often at their own risk.[18] The comparison suggests that African storekeepers were crucial in creating the conditions for consumption on which a company's success relied.

Staying up-to-date on the arrival of goods and communicating frequently with other retailers were also major parts of a storekeeper's role. He organized the transportation and delivery of goods, took special orders, and provided customers with product information. While agents were responsible for determining the type and set quantity of goods for each retail store and delivering them in a timely fashion, storekeepers often had their own ideas about the needs of their customers. They paid close attention to arrival schedules at ports and branches, even traveling to other districts to confirm if their stores had received the correct amount of stock.[19] Although the agent and the district's location determined allocations, this also depended on a storekeeper's individual initiative. In a record of his business activities, E. K. Addo, a UAC storekeeper in Nsawam, noted frequent travel to Accra to secure "sellable goods,"[20] though such travel was a practice that annoyed district agents who tried to control allocations to each store.[21] In addition to circumventing the firm's rules, Addo also described ordering goods through the postal service, which included suiting material, women's hats from England, and felt hats from Japan.[22] This also hints at the fact that, depending on customers' preferences, storekeepers stocked other goods besides those provided by the firm. Storekeeping thus required an enormous amount of energy and resourcefulness on behalf of individual storekeepers to assure a steady flow of desired goods to their districts.

Such initiative fostered a special loyalty between storekeepers and customers. While firms expected that, due to convenience, customers would shop where they lived, this was not always the case. As firms would later discover, a storekeeper's commercial ties spread beyond the immediate district in which his store was located. As one UAC director reported, a storekeeper's account books did not necessarily reflect sales for his particular district: "Trade tends to be attached to the individual storekeeper who will take it with him if he is transferred to a new store; in extreme cases the store premises seemed unnecessary, as so great a volume of the business was not derived from the local market."[23] This observation illustrated the limitations of company efforts to control trade, and it would prove especially problematic during the war years with the introduction of government quotas and the pressure to collect accurate statistics on sales. Loyalty between shopkeepers and customers manifested itself in the willingness of customers to travel far distances to buy from storekeepers they had built personal relationships with—and especially those with whom they had a good credit history. Personal relationships often trumped convenience and lower prices.

Storekeepers also colluded with credit customers to increase sales and collect larger profits from commissions. For instance, Edward Akurang Dankwa, the son of a Bawjiasi UAC storekeeper in the early 1950s, remembers that these women would tell his father "the sort of goods they would need to sell" and he would place orders on their behalf. Storekeepers took advice from credit customers on popular and fast-moving goods and admitted to splitting the commissions with them.[24] Storekeepers also supplied petty traders—who were not officially associated with the company—with goods on credit. These traders often sold merchandise in smaller quantities and split profits with the storekeeper. One could see them walking a town's streets with goods in baskets, in carts, and on trays balanced on their heads. They were also known to travel to markets in neighboring towns and villages. In a sense, each storekeeper ran his own credit customer business, offering opportunities to trusted traders who could not afford the deposit for a passbook.[25]

Because of his stable salary and ready access to goods, a storekeeper also held obligations to people outside the company—especially family and relatives. The requirement of all firms that a storekeeper secure up to four guarantors who would take responsibility for paying back any loans or debt incurred during his time of service increased this accountability. In some cases, guarantors included a storekeeper's relatives; in others, the guarantor might be a district or sales manager who had gained his trust. For example, Benjamin Heywood Okine, a UAC storekeeper in Accra, acquired a guarantee of five hundred British West African pounds based on funds received from his father, mother, and uncle and a recommendation from the UAC agent at Nsawam.[26] As a result, contracts involved an agreement not only between the storekeeper and a company but also relatives and other guarantors who had helped him secure the position. It was thus not uncommon for family members to expect goods on credit, ready cash, and a portion of the store's profits.[27]

These expectations also arose from relatives who gave nothing in the way of starting capital but made demands on a storekeeper's resources based on the understanding that any successful member of the family was obligated to care for less fortunate relatives.[28] In interviews with Kumasi storekeepers in the 1950s, Peter Garlick found that many storekeepers had struggled to fulfill multiple financial responsibilities. Examples included a man who was responsible for a particularly large store and who provided for six or seven cousins and their children; a young, unmarried storekeeper who supported his four sisters and their twelve children; and a man who maintained three wives and nine children, as well as relatives on both his mother's and father's sides of the family.[29] Financial responsibilities included housing, food, clothing, and children's school fees. Moreover, gendered household obligations shaped storekeeping practices. One storekeeper explained that where women would succeed in textiles, "men fail." "Members of the family come to the man for cloths," he explained, "which is his obligation to provide."[30] According to Garlick, male storekeepers who dealt in any kind of personal goods, like cloth, were at a disadvantage.

In addition to providing for their own families, storekeepers also supplied consumers with goods on credit, and even with small loans. S. G. Oduroh, a former UAC store assistant, revealed that he often lent cash to customers. He cited different reasons for lending, but the main reason was to help customers pay their children's school fees.[31] While some firms discouraged moneylending and credit, these tactics allowed storekeepers to build up the community's goodwill while providing poorer families with access to goods.[32] Storekeepers were still held personally responsible for any outstanding debts on unauthorized credit. Despite the risks they faced, lending money and providing credit remained an important tool for storekeepers and may have been used to appease local customers and divert any negative feelings fueled by growing nationalist sentiment toward employees who worked for European firms.

It should be noted, however, that providing relatives and customers with goods and paying their fees were not always detrimental to a storekeeper's success. While such practices could eat up store profits, fulfilling obligations also elevated a storekeeper's status in relation to his wife, children, and extended kin. In addition, it provided a ready group of individuals whom—because of their dependence—the storekeeper could ask to run errands, assist in sales, make deliveries, or watch the store in his absence. In this case, storekeeping could be understood as an avenue to obtain authority and also as a means to acquire "wealth in people" or a number of dependents who could help out in myriad—though not always expected—ways.[33] Meeting the demands of people beyond the firm was a form of social security shaped by the value placed on communal life, but it also came to being out of necessity. The instability and uncertainty of the Gold Coast economy required that storekeepers manage and fulfill outside obligations and demands. During the war, the terms of storekeeping became less attractive with the shutting down of many stores due to shortages and strict quotas. As a result, the UAC converted a number of company storekeepers from salaried positions to "aided retailers" who worked for the company on credit terms and paid rent for stores on company premises.

RETAINING ISAAC A. OGOE

Piecing together the case of Isaac A. Ogoe, a storekeeper turned manager who served the UAC and its predecessors from 1910 to 1950, offers a deeper understanding of the shifting role of African employees in mediating between firms and their customers, as well as the day-to-day anxieties produced through such relationships (fig. 2.1). Ogoe's forty-year career also provides insight as to how he was able to forward his own interests and make personal demands on the UAC.[34] While his superiors had conflicting notions about his capabilities and the extent of his loyalties, they all considered him an important asset. Ogoe not only had extensive knowledge of business in his district and close relationships with customers but also connections to chiefs and other local authorities, providing a critical link between the firm and local politics more broadly.

Born on March 13, 1890, Ogoe joined the British trading firm Miller Brothers as a wholesale storekeeper in his coastal hometown of Sekondi in 1910. After thirty-four years he was transferred to Dunkwa, about eighty miles north of Sekondi, and was appointed as a factor—that is, a person responsible for settling accounts with customers who purchased goods from the firm on credit.[35] When the UAC took over Miller Brothers in 1929, it promoted Ogoe to the position of textiles sales manager in Dunkwa. Among the firms operating along the coast, the UAC was the first to allow Africans to fill these sales positions. Depending on location, a sales manager's tasks ranged from promoting particular commodities door-to-door to seeking out new credit customers and encouraging them to buy from the UAC rather than from competing firms.[36] Duties could also include supervising junior sales staff and company storekeepers. In 1934 Ogoe was transferred back to Sekondi, where he acted as the district's hardware manager and provisions manager.

Ogoe's ability to use his intermediary position rested heavily on the fact that the last two decades of his career were spent in his hometown of Sekondi, where he had immediate and extended family as well as business connections.[37] While operating in one's hometown was not always ideal due to the demands made by family members and friends, as Garlick argued in his research on Kwawu storekeepers, Ogoe's career trajectory proves quite the opposite. His lucrative career in Sekondi illustrates how successful he was in negotiating multiple loyalties.

The UAC's general manager and district agent files are peppered with information about Ogoe. Although many of these reports are one-sided and only rarely include Ogoe's responses alongside those of his superiors, the

BIRTHDAY PICTURE

Mr. Isaac Ogoe, a Group management pensioner in Sekondi, poses with some of his children and grand children on the occasion of the celebration of his 80th birthday. Standing second from left (third row) is Mr. E. M. Ogoe, a manager at G.C.M.T. Accra, one of the sons of Mr. Isaac Ogoe.

(see story on page twenty)

FIGURE 2.1. Isaac Ogoe celebrates his eightieth birthday, Sekondi; *Unicorn* magazine, no. 16, May–June 1970. Reproduced with kind permission of Unilever from the original at the Unilever Archives.

information reveals how he navigated between what appeared to be conflicting responsibilities and obligations. Critiques of his performance through routine, confidential staff reports written and submitted at least twice a year to the UAC's general manager in Accra (and forwarded to its London office) showed what the firm expected of its African employees. Categories of evaluation and recommendation for reemployment included a man's health, conduct, ability to run a business, initiative, and ability to manage accounts. Yet when read against supplementary letters and correspondence between district and head offices, these staff reports also illustrate how men like Ogoe juggled these varying expectations.

In 1935 the district agent at Sekondi, H. Thrower, described Ogoe's knowledge of commodities as "extensive and intimate," praising him for controlling merchandise orders and stock with "great punctiliousness."[38] In the same letter Thrower recommended that the firm send Ogoe to England "for contact with buying departments." A paid-in-full trip abroad was an enormous privilege and expense that the firm did not take lightly. The next year Thrower continued with his high praise for Ogoe, describing his "painstaking" attention to detail and declaring that he was an "excellent 'commodity man'" who was able to conduct business in Fanti, Hausa, and Twi.[39]

Two years later, however, a different district agent, P. J. Brady, reported with frustration, "I am not too satisfied with [Ogoe's] services. . . . He could pass on more knowledge of local happenings than he does."[40] While these conflicting evaluations demonstrate shifting relationships between Ogoe and different district agents in charge, they also uncover the extent to which agents relied on African employees for knowledge about local markets and the community.[41] Of course, Bradley may have had different expectations of Ogoe from those of the agent who came before him, or he may have held some personal vendetta. Even so, Brady's frustrations exposed Ogoe's importance to the business in Sekondi. By controlling the flow of information that linked the UAC to Sekondi customers, intermediaries like Ogoe were invaluable to the firm's business. The discrepancies between the reports by Thrower and Bradley hint that Ogoe might have chosen to selectively disclose information over time or outwardly withhold his knowledge of "local happenings" all together.

Intermediary positions enabled men like Ogoe to use valuable local knowledge as leverage. We know from Ogoe's letters that he did so in order to secure his own interests and preserve some autonomy while working for the firm. In a 1938 letter, Ogoe wrote to the UAC's general manager in Accra requesting a car allowance of two to three pounds per month.[42] In this letter Ogoe described his travels to different areas surrounding Sekondi to promote

UAC business with potential customers: "I am submitting my application to you for your consideration for a small car allowance for my Vauxhall car which I have had since May 1937. . . . I have been using my own car at my own expense to [visit] stores and beads customers when the district manager's car is engaged and sometimes I go to villages with my own car to get in touch with chiefs about the gunpowder trade." In explaining his activities Ogoe used the letter to place himself at the center of commerce in Sekondi. He reminded UAC authorities of his relationships with the local authorities, like chiefs, and used these connections to make demands for more money. Ogoe's car allowance request also revealed his desire for more independence. Although the firm provided each district branch with a vehicle, the district manager or agent controlled permission to use it. Using his own vehicle, rather than a company car, offered Ogoe freedom to come and go as he pleased, away from the district manager's watchful eye. A subsequent letter submitted by P. J. Brady, the same district agent who wrote an unfavorable review of Ogoe a year earlier, attempted to undermine Ogoe's request by suggesting that his car has "always been" at Ogoe's disposal and at the disposal "of any member of staff for business purposes." While there is no record that Ogoe's particular request was ever granted, some of his other requests surely were.

Throughout his career Ogoe requested greater amounts of money. In 1949 he was able to secure a five hundred-pound loan to construct a building, most likely a family compound, in Sekondi. The firm agreed and offered him the full amount under the conditions that he repay the loan at the rate of twenty pounds per month.[43] Building a house in one's hometown for many Ghanaian men, as Stephan Miescher has shown, was one of the most important achievements in life.[44] It was significant physical marker of becoming an *ɔpanyin*, a respected and trusted elder—"a status that was not self-ascribed but granted by society" through a process that could extend over years. Beyond his own nine children and three wives, Ogoe was most likely responsible for supporting a number of other kin, and the building was thus an investment meant to protect his and his family's well-being, a residence to be passed down to younger relatives through inheritance.

During the last three years of his career, 1947–50, Ogoe worked as the Sekondi credit sales manager and as an assistant to the district manager. In 1944, UAC's general manager, S. C. W. Cruickshank, described Ogoe at the age of fifty-four as "another old and loyal servant with wide experience but no longer possessing the vigor and initiative necessary for post-war trading."[45] One year later, however, a Sekondi district agent named Hockley responded to the general manager that while Ogoe may be unsuitable for his present position in sales, his "knowledge of the District, customers, and people is, of course, extensive, [and] correctly applied it can be extremely useful to the Company."[46] He also reported on Ogoe's excellent health, and suggested alternative positions for Ogoe as a credit sales manager, a produce manager, the person in charge of the UAC pension fund, or an assistant to the district manager, where he could provide current information on "native affairs, local politics, etc."[47]

Maintaining Ogoe's services was of immediate concern to the Sekondi district manager. In his assessment, general manager Cruickshank, who conducted business from company headquarters in Accra, may have underestimated Ogoe's crucial role in facilitating local business, viewing him as a loyal but aging employee on the brink of retirement. By suggesting other positions for Ogoe, reporting on his excellent memory and health, and praising his ability to "hold down the fort in any department," district agent Hockley went to great lengths to defend Ogoe's retention at the Sekondi branch.[48] Frequent justifications for keeping Ogoe on staff were necessary, as he required a higher salary due to his long years of service. By 1948 his annual pay had reached £750 per month. In a letter to headquarters, Hockley noted that, "though expensive," Ogoe remained "a most useful contact with political and municipal affairs" and assured Cruickshank that "we are convinced that he places his loyalty to the company first."[49] Apparently the agent convinced his superiors; the UAC kept Ogoe on in a managerial position until 1950.

In June 1951 the UAC held a ceremony at the Sekondi district branch honoring Ogoe and celebrating his retirement. The *Gold Coast UAC News* described it as an "impressive gathering" of both European and African staff, credit customers, local politicians, and Ogoe's relatives and friends. The celebration was followed by a "drinks party" at the "Swanmill Bungalow."[50] Uncertainties surrounding the planning of the event also demonstrated efforts by the UAC to stay on Ogoe's good side even though he would no longer be officially employed. Prior to the ceremony, Patrick H. Fitz-Gerald, the UAC's general manager, wrote to the head office in London asking the UAC to rewrite its official appreciation letter and for permission to present Ogoe with a special gift. He pointed out that the usual signed certificate by UAC chairman Lord Trenchard was inadequate and feared that Ogoe might consider an ordinary letter not appreciative enough. "I am wondering if we could make a special case by presenting a silver cigarette box or tray," he suggested. "He is still quite an influence in Sekondi, and it would do us no harm."[51] Ogoe's European supervisors were not only eager for insider knowledge from people like him but were also afraid of offending him. In fact, Fitz-Gerald's letter alludes to the fact that it was Ogoe who may have asked him for a more substantial sign of appreciation: "He was very keen to have some sort of Testimonial to show his grand-children and also junior members of the staff." In the end, the head office granted Fitz-Gerald's request; at the ceremony he presented Ogoe with an extended letter recounting his years of service and a solid silver tray inscribed in capital letters with the following message: "Presented to Mr. Isaac A. Ogoe by the Board of Directors of the United Africa Company, Limited, on the occasion of his retirement on the 31st December 1950, after forty years of faithful service."

But Ogoe's connection with the UAC did not end after his retirement. He continued to make demands on the firm for additional loans, special terms for purchasing large household items, and personal favors. In 1951 he insisted that the firm provide him with an additional construction loan and remarked that the initial five hundred pounds was insufficient. He also asked for a second Electrolux refrigerator on credit terms reserved for current employees, and the company agreed to his request.[52] Two years later, in a remarkable demonstration of the influence he still held over the firm, Ogoe convinced the UAC's London office to reserve him a seat at Queen Elizabeth II's coronation ceremony, which he would attend as part of his visit to the United Kingdom in 1953. His attendance at the coronation, and the willingness of the UAC to reserve him a private seat at such a high-profile ceremony, illustrated that Ogoe's reputation transcended the town of Sekondi. It also showed how carefully the UAC treated men like Ogoe and how willing it was to appease such an important man in the name of business.

Although it would not entirely disappear, the authority of men like Isaac A. Ogoe would fade in the second half of the twentieth century. Africanization policies of the 1950s, combined with the onset of Gold Coast independence, forced trading firms to reevaluate their hiring practices and appoint more Africans to managerial positions formerly held by Europeans.[53] During his career Ogoe was one of very few African managers. By the time the UAC transferred him back to Sekondi in 1934, he was only one of about thirty working for the company in the colony.[54] Africanization policies increased the number of African managers and thus diluted the authority that men like Ogoe once had; they were no longer exceptional.[55] As more African managers filled supervisory positions and managed other African staff, the exclusivity of their role as intermediaries slowly diminished. Yet Ogoe's story reveals how one UAC employee used his intermediary status to successfully navigate among different interests, both inside and outside the company.

AN ALL-WOMEN SALES FORCE

While coastal cities and towns had been the main centers of wholesale and retail trade, the UAC relied heavily on credit customers to distribute and sell goods in areas where company stores did not exist. According to UAC records, the credit customer system was established by the British firm F. & A. Swanzy around 1850.[56] Through this system, firms allowed Africans to buy bulk merchandise at wholesale, interest-free prices. All credit sales were accounted for on a monthly basis, and only after settling one's account could a credit customer stock up on new supplies for the following month.[57] Most firms expected credit customers to put down a deposit in the form of cash or valuables. For instance, in 1933, Rosina Ocansey from Kumasi deposited one gold chain, two hair pins, two pairs of bracelets, two brooches, and thirty-three gold nuggets to secure her passbook.[58] To record account activity, firms provided each of their credit customers with a passbook containing a black-and-white photograph of the holder, the district he or she was allowed to sell in, rates of commission, credit limits (which could fluctuate over time), and the recurring dates when goods were to be supplied (figs. 2.2, 2.3);[59] the term *passbook trader* was synonymous with *credit customers*.[60] Longtime, trusted customers could receive as much as £300–400 worth of goods in one month without a full deposit, though most were only able to take goods against the amount of their original deposit.[61] While some men were credit customers, African women dominated this system.

Regardless of their pivotal role in facilitating the movement and sale of goods throughout the Gold Coast, we know very little about the lives and businesses of credit customers. While literature on market women in Ghana is extremely rich, this scholarship often presents credit customers as merely appendages or dependent clients of European firms.[62] This portrayal has obscured the diversity of business practices these women manifested and the ways—both large and small—in which they attempted to establish independence from firms. It also limits our understanding of credit customers themselves. Among these women, levels of education, autonomy, experience, and age varied widely; for example, the youngest UAC credit customer recorded in the archives was Ellen Mensah Segbefia, a seventeen-year-old girl from Akuse.[63] Credit customers specialized in different types of goods, and profit levels varied considerably; as one UAC merchandise director noted, "[credit] accounts ranged from the humble trader turning over of a few pounds a month to the biggest account of £30,000 a month."[64] While credit customers were by no means a homogeneous group, the fact that a woman held a passbook, paid a deposit, and had security with a firm elevated her above other retailers; she was known within local business circles as a "first degree trader."[65]

To some extent, all credit customers operated as wholesalers and retailers, controlled networks of subdistributors, and had their own clients, or "second degree traders," who sold on their behalf. One trader, Agatha Blewor Borti Tamakoloe of Keta, described a typical week of business:

> I am all-round trader, that is to say, I deal with the various departments of the Company, taking keen interest even in the smallest articles up to the retailing of Pigs Feet and Matches. I have many sub-traders who tour the district between the Keta Market-days, Denu, Aflao, Dzode and Wudoaba. My main store is in one of the Company premises, where I am charged, of course, monthly rent. My busiest day is the Keta Market-day and in order to alleviate the day's pressure on me, I have arranged for four stalls distributed throughout the market where my wares are displayed.[66]

FIGURE 2.2. UAC passbook belonging to Madam Amba Otwiwa, ca. 1950–1960, UAC of Ghana Ltd. financial records. Reproduced with kind permission of Unilever from the original at the Unilever Archives, UAC/2/20/2/9/1.

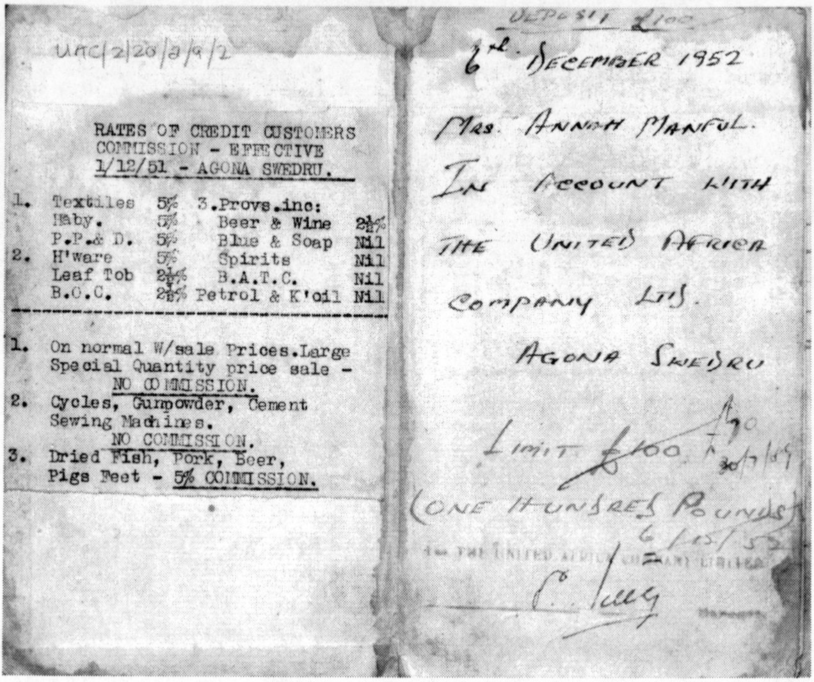
UAC/2/20/2/9/2

RATES OF CREDIT CUSTOMERS
COMMISSION - EFFECTIVE
1/12/51 - AGONA SWEDRU.

1. Textiles	5%	3. Provs. inc:		
Baby.	5%		Beer & Wine	2½%
P.P.& D.	5%		Blue & Soap	Nil
2. H'ware	5%		Spirits	Nil
Leaf Tob	2½%		B.A.T.C.	Nil
B.O.C.	2½%		Petrol & K'oil	Nil

1. On normal W/sale Prices. Large Special Quantity price sale - NO COMMISSION.
2. Cycles, Gunpowder, Cement Sewing Machines. NO COMMISSION.
3. Dried Fish, Pork, Beer, Pigs Feet - 5% COMMISSION.

DEPOSIT £100

6th. DECEMBER 1952

MRS. ANNAH MANFUL.
IN ACCOUNT WITH
THE UNITED AFRICA
COMPANY LTD.
AGONA SWEDRU

LIMIT £100.
(ONE HUNDRED POUNDS)

FIGURE 2.3. UAC passbook belonging to Mrs. Annah Manful ca. 1950–1960, UAC of Ghana Ltd. financial records. Reproduced with kind permission of Unilever from the original at the Unilever Archives, UAC/2/20/2/9/2.

Credit customers mixed and matched their use of selling spaces depending on factors that ranged from customer demand to day of the week. They rented physical stores and market stalls, set up temporary neighborhood or roadside kiosks, and hawked goods from place to place on foot.

Such tactics could also have larger business aims and serve as examples of women's business acumen. Credit customer Mary Baiden described how she relied on smaller retailers to move popular lines such as boneless beef, pig's feet, and stockfish while she concentrated full-time on her more profitable tobacco business, and her delegation of safe selling to assistants and steady profits on smaller lines allowed her to invest further in the tobacco trade. By the early 1950s she was known in Kumasi as the Tobacco Queen, though she continued to deal in other types of commodities.[67] By fluctuating between wholesale and retail activity, Baiden maintained the flexibility to both invest in products that would maximize her profits and collect commission on safe lines delegated to others, depending on the market. In managing a number of smaller retailers, it is likely that Baiden also provided credit herself and managed her own group of credit customers—a strategy similar to that of company storekeepers and not uncommon among "first degree traders."

Other credit customers conducted business from their private homes and traveled to different districts. Accra credit customer Esther Mensah, for instance, rented two different stalls in the city's largest market, Makola, and hired assistants to push handcarts around various Accra neighborhoods displaying goods and spreading information about her products (fig. 2.4). She also ran a samples viewing room in her own home, where she welcomed customers to try different hair pomades and talcum powders, view the latest cloth designs, inspect the quality of new leather sandals, and ask questions about an array of household durables and products from cooking pots to Dettol.[68] Many credit customers also traveled frequently. Catherine Botchway described going between Obuasi and Dunkwa, a round-trip distance of almost forty-five miles, and selling in both towns and in between.[69] This strategy reached a wider number of customers and was used to sell older stock. As former UAC credit customer Agnes Kwa Kwa from Cape Coast explained, if goods were not moving in the city, she would sell them in nearby rural areas. Some farmers were not aware of new trends so they would be more likely to buy, not knowing that a particular style was from "last season."[70]

While women's sales strategies helped the UAC profit, their skills also provided them with opportunities to invest in other types of business. Like Baiden, who invested her retailing profits in the tobacco trade, other credit customers became property owners, transporters, and moneylenders.[71] As J. F. Enninful, a former UAC clerk turned manager recounted, "They were making money, some of them were able to put up houses and other things. Apart from the commission earned on their purchases [,] they sell at a price which also gives them a margin of profit at the market . . . especially when you go to Takoradi, you see the mighty mighty buildings owned by women."[72] Business reputations also translated into social capital and leadership positions in communities. One "first degree trader" in Accra became a leading member of the Market Traders Association, the Federation of Gold Coast Women, and the Presbyterian Church.[73] Similar to men like Ogoe, women credit customers sought to establish reputations by constructing houses and undertaking community leadership roles.

To better control the terms of their relationship with firms, some women also secretly held passbooks from multiple firms, a practice that the firms strongly discouraged.[74] Multiple passbooks, the UAC argued, allowed credit customers to evade debt and prevented company loyalty. But the strategy allowed customers to negotiate better sales terms and avoid dependency on

FIGURE 2.4. Esther Mensah (seated, second from right) with hardware sales manager J. E. Boakye-Mensah and other Accra credit customers, UAC Swanmill, Accra, August 3, 1950. Photo courtesy of Madam Beauty Boye.

one firm. For instance, if a firm's wholesale price on a carton of milk was not favorable, a credit customer with multiple passbooks could try to obtain a carton for a lower price at another firm's district branch. Furthermore, multiple passbooks allowed credit customers to check wholesale prices at different firms and to protect themselves from being cheated. Such tactics allowed credit customers to use the system to their advantage. Of course, these strategies were only successful during times of abundance. As we shall see later in chapters 3 and 4, scarcity and shortages created a seller's market where demand far outstripped supply. Such conditions diminished credit customers' bargaining positions considerably.

A number of the UAC's first credit customers were from long-established trading families and had held accounts with the company's predecessors.[75] As they reflected on their careers, credit customers described apprenticeships or learning the merchandise business from grandmothers, mothers, and aunts.[76] Helena Adzowor Tengey of Korforidua credited her aunt Delina Acolaste, a top trader in Saltpond, with teaching her the business. "I always used to go with her to [Miller Brothers, F. & A. Swanzy, and John Walkden] for her monthly supplies," she explained. "Sometimes I would go alone and then I would grumble to myself that she was much too troublesome, not realizing that she was putting me on the right path."[77] This familial connection is not surprising, as passbooks could be passed down from generation to generation.

For others, life as a credit customer was a second or parallel career that came after or simultaneous with formal schooling and professional training. Esther Mensah went to the Accra Government Girls' School at age five, passed standard level 7 in 1929, and trained as a nurse the following year. In 1938 she resigned from the hospital to trade, securing herself a UAC passbook.[78] In a related example, all three Igbo credit customers Gloria Ifeoma Chuku interviewed in Nigeria attended primary school, and two of the three had secondary school education and trained as teachers. Chuku argues that retailing offered flexibility, which enabled many women to care for their children and tend to household responsibilities.[79] While this option was certainly the case, many women also established themselves as professionals and made a lucrative career out of passbook trading.

Some of the more profitable passbook holders were wives and relatives of UAC employees; although many of these women began retailing before marriage, their husbands' positions no doubt played a part in their later business success.[80] Wealthy husbands and influential male relatives provided the cash deposit needed to gain a passbook and often set up female relatives with a small store, and they collected a portion of the profits in order to pay back whatever cash deposit they had contributed to the women.[81] Yet some credit customers purchased or inherited passbooks from other women and maintained entire households of immediate and extended family (which for one woman was thirty dependents) on their own.[82] Beauty Boye, stepdaughter of prominent Accra credit customer Esther Mensah, revealed that many of her stepmother's business associates never formally married. She described that some of these women were wealthy, owned property, and had built their own homes, implying that their status had intimidated potential suitors.[83] Others may have simply not seen the sense in formally marrying.[84] While it might be tempting to categorize the power of this group of women as a form of feminism, we must remember that their prized position in Gold Coast society often rested on the labor of many other women—and men—who were not as privileged. Such a reality does not undermine their business intelligence, however. Within an increasingly restrictive colonial context, credit customers provide an intriguing example of women who were able to maintain a certain amount of autonomy and carve out meaningful lives for themselves.

While European agents frequently complained about the "dangers of the credit business," details about their relationship with credit customers remain spotty. Instead of identifying this absence as a gap in the corporate record, however, what is most revealing in the case of women credit customers is how and when they do appear and what these moments might reveal about commercial spaces as sites where ideas about gender, race, and power are produced. An analysis of managers' correspondence and staff circulars suggests that the demands of these successful retailers caused anxiety among British, exclusively male, management. Not only did these women's public visibility and economic independence challenge the bourgeois ideas of femininity to which many of these men subscribed, but their practices also disrupted the racial logic that figured Africans as inferior and in need of guidance. How, then, did company management reconcile these contradictions and make sense of its dependency on credit customers?

One way was the firm's use of pejorative stereotypes that masked credit customers' crucial role in the merchandise business. Company publications often referred to a credit customer as a "market mammy," a "bush mammy," and collectively as "mammy traders."[85] To use the term "bush" meant that these were simple and uneducated people lacking any type of sophistication, while the term "mammy" was in the US South used to describe black women, often enslaved, who worked for white families and cared for white children. The happy-go-lucky mammy character was portrayed in film and advertisements as a loyal servant, and such images were offered as evidence of the supposed humanity of the institution of slavery. Furthermore, persistent depictions throughout the twentieth-century United States both represented and maintained a white fantasy of harmonious race relations.[86] In the British colonial context, the term "mammy" negated any understanding of credit customers as serious business associates or colleagues. Evoked by European managers and staff, the term implied a mother or someone with a familial type of connection, thus also rendering invisible a capitalist relationship and the exploitative potential of such a system. Furthermore, by constructing businesswomen as "mammies," their work is figured as both domestic and obligatory rather than a form of labor that should be valued and compensated in market terms.

Staff narratives fluctuated between viewing such women as intimidating forces to be reckoned with and as sources of amusement. For instance, as a 1950s British-American Tobacco employee explained in his memoir, "market mammies are powerful, apart from their sheer physical presence.

Raucous, impetuous, bawdy and full of fun."[87] As Ann Stoler reminds us, "imperial authority and racial distinctions were fundamentally structured in gendered terms."[88] Through depictions of credit customers' appearance and behavior, black femininity is then figured as an opposite to white womanhood within a racial logic that imagined European women as delicate "domestic angels," however stereotypical those categories might also be. By describing their bodies as intimidating, yet exciting and powerful, such an account also fetishized African women.

British managers also seemed fascinated with what they described as a mix of "matronly kindness" and "ruthless arrogance."[89] While male staff often remembered these women humorously, their erratic behavior, wavering between the two extremes "kind" and "ruthless," painted them as objects of suspicion. Such caricatures perpetuated the belief among male staff that African women needed to be managed.

These representations also had implications for how firms understood credit customers' practices. Managers often rendered the customers' business skills as a form of trickery or even deception.[90] In December 1954, the general manager of G. B. Ollivant, a company owned by the UAC, circulated a letter to all stations concerning loss of sales on 110 cases of Dutch Silver Fish. Whereas the correct selling price should have been sixty-six shillings, a district agent sold to customers for fifty. This "fatal blunder," the general manager argued, cost the company £80. Clearly irritated with the agent, he stated, "I can accept no valid excuse . . . it is a question of not looking at the goods and not showing much intelligence in trade. . . . We cannot afford to be fooled."[91] The general manager reduced credit customers' informed buying to a form of trickery rather than a testament to their superior market skills. While the manager faulted the agent for poor management, his warning about being "fooled" also suggested that the agent was a victim of a scam. Most likely credit customers paid the lower price knowingly and did not inform the agent he was in the wrong.

In a similar case, one goods manager of the Swiss African Trading Company, another UAC-owned firm, described being outsmarted by two experienced credit customers during his first buying trip to Manchester. He remembered, "I was taken around several textile factories . . . to select saleable materials, assisted by two 'market mammies.' . . . Of course they picked the cream of the available designs for themselves." They left him, as he later found out when he returned to Kumasi, with what were "second-rate styles."[92] Because of their intimate knowledge of local style and changing consumer tastes, women credit customers, especially those dealing in wax prints, were often invited as guests to England to consult on designs. Although he later recalled this incident with a sense of humor, the goods manager's narrative positions the act of the women taking the best designs as an underhanded move to trick him; thus, the same women who the company invited to England because of their perceived skill in identifying popular designs are still presumed to be untrustworthy.

While European male management drew on preexisting racial and gender ideologies, they also constructed notions about race, gender, and ability through their everyday business interactions and correspondence. In many ways narratives that cast credit customers as sneaky "market mammies" and "tricky traders" maintained "colonial authority and a particular set of relations of production and power" that preserved the firm's image at home and among staff on the coast.[93] These stories also justified treatment of these women as a cheap form of disposable labor. That international audiences were presented with the generic and stereotyped figure of the market mammy instead of actual businesswomen like Mary Baiden or Esther Mensah suggests that the company had a stake in representing African women as in need of company guidance.

RELIABLE WOMEN?

In the postwar period, tensions between the UAC and its credit customers came to a head in discussions about corporate restructuring. World War II brought serious commodity shortages, introduced government price controls, and increased pressure on firms to ensure fairer distribution, mostly by regulating district allocations. After the war restrictions eased, and there was a substantial growth in African spending power as the price of cocoa, timber, and gold—the Gold Coast's main exports—rose on the world market. The period after 1945 was a time of economic expansion and returning prosperity; it was also a time of intense competition among firms.[94] To keep its top position, the UAC stepped up its merchandising strategies and attempted to restructure business. Increasing public criticisms and nationalist activities, as well as new rhetoric about economic development and colonial rule, further shaped changes in corporate policy.[95]

To gain a competitive edge, two of the UAC's initial strategies were to increase credit limits and build women's trust. For example, in March 1950, UAC general manager Patrick H. Fitz-Gerald sent instructions to district managers noting that "we shall have to give our credit customers a higher limit of credit . . . if you are satisfied that the woman is reliable, it is to the benefit of the company to extend credit."[96] By increasing credit the UAC hoped to secure credit customers' loyalty and ensure that they would not work for competing firms.[97] UAC correspondence also discussed how to gain the favor of female credit customers in order to outsmart competitors. In February 1953, G. B. Ollivant's general manager H. Schiess instructed agents in Kumasi, Sekondi, and Accra to choose ten customers with turnovers of five hundred pounds monthly and to visit them and conduct monthly interviews. The main purpose was to "keep fully alive to local trade developments" and to offer the "right" ones more credit to expand their business.[98]

Such top-down efforts, however, may have been a sign of desperation rather than innovation. After 1950, merchandise circulars sent by the general manager to each district agent took on a repetitive and frantic tone suggesting that agents were in fact unable to cultivate personal relationships and trust.[99] For instance, Scheiss declared, "I have for some considerable time been pressing for a better building up of a handful of clients [credit customers] to be given the personal attention of the agent . . . very few [branches] have made a satisfactory progress. I have written enough on this subject and from now onwards it will simply mean that where this progress is below expectations the agents own ability . . . is to be questioned."[100] The failure of agents to extract valuable market information from credit customers led to aging stock and slow-moving and unsuitable lines that cost the company "unnecessary losses."[101] The company also grew increasingly annoyed with "upcountry traders" who were not satisfied with their district allocations and traveled to Accra for a better selection.[102] Well into the 1950s there was still a gap in the UAC's knowledge about local markets, consumer taste, and demand—precisely those areas of operations in which credit customers were most expert.

Whether credit customers ever strategically withheld market information is unclear. Nonetheless, the company increasingly considered credit customers, and particularly its top sellers, as unreliable sources of market information.[103] In 1955, even as the UAC was trying to deepen relationships with credit customers, directors in London and its general manager in Accra began discussions about how to break down the customers' power.[104] While these efforts were part of a larger shift in postwar UAC business that focused on prioritizing the firm's identity as a wholesaler, this change also stemmed from the fact that some large credit customers had become powerful wholesalers who directly imported goods, circumventing the UAC.[105] The ability of top-selling customers to create alliances that forced down buying prices and pressured firms to offer better terms also affected the firm's selling margins.[106] As a UTC agent at Akuse observed in 1938, "Today almost all the cotton income is carried out by two mammy customers, F. M. Adodoadji and Selina Melenja. We absolutely respect the liveliness of both mammies, especially of Adodoadji, but we cannot let them ever dictate our prices."[107] The difference, however, was that under intense competition alliances between women like Adodoadji and Melenja posed more of a threat. According to the UAC, distributing passbooks to a larger number of new credit customers would in effect diffuse the power of the larger, more established ones.

In a confidential letter to the UAC's general manager, merchandise director A. C. C. Baxter wrote, among other things, "We are seeking a larger number of new customers, many of whom will be in a smaller way of business." He further instructed that larger customers should be "sold smaller quantities than have been customary." He was cautious, in noting that "we are not trying to eliminate our big customers or to take their customers away from them," instead claiming "we are seeking new customers and in doing so we shall be coming closer to people, who are themselves retailers but we remain wholesalers."[108] His careful delivery suggested that this policy might not have been popular with those actually working on the ground. While agents most likely preferred to deal with a few large customers, they also probably found it equally difficult to withhold goods from women who wielded a considerable amount of authority in their districts. Either resistance to this top-down policy, or the inability to enforce it, is evident in a letter three years later, in which the general manager reprimands district agents for lack of compliance.[109]

The UAC's efforts to break down large credit customer business should also be understood as a part of its shift to a more "scientific approach to selling." A 1955 merchandising meeting in London established an urgent need to recruit and train a force of young African salesmen as "researchers" to act as the company's "eyes and ears."[110] While this was an attempt to close the gap between the firm and everyday consumers, directors also agreed that they could not rely on large credit customers to develop new lines or to provide consistent consumer feedback; instead they wanted "objective research and the continual passing back of information on consumers' reaction to our lines, competitors' activities, [and] ideas for new lines."[111] Corporate language renamed and reshaped cultural competence in business, a competence that many female credit customers already possessed. By de-emphasizing the role of credit customers, salesmen were positioned as more "reliable" (more "scientific") in their assessments of consumer taste than the women who had been doing this work all along. The talk about making selling more professional, and more scientific, is perhaps the best evidence of the UAC's inability to fully control the local market. After all, as A. C. C. Baxter would explain to an audience full of business students and professors at the City of

London College in 1960, after his thirty years of experience in the field, he was certain that "nearly all African traders" were still "ignorant of progressive retail techniques" and needed proper guidance.[112]

While global economic and political issues influenced the flow of commodities into West Africa, shifting relationships between and among the UAC and its employees, storekeepers, and credit customers also shaped the development of twentieth-century Gold Coast consumer markets. Individual responsibilities and obligations influenced selling practices, and the extent to which intermediaries were able to navigate among competing loyalties to the company, their communities, and their families determined their success. The coming of World War II, however, was a major turning point in how foreign firms and local intermediaries would navigate an already fragile relationship. Tensions and suspicions between groups escalated during the 1940s as goods to West Africa, as elsewhere, were increasingly limited due to wartime conditions. European agents increasingly found themselves "weary and nervous," as J. Lenggenhager expressed in 1941. Commodity shortages, as well as growing nationalist activities, also forced firms to rearticulate their role in a future independent Ghana. The UAC, for example, attempted to restructure its merchandise business by pulling out of retailing and focusing more on wholesaling. A government report from 1943 noted that seventeen out of thirty-four retail stores were shut down in one district, while in another, 114 out of 150 had disappeared. The colonial state estimated that about twenty "petty traders" would be necessary to absorb the trade of one closed retail store with a monthly turnover of one hundred pounds.[113]

By closing down many African-run retail stores and diverting the power of storekeepers and large-scale credit customers to several smaller customers and petty traders, the UAC ended the autonomy of district branches. This move also diluted the authority once enjoyed by salaried storekeepers and the larger credit customers. Postwar changes, together with corporate language stressing the need for professionalization and objective market research, would further lead to new company public relations strategies that sought to understand and connect more directly with African consumers. As we shall see in chapter 3, however, Kwame Nkrumah, Ghana's first prime minister and later its president, had his own motivations for maintaining ties with the UAC in the years leading up to and immediately after independence. Framed by nationalist discourse, a new relationship with foreign firms that combined past colonial experiences with future aspirations was forged.

3 "In Time for Independence"

Kingsway Department Store, Modernity, and the New Nation

On December 23, 1957, the *Daily Graphic* reported that a Kingsway Department Store security guard had apprehended "an Irish housewife" named Bridgett Mary Ryan for stealing "two packets of ice-cream, half a pound of butter, meat, ham bacon, pork sausage and cake, valued at a total of £2 2s. 1d."[1] According to F. Kwaku Setrena, the security guard on duty, Ryan went from aisle to aisle piling items into both her shopping cart and a separate bag she had placed inside it. When Ryan arrived at the cash register, she removed the bag and paid only for the items in the cart. Before she could exit the store, Setrena approached Ryan and asked her to accompany him to the store manager's office. Ryan claimed she was simply "putting the items aside" and begged to pay double the price of the goods if the manager released her. The manager refused Ryan's plea and handed her over to the police. At her court hearing, Ryan denied the charges and argued that she was on her way to collect money from her husband, and fully intended to return and pay for the items. The senior court magistrate, E. A. L. Bannerman, argued that Ryan had been in Ghana for almost a year and "should be quite conversant with the self-service operation at Kingsway." To prove to the public that shoplifting "does not pay," Bannerman sentenced Ryan to three months' imprisonment with hard labor.[2]

Ryan's case was not unique; similar stories about shoplifting expatriate housewives appear occasionally throughout the late 1950s. A month after

Ryan's case, an Accra court found thirty-four-year-old Welsh housewife Dorothy Gwendoline Elliot guilty of stealing a pint of gin valued at twelve shillings, ten pence.[3] While Accra appellate courts ended up reducing the sentences of both women to one day in prison and fines, these incidences stirred up angry debates in the local press.[4] Local journalists criticized the presumptuousness and latent racism of white shoppers who believed they could easily swindle what they considered unassuming and unobservant Ghanaian employees. *Daily Graphic* contributor Gloria Lamptey wrote, "It is unfortunate that most of these housewives, particularly the white ones, tend to use their seemingly superior social standing to play all sorts of dirty tricks in the hope of evading challenge by the naturally friendly and accommodating Ghanaian salesman and saleswoman. . . . This is not an idle accusation. It is a trick which has been seen through. The sooner this nasty practice is stopped, the better it will be for good relations. Ghanaians are not so credulous as they seem."[5] Lamptey's article conveyed not only a sense of disgust at white shoppers' behavior but also revealed a determination to shed any colonial holdover that devalued Africans' abilities as workers and trustworthy consumers.

This chapter examines Kingsway Department Store as a site of political and social tension in Ghana's capital city, Accra, in the period leading up to and following the country's independence on March 6, 1957 (fig. 3.1). Although the city was home to other department stores, such as Glamour, the Union Trading Company Department Store and, later, Ghana House (opened by the Ghana National Trading Corporation), the new Accra Kingsway was one of the largest and most impressive. While the United Africa Company (UAC) owned and operated the new Kingsway, the history of its construction was notably shaped by nationalist politics.[6] During British rule, as we have seen in chapters 1 and 2, the UAC and the Union Trading Company (UTC) attempted to impose their selling and distribution systems on local markets for profit. But this was not the motivation behind the building of the new Kingsway; in fact, private letters between the UAC executive director Frederick Pedler and general manager Patrick H. Fitz-Gerald reveal that the company considered the department store project a huge economic liability.[7]

Plans for the construction and opening of Kingsway were fueled by competing political and economic interests and were intimately intertwined with debates about what constituted "the modern" and what postindependence modernization should look like. As scholars have argued, in colonial societies technology and infrastructure were not neutral concepts but were invested with dense—if unstable—symbolic meaning.[8] For the UAC, the building of Kingsway was a sign of goodwill and an opportunity to shed its identity as an old colonial trading firm. Prime Minister Kwame Nkrumah

FIGURE 3.1. Exterior of Kingsway Department Store, Accra, ca. 1957. Reproduced with kind permission of Unilever from the original at the Unilever Archives, UAC/1/11/9/46/1.

positioned the department store as a symbol of the new, independent nation, as well as a sign of overseas confidence in his Convention People's Party government. In addition, he hoped that Kingsway's modernist architecture would contribute to Accra's image as a major international hub and popular travel destination.[9] Local residents and government officials also weighed in on debates about Kingsway's construction and location. While residents had been pressuring the UAC to update Accra's shopping facilities for years, local officials rejected the idea that a department store should be a central feature of any developing city.

As historians Stephan F. Miescher and Dzodzi Tsikata have argued, the promise of modernity and the route to it—modernization—was one of the most powerful and popular discursive strategies for emerging African nations in the 1950s and 1960s.[10] Yet, rather than "setting straight or correcting modernization discourse," this chapter demonstrates what scholar James Ferguson called for almost two decades ago, "an analysis that shows what it does."[11] In doing so I borrow from Charles Piot, whose study on postcolonial Togo asks us to reconsider modernity less as a historical condition and more as a political project whose aim has always been to "center the West and marginalize the rest."[12] Focusing on consumer politics, however, shows us how modernity was also evoked and deployed by African politicians, bureaucrats, and businessmen, and how its terms were contested in the cultural realm. As Andrew Ivaska demonstrates in his study on youth culture in postcolonial Dar es Salaam, "the modern" became a "claim-making category" used in social struggles over gender, generation, and wealth.[13] The present chapter thus addresses how the promises of modernity and modernization intersected with commercial developments in the 1950s and early 1960s, and how those promises appeared both along with and in opposition to the rhetoric of decolonization and nation building.

In Ghana, as elsewhere, urban department stores often highlighted and exacerbated the social, political, and economic debates of the time.[14] These embodiments of conflict are regularly ignored in studies of African consumption, or they are briefly acknowledged, only to then be dismissed as either the preserve of European expatriates or as catering exclusively to African elites. To some extent, both these statements are true. Kingsway advertisers and marketers did target mostly urban elite and middle-class consumers. The store's employees, including then manager Deborah Quartey, considered "regular customers" to be people like lawyers, judges, and housewives.[15] Similarly, G. A. Attoh, a former employee, explained that the store's location allowed it to construct its identity as a "first-class shop." According to Attoh, shoppers considered other stores, like the UTC, to be "second-class" because they were closer to the city's central market and High Street, and therefore very popular with market women.[16] These descriptions suggest what we already know, either intuitively or from our own experiences today: that the city as a whole is often crucial to the construction of each of us as consumers—in this case, the "African consumer"—but also that this process of becoming a consumer is always more complex and more specific. Within a given city there can be significant variation in the meanings of different spaces; in Accra, as we shall see, certain places encouraged certain types of consumption. Yet as Abdoumaliq Simone argues, no matter how hard planners and policy makers might try, "at the heart of city life is the capacity for its different people, spaces, activities, and things to interact in ways that exceed any attempts to regulate them."[17]

This chapter therefore examines the tension between the development of postcolonial urban space and the construction of consumer identities, as well as the multiple strategies undertaken by all types of local residents to include themselves in these discourses. It also explores how these tensions played out inside the store. Here I follow the lead of department store historian Susan Porter Benson, who argues that the ways in which salespeople, customers, and managers "jousted for power on the selling floor" offer a window on a society increasingly pervaded by consumer capitalism.[18] Kingsway, the modern department store that valued convenience and technological know-how, as well as order and efficiency, was a site of chaos and conflict. Salaried women on staff, younger managers supervising older employees, and incidents like the shoplifting Irish housewife disrupted cultural norms that in the past had granted authority based on established hierarchies of gender, age, and race. The last section of the chapter shifts attention onto Kingsway's broader, and at times unintended, audience. Information and news about Kingsway circulated beyond the urban elite imagination through news, advertisements, store exhibitions, and word of mouth. Kingsway was more than just a place to shop; the store became part of everyday discourse in socially meaningful ways. To cite one of numerous examples, attractive, well-behaved children became known as "Kingsway babies" among Ga women in Accra.[19] Therefore Kingsway was never neatly set off from daily life, but intricately bound up in its fabric.

"TIMES ARE CHANGING"

Claiming to carry the "latest and best" from London, Kingsway stores began as a chain of department stores for Europeans to maintain, as closely as possible, their "home" lifestyles in a West African environment.[20] Opened by the Miller-Swanzy Group in 1920, the first Kingsway Department Store was located on High Street in Accra and was named after the location of the company's headquarters on Kingsway in central London.[21] In 1929, the UAC took control of Miller-Swanzy, expanded its operations, and used the name Kingsway to start a chain of department stores throughout major British West African cities, including Freetown, Ibadan, and Lagos. Where Kingsway stores did not exist, the UAC opened smaller versions known as EDs (European department stores). Depictions of Africans visiting Kingsway in commercial guidebooks published for European businessmen and travelers focused on African amazement at and "misuse" of Western goods. One description notes that "facing the main entrance is a large mirror, which is in the nature of a Ju Ju to primitive people from the bush who have never before beheld themselves in so extensive a looking-glass."[22] As Brian Larkin argues, colonial officials seemed eager to have Africans react to technology as a sublime force and equally eager to make sure those reactions were recorded and circulated. Thus, what he terms the "colonial sublime" was based on maintaining ideas about racial difference and white supremacy.[23]

Although originally aimed at European colonial bureaucrats and their families, EDs and the Kingsway stores increasingly attracted African shoppers—both members of the elite and the emerging middle class. By 1954, the UAC's general manager Fitz-Gerald observed that "almost as many Africans are customers of this type of store as Europeans." Further recognizing that "politically times are changing," he ordered all UAC district managers to replace the term "European Department Store" with the name "K store" that same year.[24] That shift was one small example of the ways that British businesses began to understand (or at least acknowledge) the changing desires of its West African customers in the decade after World War II. This recognition was closely linked to the emerging status of Gold Coasters as citizens of a newly independent nation rather than as colonial subjects, which soon became visible in the company's advertising campaigns and employment practices.[25] The opening of the new Kingsway store in 1957, the exact year of Ghanaian independence, reflects not only transformations in UAC retail policies but also an effort to appeal to African audiences and promote goodwill between the company and the new nation.

With self-rule quickly approaching, UAC executives agreed that the new Kingsway in Accra should directly target African customers. This aim, however, was not universally accepted. A presentation years later to the board of directors of Unilever, the UAC's parent company, clues us into some possible pushback. "Kingsway Stores, *in spite* of its modern approach," the UAC's chairman explained, "was intended to serve Africans."[26] At the time, investment in a modern department store that catered to African customers may have seemed inappropriate. Of course, concerns about Kingsway's potential as a moneymaker drove criticisms. Yet the chairman's insertion of "in spite of" also reveals persistent assumptions among firm executives about the African marketplace as primitive and hesitations about African consumers as a group worth courting through modern approaches. Nevertheless, in a private letter, Fitz-Gerald acknowledged that while department stores in Africa were not the most profitable system of retailing, the project was in the UAC's best interests because "a business of this nature, properly conducted will bring prestige and goodwill to the Company from the particular section of society where the greatest influence is going to lie in the future. . . . African Ministers and their wives and families, senior African Civil Servants, [and] the ever-increasing class of professional men of all kinds, will provide the main section of society from which our customers will be drawn."[27] The building of Kingsway was thus part of larger public relations efforts to combat negative criticisms and assure members of the African elite that the company was committed to supporting an independent Ghana. In fact, the new Kingsway was one of several large development projects undertaken by the UAC to promote itself as a socially conscious firm in the years leading up to independence. In addition to the department store, which cost approximately £500,000 to construct, the company financed £65,000 to build a sports stadium in Kumasi, constructed the Accra Community Centre, and donated large amounts to public charities, scholarships, and various community development projects.[28]

The aim to appeal to African shoppers, as well as plans to update existing Kingsway stores, initiated a series of research visits to popular department stores in cities around the world.[29] The UAC also hoped that by adopting the "improved techniques in buying and selling" used at other stores—such as the regular use of modern equipment like accounting machines, cash registers, and refrigerators; self-service; merchandise displays; and staff training courses—it could update its corporate image.[30] Frederick Pedler, the UAC's executive director, led these investigations by observing and interviewing store managers and supervisors throughout Britain, Germany, Switzerland, and the United States. In Britain, Pedler's itinerary included Bentalls, Harrods, Jessops, John Lewis, Kendal Milne, Marks & Spencer, Sainsbury's, and Selfridges, and took his team to urban centers including Eastbourne, London, Manchester, and Nottingham. In Germany, he visited Frowein & Nolden in Dusseldorf and Kaufhalle in Cologne. In Switzerland, Pedler spent time in Zurich and visited St. Anna Co-op and Migros. In the United States, he toured Marshall Field's in Chicago, Bloomingdale's and Abraham & Straus in New York, and Wieboldt's in Evanston, Illinois.[31] In addition to visiting these stores himself, Pedler arranged for Kingsway managers, both European and African, to spend time at selected sites. For instance, David Aninakwa—who would later become the first African general manager of Kingsway Stores of Ghana—spent a year working in and observing the daily functioning of the John Lewis stores in London. To further pursue his goal of making the UAC's department stores in West Africa top-notch, Pedler also studied retail stores and potential competitors in other African cities, including Dakar, Leopoldville, Mombasa, and Nairobi.[32] In many ways Kingsway was the culmination of postwar efforts toward the more scientific approach to selling that had come about (as noted in chapter 2).

Pedler's major areas of research included advertising, market research, and self-service. But an analysis of his observation notes and interviews reveals that security procedures in London's John Lewis stores, as well as African American consumers and staff in US department stores, interested

Pedler the most. Prior to the development of Kingsway, African consumers were not allowed to select, or even touch, goods on their own; at company-owned retail stores a shopkeeper and his various assistants mediated purchases of even the smallest items, and the large wooden counter that separated the customer from the goods guaranteed this distance. Pedler's preoccupation with security procedures suggests a tension between the company's desire to adopt "modern selling techniques" and its inability to fully trust African customers and staff with self-service. At John Lewis, Pedler met with management to discuss not only the prevention of general shoplifting but also how to monitor customers and staff.[33] He noted that John Lewis hired an outside firm that specialized in "store detection" to visit periodically, but also employed its own "in-store detectives" or plainclothes security guards. Pedler concluded that John Lewis's policies should be applied to Kingsway stores and advised managers to employ "intelligent African boys with Standard VII certificate" as in-store detectives. These "boys," he wrote in his final report, were to spend their time watching both customers and sales assistants.[34]

Another major area of interest was the presence of "black employees and many black customers" in US department stores. While Pedler initially approached these stores as a potential key to unlocking the needs and wants of African American consumers, he was surprisingly mistaken. After his 1952 US tour, he wrote, "I enquired everywhere whether goods are bought specifically for black customers, and whether conscious effort is made to develop a special appeal to draw in black people. This possibility had not crossed the mind of any of the persons to whom I addressed my questions."[35] US department stores like Marshall Field's and Bloomingdale's did not feel any special need to seek black consumers, possibly because white buyers did not envision their potential clients to be anything but white consumers. It is important to note that all of Pedler's US visits were made to department stores in the North. In southern stores, African Americans faced tougher challenges as a result of Jim Crow legislation: black customers were often banned from entering certain department stores and restricted from trying on items like hats or shoes that could potentially later come in contact with white customers' skin; additionally, department stores refused to serve black customers at their lunch counters and in their restaurants.[36] Despite later attempts in the 1960s to attract upper- and middle-class black women with certain lines of beauty products, most US department stores were not interested in making special appeals to African Americans.[37]

Investment in department stores further allowed the UAC to combat criticism and to publicize its new commercial policies. As a direct result of ongoing allegations that it was monopolistic and was forcing African retailers out of business, the UAC began to withdraw from the retail sector.[38] Company publications during the late 1940s and throughout the 1950s, such as the *Statistical and Economic Review*, as well as the UAC's in-house employee magazine the *Unicorn* were also part of this effort.[39] Articles stressed the company's emerging identity as a wholesaler and "specialty dealer" and claimed that the Kingsway stores were part of its withdrawal from general retailing.[40] "Department stores formed no part of the indigenous system of trading in West Africa," one company publication reasoned, and thus did not "trespass in the field of the African trader."[41] Whether this was a genuine approach or merely an excuse to find new ways to make a profit, this justification located Kingsway at the intersection of decolonization and consumer politics. As such we must consider that the construction, promotion, and everyday operation of the department store represented more than simply the will of foreign capital.

"WE REALLY WANTED TO SHOW THE WORLD"

Demands from nationalist leaders, pressure from Accra residents, and opposition from local officials also surrounded the construction of the new Kingsway store. In his personal papers, Pedler noted that several Accra residents had been urging the company to build an "up-to-date" retail facility for years.[42] According to Pedler, Gold Coasters had become jealous of the UAC's investments in Kingsway, Lagos in Nigeria and felt neglected. This was a rather crude assumption. While unequal distribution of UAC funds between the Gold Coast and Nigeria may have sparked some attention, ongoing public pressure to build a new department store in Accra also suggests an increasing sophistication among Gold Coast customers who had come to expect a larger variety of higher-quality goods. This correlation is backed up by UAC merchandising reports: in 1950, for example, the company reported a marked improvement in the sales of consumer goods, including sheets, blankets, children's wear, and leather footwear.[43]

In the decades following the Second World War, Accra's landscape also changed dramatically. Its population more than doubled, increasing from 133,192 in 1948 to 337,828 in 1960, and a number of new landmarks and buildings had been completed.[44] As historian Nate Plageman has demonstrated, enthusiasm for infrastructural development also filled the pages of local newspapers. Through published photographs, reader's letters, and editorials, "the city rather than the countryside" was positioned as a "blueprint for national prominence," whereas prior to the 1950s cocoa production in more rural areas dominated the discussions about development among Europeans and Africans alike. According to Plageman, local employees of the *Daily Graphic* (the most dominant newspaper of the period) used the newspaper to "vigorously promote an urban ideal that could become the basis of the entire nation."[45] Likewise, images, articles, and advertisements featuring Kingsway Department Stores appeared frequently in the *Graphic*, further linking ideas of national prestige with commercial buildings and consumerism among readers.

Local residents were not the only source of pressure on the UAC. In public speeches and private conversations, Kwame Nkrumah, who was then Leader of Government Business, rearticulated the historical relationship between the UAC and the Gold Coast, and strategically used it to make demands on the company. As Pedler explained in 1954, "Nkrumah told us that it was the duty of the United Africa Company to provide a fine department store in time for independence celebrations."[46] He further demanded that the store should be the best in all of Africa and that all distinguished visitors should "go back home saying that Accra had shopping facilities that were equal to anything in the world."[47] By doing so, the UAC would be helping to transform Accra into a modern international city.

The UAC agreed to the demands of Nkrumah and the desires of the public, but received little support from local authorities. Initially, Minister of Local Government Edward Asafu-Adjaye, supported by the permanent secretary at the Ministry of Works and the commissioner of lands, rejected the UAC's site proposals and plans. Pedler commented that plans to construct a Kingsway store in downtown Accra toward the city center with a large parking lot "horrified them." According to Pedler, local planning authorities did "not recognize retail trade as a facility which deserved consideration" in the development of an expanding city.[48] After learning of his failed attempt, Nkrumah contacted the ministry and took it upon himself to secure a large hilltop property in Accra called Adjabeng Lodge where the UAC could start the project. Set off from the center of town, the area was to be part of a new major development project through Accra that would connect Station and Nsawam Roads; this new road was to become the principal thoroughfare of the town, bearing the name Independence Avenue. Pedler recounted that "the planning office [was] in a state of consternation" at Nkrumah's insistence.[49] A modern department store strategically elevated above a new urban thoroughfare (what is today known as Kwame Nkrumah Avenue) guaranteed that pedestrians, buses, lorries, and other vehicles would pass by regularly. In turn, the structure would become a recognizable part of Accra's skyline. For Nkrumah, department store shopping was a central component in transforming Accra into a desirable destination for foreign and local visitors alike.

After almost four years of negotiating plans and two years of construction, the Kingsway store officially opened its doors on January 31, 1957, about a month before independence. According to the press, the store would usher in "a new era of shopping luxury."[50] As opposed to large outdoor markets where customers haggled with sellers over prices, Kingsway promised Ghanaian customers "*the* modern shopping experience" through self-service, a friendly sales staff, and a wide variety of quality goods.[51] Invited to give the inaugural speech at the store's grand opening, Nkrumah argued that the new store would represent the country's "future peace, progress, prosperity and stability." Nearly in the same breath, he declared that it was a place where Ghanaian citizens could have their "every want met."[52] Nkrumah's speech was not entirely celebratory, however; to an audience of European executives, future political leaders, and a packed crowd of eager shoppers, he offered a searing critique. Although it was omitted from the firm's official publications, Nkrumah's original speech included the statement, "It is idle to pretend that the people of the Gold Coast . . . [have] always been on the friendliest terms with such a mighty financial power as Unilever. But times have changed . . . my government like myself and the people of the Gold Coast, does prefer the devil it knows to the devil it does not know."[53] In a single speech Nkrumah captured the conflicting and contentious history of consumer politics in Ghana; while he hoped that consumerism on display would help legitimize the country as a new nation, it was—in his own words—a deal that had been struck with the devil.

An analysis of Nkrumah's private papers reveals that he shopped avidly at UAC stores and ran up huge tabs on items ranging from fine suits to silk socks.[54] Yet his conversations with UAC executives and his inaugural speech suggest that the store represented more than just a place for Ghanaians to fulfill consumer desires or become more like the West. This was an important shift from the past, when the colonial government had used technology and infrastructural projects to demonstrate colonial authority and produce a particular sort of modern African subject. In contrast, Nkrumah considered new large-scale development projects as tools to refashion modern Ghanaian citizens.[55] The Kingsway store was part of this effort, along with his other projects: the Akosombo Hydroelectric Dam, the Accra-Tema Motorway, and the Adome Bridge. Such achievements, he hoped, would help shed Ghana's image as a colonial dependent, attract further foreign investment, and assert a sense of global membership.[56]

In many ways the four-story state-of-the-art Kingsway building, with its parking lot that occupied just over two acres, lived up to its promises; it not only surpassed the Lagos Kingsway store in size but offered twice the number of services. In addition to the supermarket and three floors of retail space, the Accra store housed a restaurant, a barbershop, a pharmacy, a hair salon, and a post office as well as photographic, laundry, and shoe repair services.[57] Other departments included women's and children's clothing, cosmetics, furniture, textiles and materials, menswear, hardware, stationery and books, floor coverings, electrical items, toys, food and provisions, and an air-conditioned cold store selling fresh meat and fish (figs. 3.2–3.4). Modern technologies and an abundance of goods attracted many, and visitors flocked to the new store out of both curiosity and excitement. One of the most memorable features was the store's escalator, the first in West Africa. "My family lived close by," Esther Addai remembers, "and after school I would come here with my cousins and play on the escalator. One of my cousins was afraid, and I would hold her."[58]

Looking back, older men and women speak of the thrill of traveling to Accra and visiting Kingsway for the first time. Alice van der Staaij-Ghartey, originally from Takoradi, remembers her first visit: "We just had independence . . . in those early days, my goodness, you had people coming from the bush who had never been to Accra before, and they want to come and

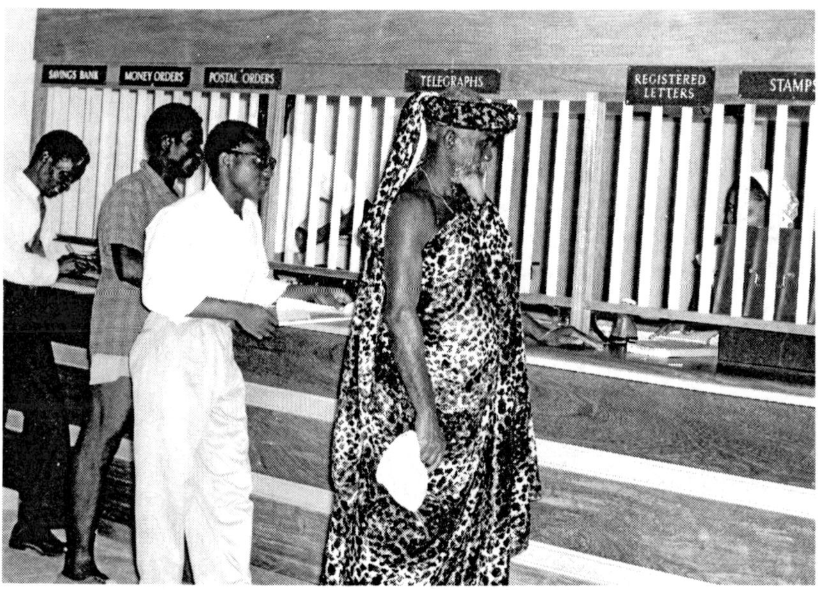

FIGURE 3.2. Post office counter, Kingsway Department Store, Accra, ca. 1960. Reproduced with kind permission of Unilever from the original at the Unilever Archives, UAC/1/11/9/46/7.

FIGURE 3.3. Hat sale, February features, Kingsway Department Store, Accra, February 1960. Reproduced with kind permission of Unilever from the original at the Unilever Archives, UAC/2/10/B1/8/1/15.

FIGURE 3.4. Cosmetics counter, Kingsway Department Store, Accra, ca. 1960. Reproduced with kind permission of Unilever from the original at the Unilever Archives, UAC/2/10/B1/8/1/15.

see, even those of us from Takoradi, we came to Accra."[59] The various departments and variety of services offered first caught Emmanuel Idun's attention: "[It had] everything from food—you could get your hair done in a proper salon. It was fantastic, everything was on display—furniture, you name it, it was all there."[60] Moreover, the quality of goods and brand names carried attracted Kwesi Akumenya Cato: "When you wanted to be a best-dressed chap, you went and bought a suit from Kingsway . . . Austin Reed, Van Heusen shirts . . . shoes from Burton's."[61] This sentiment resonated with other customers years after Kingsway's official opening. As a commercial school student in the mid-1960s, Nana Anwasi Agyemang remembers: "I went to Kingsway in Accra to buy some [suiting] material for myself. I'm from the Eastern Region, and I want to know Accra, you know, as a young guy from school to go to the city, to buy something."[62] For the young Agyemang, Kingsway represented a place of possibility and opportunity to "know" city life. Esther Addai fondly recounts a similar adolescent memory: "It is where I bought my first brassiere." Kingsway became a symbol of the city, and after independence, people from all over Ghana came to visit. As the memories of these elders illustrate, Kingsway was more than a place to buy goods; it was also an experience.

For many Ghanaians, Kingsway symbolized not only promises for a better future but also opportunities to improve their standard of living. Nkrumah himself, as a personal favor, requested that the store always be kept illuminated. According to Pedler, Nkrumah "loved to look over the roofs of Accra and see it, brightly lit on its hill."[63] As one of the many manifestations that modernization could take, a brightly lit department store on a hilltop became a symbol of prosperity: excess electricity and enough capital to keep the store lit throughout the night symbolized the potential of Ghana as a new nation. Electricity was, according to Nkrumah, also the basis for industrialization, a element central to his political agenda.[64] In addition, the building itself, specially designed by T. P. Bennett and Son of London, reflected a type of architectural modernism that, art historian Janet Hess has argued, "emphasized volume, avoided ornamentation, and was constructed in an international style."[65] She notes that while Kingsway's modernist design underscored the central aim of Nkrumah's government—to construct a unified "homogenous community"—it also exhibited a sense of national pride.

In its initial years, Kingsway was a popular destination for local and foreign visitors as well as commercial competitors. Photo shoots of local celebrities browsing the store were common. In one image, photographers snapped Monica Amekoafia, Miss Ghana 1957, making her selection at the haberdashery and handbag counter assisted by two Kingsway saleswomen. As Ghana's first beauty pageant winner, the twenty-two-year-old would travel internationally and became the face of Ghanaian independence.

Images and descriptions of Kingsway featured in tourist handbooks and government ministers brought visiting politicians and other dignitaries to the store for tours. In 1960, Nkrumah's Pan-Africanist vision literally took shape on Kingsway's shop floor through a well-publicized visit by Princess Aida Desta, the eldest granddaughter of Emperor Haile Selassie I of Ethiopia.[66] Two years earlier, Nkrumah had been the first African leader officially invited to Addis Ababa by Haile Selassie. Together, both men played prominent roles in establishing the Organization of African Unity in 1968.

The UAC's competitors also encouraged their staff to visit Kingsway for market research. At a merchandise meeting, UTC's vice director lamented: "The comparison to Kingsway is always an impressive, but also depressing event. We cannot recommend more to go there to see 'how it's done.' Our designers are influenced by the 'Swiss school' . . . the shop windows are not filled with enough goods," he further complained.[67] Compared to Kingsway, the UTC's department store aesthetic was considered too sterile for Ghanaian shoppers.

Among elite and middle-class Ghanaians, Kingsway also became a place to socialize and be noticed. Alice van der Staaij-Ghartey remembers socializing at Kingsway's restaurant and that she and her friends would dress up specifically to go shopping: "[B]ecause the shop is beautiful you would . . . you are not going to the market, so you put on something real nice . . . in those days we wanted to be seen."[68] She adds that looking good was also a strategy to counter imperial and racist assumptions about Ghanaians: "Look, here was a nation where the ideas [were] that we are primitive, we are uncivilized . . . but in that short period of time we really wanted to show the world that we are capable of doing things better . . . hence, dressing up."[69] By stating that "we really wanted to show the world," Van der Staaij-Ghartey situates her sartorial elegance within a larger, global framework; dressing up and shopping at Kingsway was her version, however small, of subverting colonial ideas of African inferiority.

Yet not all people enjoyed visiting Kingsway. For some—namely, poorer or less educated customers—fixed pricing, self-service, and written product information exacerbated anxieties about shopping. As Sadiku Musah, a former UAC driver, explains, "[Literates] have book knowledge when they enter a shop, they know what to do, but the illiterates most of the time fear to enter the shop. When you are illiterate, there are some places you want to go, but your conscience will tell you it's only big men that go there. [For example,] anyone who has been to school, he knows what a bank does . . . the UAC was also like that."[70] Literate customers who could read product information and pricing navigated large department stores comfortably, while the less literate felt shut out. Fixed pricing and unfamiliar goods could deter illiterate shoppers from entering larger stores where most information appeared in writing. Similar to other urban spaces, Kingsway became a popular site of postcolonial "elite culture." In the first decades of independence, historian Emmanuel Akyeampong argues, divisions between "commoner and elite cultures" sharpened; department stores like Kingsway intensified notions that where one shopped and what items one bought were accurate indicators of class status.[71]

"THE CUSTOMER WAS KING," AND CONFLICT ON THE SELLING FLOOR

Kingsway also tried to assert its up-to-date image through its employment practices and staff training. Although Kingsway employees comprised a small section of Accra's population, this group of about four hundred men and women were themselves part of the store's main attraction.[72] The UAC intentionally promoted what it defined as modern salesmanship and customer service (in opposition to African selling practices it deemed outdated and inefficient) and placed its management and sales staff at the center of the shopping experience. According to the firm, Kingsway was to act as a model for modern methods of selling and provide a "general standard of shop keeping" for the entire country.[73] Former UAC shopkeeper George Darkwa Kwakye's most vivid memory of Kingsway was that "there were *so* many clerks." He read the abundance of clerks as a sign of the wealth and grandness of Kingsway; to be able to hire and pay that many employees, when the average shopkeeper had a single paid assistant at best, was impressive.[74]

Furthering that image of grandness was Kingsway's hiring of high-profile personalities. Emmanuel Chris Briandt, the first captain of Ghana's national football team, the Black Stars, became an Accra store manager.[75] The company also hired the children of prominent Ghanaian politicians; in 1961 all three major local newspapers reported that Miss Marian Asaufu-Adjaye, the daughter of Ghana's high commissioner in London, was appointed to a management position.[76] These popular and well-connected young men and women could both assist with the store's promotion and be used by the UAC to gain favor with the Ghanaian elite—especially as those families became newly influential, both politically and economically, after independence. Of course, employment at Kingsway also came with various benefits. Stable salaries, discounts, hire-purchase or layaway privileges, and staff dances and social functions were attractive incentives for workers.[77] The social cachet associated with working at Kingsway and being surrounded by luxury was also a draw. In the years following independence, a Kingsway staff position was an elevated social status unto itself.

From its beginning the UAC focused on providing its African clerical staff and managers with professional training and certifications, but these efforts increased significantly after World War II. In the 1950s the company invited local and foreign instructors to teach formal courses on salesmanship; staff trainers screened instructional films taken in US and British department stores and organized role-playing exercises to demonstrate techniques for increasing sales and displaying merchandise (fig. 3.5).[78] By the 1960s methods were refined further, and Kingsway's staff training room hosted a number of ten- to twenty-week courses including bookkeeping, commercial arithmetic, elementary economics, business law, and personnel management; the company provided textbooks and held exams at the end of each term.[79]

This new attention grew out of broader transformations in retailing, especially in the United States, that positioned salesmanship as "the science and art of creating demand."[80] Former Kingsway manager Deborah Quartey recalls, "We had in-service training . . . so all these checkout operators, sales-

FIGURE 3.5. Salesmen preparing a display for electric Singer sewing machine, Kingsway Department Store, Accra, ca. 1960. Reproduced with kind permission of Unilever from the original at the Unilever Archives, UAC/1/11/9/46.

girls, salesmen, everybody went through training before you were given a little place of a department to handle. You even learnt how to operate a machine, you learnt customer service—how the customer was king, you needn't argue or fight with the customer, the customer was king; without him you wouldn't be there."[81] These instructions were reinforced in the staff sales manual, which contained detailed scripted responses to customer queries. Customer service required being alert, smiling, and properly greeting customers. Moreover, the manual covered such issues as how to talk about your merchandise, how to increase sales, and how to ask customers essential questions. Above all, as Quartey notes, the firm emphasized that the customer came first.[82] While ideas about service and salesmanship were nothing new in Ghana, what was new at Kingsway was the enormous authority given to the customer and the deferential selling techniques that the UAC turned into classroom lessons and lectures.

In addition to emphasizing sales skills, company training stressed the importance of personal appearance and hygiene. Kingsway employee handbooks established further the connection between physical appearance and salesmanship, implying that the more attractive a salesperson appeared, the better his or her ability to sell. The company instructed women on how to apply make-up and fingernail polish and reminded them to wash their hands and feet. Women's shoes were also a point of strict instruction: "If your shoes have straps see that they are fastened, if your shoes have buckles please see that one is not missing."[83] Men were encouraged to shave daily, wear leather shoes and "crisp white shirts," and keep their hair short. The staff manual also provided detailed guidelines on how to wash the store uniform; soaking it in Omo or Surf soap (products sold at the store) was preferred, and all items of clothing required ironing. Frequent customer Van der Staaij-Ghartey recalls the impeccable appearance of Kingsway sales staff; she was especially taken with the women, whom she remembers had "excellent style."[84]

The store also used Kingsway staff as models for in-store fashion shows and as subjects of market research. Hired by the company in 1959 to study African female consumers, Eleanor MacDonald commented that when she needed ideas for developing new lines, she would "go around each department and ask the opinions of African staff."[85] It is ironic that British and Ghanaian newspapers referred to MacDonald as the UAC's "fashion expert" when she was, in fact, receiving her cutting-edge fashion advice from African women, including Kingsway's saleswomen.[86]

While being praised for their fashion sense and style, Kingsway staff also found themselves at the center of gender and generational conflicts. In the local press, saleswomen in particular received much public attention; young, beautiful, and decked out in the latest fashions and hairstyles, they became objects of both desire and disgust. A 1958 *Ghana Evening News* article captured some of this sentiment; as one customer noted, "[There was a time] when employees in all the shops had to be reasonably well-mannered. If they failed to live by that they got their sack . . . I have seen attractive but overbearing girls in shops order customers to form a queue in the most objectionable manner. I have seen respectable customers, including myself of course, waiting patiently to be served while a pair of sale girls finished their talk about the boyfriend [*sic*]."[87] Clearly annoyed about the lack of personal attention and the tactics used to command shoppers, this customer depicted saleswomen as attractive, yet disrespectful and frivolous. A 1961 open forum in the *Sunday Mirror*—"Are Ghana's Salesgirls Courteous?" delivered similar complaints. While one younger man claimed that saleswomen needed more training, another commented, "Damn those salesgirls . . . they are real thorns in the flesh of customers. Why, they find it lip-splitting to smile at a customer. All these girls should be drafted to the kitchen. That is the place for them."[88] This shopper believed that saleswomen's refusal to greet him with smiles was an intentional act and grounds for dismissal. In another response, a younger woman, perhaps a saleswoman herself, wrote that it was often "the ungentlemanly behavior of some of the customers" that was intolerable.[89] After compiling dozens of letters, forum editors concluded that although the average saleswoman was beautiful and smart, most were rude and discourteous.[90]

Although not focused solely on Kingsway staff, these articles, and especially the newspaper forum, illustrate how Ghanaian shoppers employed gender tropes to criticize the behavior of female sales staff and question their abilities to hold such positions. The most critical voices against saleswomen were young male customers, which gives a hint at the disruption of gender roles that came with the elevation of these young women into desirable, and surprisingly powerful, positions of employment. The young saleswomen who had at least secondary school educations, and the sense of accomplishment that came with stable wages, likely threatened some young men.[91] These educated women may also have resisted young male shoppers who pushed the "customer was king" ethos too far by ordering them to fetch items or demanding certain services. The department store, like so many public spaces in a rapidly changing country, became a space where men and women attempted to define proper gender roles. The discourse surrounding "customer service" was both informed by and an influence on sexist attitudes toward young working women.

Generational conflict also came to a head on the selling floor. As early as the 1950s the UAC personnel department began initiating plans to hire young Africans who had graduated from its training program rather than promoting currently employed Africans who had not.[92] This move caused significant tension between younger managers and older staff—particularly those who had served the company for decades and now found younger men and women as their superiors. Moreover, this shift caused a rift between what the company categorized as "old school" and "graduate" employees. While the UAC considered "old schoolers" to be loyal, reliable, and very enthusiastic, they did not expect them to "rise to any greater heights." The company described graduates, on the other hand, as "young, energetic, well informed, and articulate."[93]

Generational roles and expectations were challenged by Kingsway's hiring practices. Deborah Quartey, who was hired through the UAC's recruitment program after graduating from college, emphasizes the difficulties working with older women who had different job expectations and did not see her education as trumping their work experience. "We had a lot of staff who were nongraduates," she remembers. "They had worked for maybe twenty to twenty-five years before I joined and I was earning more, by virtue of going to university, so all those elderly women who could pass for my mother were already there and I was this little girl earning more than they were."[94] As a young manager, Quartey faced challenges in acting as a superior to older saleswomen. Although she admits to having reported some of the difficult older employees, Quartey, who was then in her early twenties, often opted to diffuse conflicts by simply doing their jobs herself. She notes that she often chose to operate checkout machines and attend to customers when older staff refused to take directions from her: "I had difficulty giving them instructions, and they didn't want to take it, so you had to do the job yourself at times. So if you felt too old, and you didn't want to take instructions from me, I would do it. I remember I used to tell them, 'You wait till your son or daughter comes out from the university and then see if you will like it if he or she is treated the way you are treating me.'"[95]

Quartey's experiences emerged directly from cultural norms about age and life experience; in some sense she submitted to the dictates of older staff even though she was in a senior position. In addition, Quartey's age was compounded by the fact that she was both well-educated and unmarried—two strikes against her in the minds of many. For Ghanaian women, marriage and motherhood brought a certain amount of social prestige and also signified a woman as a legitimate adult. As Carmel Dinan argues in her study of white-collar women workers in Accra in the 1970s, unmarried working women were suspected by men of being harsh and selfish, and by other women of being immoral and a lure to their husbands.[96] For many of the older women she supervised, Quartey's position as a manager was also a blatant reminder that they were being passed over for promotions. Many of these women had faced difficulties breaking through racial, gender, and generational barriers when they began working for Kingsway. This recognition may have also played a part in Quartey's response to what seemed like acts of insubordination on the surface. Nevertheless, she sympathized with the older women she supervised; by referring to herself during that time as a "little girl," Quartey ultimately legitimized the attitudes of the same women about whom she complained.[97]

SHOPPING ASPIRATIONS, REMAKING, AND RESELLING

Kingsway print and radio advertisements from the mid-1950s not only targeted elite and middle-class customers but also promoted Kingsway in association with a specific type of lifestyle. An advertisement titled "Your Way" featured a beautiful couple posed arm in arm opposite Kingsway's self-service section (fig. 3.6); we can assume that the couple is married and that the woman—who wears a white kaba and slit ensemble accessorized with jewelry and a handbag—is a new mother. (A Ghanaian mother traditionally wears white for several months after the birth of a child.) The man who appears at her side wears a three-piece suit—a sign that he is either a senior civil servant or a manager at a commercial firm. His look is rounded out by a tie, hat, and leather shoes. Behind the couple is a scene of plenty; the shelves and shopping carts are full of imported food items, and people leisurely select from the variety of goods. By juxtaposing the happy couple to fully stocked shelves, this advertisement celebrates consumer choice and abundance in association with a nuclear family model.[98]

The "What We Like about Kingsway" campaign sent a similar message to viewers and readers while also focusing on the store as a "one-stop shop" and on the various services it provided (fig. 3.7). Together, the family sends mail at the post office, orders medicine from the dispensary or pharmacy, and eats a tasty meal in the restaurant. In this rendition, the various service sections are presented as spacious, orderly, organized, and efficient.

Both advertisements present the consumption of goods and services as a crucial component for attaining and maintaining a modern, respectable middle-class lifestyle.

By promoting shopping as a joint activity for couples and families, advertisers also constructed Kingsway as a gender-neutral space. For men, shopping at Kingsway was deemed more acceptable than local outdoor markets, which in most Ghanaian cities were predominantly female spaces. While men sold specific items like electrical goods, hardware, and shoes, women controlled the majority of retail trade in essentials like foodstuffs, toiletries, and

FIGURE 3.6. "Your Way," advertisement, ca. 1955, UAC Public Relations Department. Reproduced with kind permission of Unilever from the original at the Unilever Archives, UAC/21/10/B1/8/1/10-d.

FIGURE 3.7. "What We Like about Kingsway," advertisement, ca. 1957. Reproduced with kind permission of Unilever from the original at the Unilever Archives.

various domestic products. This gender division is clearly described in Christine Oppong's study of middle-class marriage in the 1960s, in which interviews with husbands and wives about the division of household labor revealed that most men dreaded market shopping, especially for food. As Oppong notes, "Some of the wives laugh about this saying that their husbands are only willing to shop in the market when there is no one around to see them. If they go they may be teased by market sellers."[99] The Kingsway environment and self-service system worked to neutralize the gender of shopping: the modern man could now also be a shopper. To attract male customers, Kingsway held contests like the Smart Man competition and awarded prizes, including clothing valuing up to twenty-five pounds, to the best-dressed contestants.[100] In addition, the "Your Way" advertisement depicted two distinguished men, one confidently holding a shopping basket, one browsing food items in the self-service aisle with ease. The local press jumped at opportunities to snap photos of Kwame Nkrumah during Kingsway shopping trips. Despite his expensive tastes, what the press emphasized was the normalcy of the male leader of the country popping into Kingsway for a new pair of glasses; indeed, the *Evening News* labeled him "citizen among citizens."[101]

For most men and women living in Accra, regularly shopping at Kingsway remained an aspiration. This held also true for other Ghanaian cities as smaller versions of Kingsway existed in Cape Coast, Kumasi, Sekondi,

Takoradi, and later Burma Camp, Tamale, and Tema. Household surveys conducted in the 1950s, for all their flaws and shortcomings, do offer some insight into the consumption habits of the day and how people chose to spend their money.[102] Produced by the Gold Coast Office of the Government Statistician, which had been established by the colonial government in 1948, household surveys emerged as a tool for measuring standards of living and welfare conditions in the colonies, as well as in Britain itself.[103] A comparison of four major surveys compiled from interviews with hundreds of urban residents in Accra (1953), Akuse (1954), Kumasi (1955), and Sekondi-Takoradi (1955) revealed that the highest percentage of workers' income was spent on food.[104] Locally grown food accounted for almost half or more of a worker's monthly wages, about 49.2–52.3 percent, while imported foods accounted for only about 5–9 percent, with the highest percentage consumed in Accra. Local foods included meat, fowl, fish, eggs, oils, nuts, cassava, cocoyam, plantains, and various other fruits and vegetables. Imported foods included biscuits, butter and margarine, milk, sugar, sardines, and tea. After food, the next largest expenditure category in all cities was clothing, at about 12.1–17.3 percent. Coveted items for women included cotton prints, head ties, and sandals, and for men cotton prints, ready-made shirts, shorts, socks, and shoes. Both percentages include amounts spent on tailoring charges, as most people took advantage of the numerous skilled tailors and designers who flocked to the city for work. Other categories included fuel and light (candles, charcoal, kerosene, matches); services (school and church fees, books, transportation, entertainment, shoe repair, and haircuts); durable goods, including furniture; dry goods (blankets, sheets, and towels); buckets and kerosene tins; cooking utensils; axes, cutlasses, and cutlery; coal pots and cookers; glassware; carpets and mats; and lamps and lanterns.[105]

Because of the financial realities of many urban workers, who spent most of their money on local food items rather than on imported goods available at Kingsway, advertisements promoting shopping as an activity for couples or the family were not conducive to the lifestyle of most people. Urban studies from the 1960s show that the majority of consumption decisions took place outside the household. Women tended to spend money on clothes and wigs to attend community and church functions, and men on going out to places like bars, football matches, and nightclubs. Husbands and wives had individual incomes and separate sets of friends; they made separate decisions about consumption activities. In addition, as other scholars have shown, conjugal partnership was not the norm or was only temporary in a couple's early years of marriage, and many married couples lived apart.[106] While the emerging elite, new politicians and senior civil servants who took charge after independence, "popularized the concept of the single family home or self-contained home or flat after independence,"[107] household studies and surveys showed that the majority of urban residents lived in multihousehold buildings or compounds that contained from four to forty rooms rented out by landlords. While wealthier families could afford multiroom apartments furnished with larger domestic items like televisions and refrigerators, and some among the lower-middle and working classes had electric irons, fans and phonographs, "most live[d] in a single room about twelve feet square, with only a bed, storage containers, chair, table, cooking utensils, and perhaps a radio."[108] Additionally, cooking areas (mostly located outdoors), bathrooms, and latrines were all communal.[109] Even though Nkrumah arranged the construction of new single-family developments in places like Tema, a 1959 survey showed that tenants converted extra rooms intended to divide sleeping, eating, and living space into places of business: provision stores, bars, and chop bars (places to buy prepared meals).[110] The financial realities of most urban residents did not give way to the consumption patterns promoted in Kingsway advertisements and through the press.

The point here, however, is not to show how disconnected Kingsway was from ordinary life and consumption patterns. We know that, even today, most advertisements promote aspirational lifestyles rather than reflect realistic ones. Instead I hope to paint a more dynamic picture of shopping culture, of which the department store was a part. Kingsway catered to elite and middle-class customers, but entrance and admission to store events was never limited to just them. Every aspect of the store, from beauty contests to cute baby competitions, fashion shows to home demonstrations, was free and open to the public. A photograph taken at Kingsway's "Modern Living" promotion in 1961 depicts a diverse audience including professional women, mothers, schoolchildren, and curious youngsters attending the "Lovely Babies" competition (figure 3.8). Free samples, special discounts, and opportunities for people-watching also drew crowds to these events.[111] Further support for this claim comes from G. A. Attoh, who was hired in 1957 as one of the store's first salespeople in the photography department. He recalls that all types of people passed through Kingsway's doors in those early years, and cites numerous elevator injuries to bare feet to emphasize his point; this suggests that the crowds at Kingsway were far more varied than those depicted in advertisements and promotional photos.[112]

Despite the UAC's efforts to promote department-store shopping, divisions between newer and older consumer spaces remained fluid. While Kingsway presented itself as a one-stop shop, both a department store and a supermarket, this concept proved impossible to realize in practice. In its initial

FIGURE 3.8. Lovely Babies competition, Kingsway Department Store, Accra, May 29–June 10, 1960. Reproduced with kind permission of Unilever from the original at the Unilever Archives, UAC/2/10/B1/8/1.

years of operation, Kingsway sold only imported food items. Upper-class women like Alice van der Staaij-Ghartey, who had the means to purchase goods at department stores, remembers still needing to shop at local markets: "We went to the market to buy our indigenous foodstuff, plantain, fresh tomatoes, cassava, smoked fish, kontomire, garden eggs, anything to do with Ghanaian cooking. . . . So sometimes we went to the market to buy these things because they are there and they are cheaper. And fresh."[113] Her explanation suggests fluidity among urban shopping spaces: although she shopped at large department stores like Kingsway and UTC, she also shopped in Accra's main local market, Makola (about a fifteen-minute walk from Kingsway) to buy food and to compare prices. The main market, a prominent feature in almost every Ghanaian city, was located outdoors, sprawled several city blocks, and housed hundreds of vendors. As we saw in chapter 2, many successful credit customers operated at least one stall, and sometimes dozens, in city markets.

Creating and selling knockoffs of imported fashions and goods was another strategy used by those who did not have the money or time to shop at places like Kingsway regularly. Such tactics were essential for many groups in fashioning modern urban identities. Nate Plageman notes that financially marginalized groups like laborers, students, and migrants found ways to participate in the commercialized leisure and nightlife of the city by producing their own versions of the gowns and suits sold in large department stores. Young women, in particular, sewed their own dresses; this was cheaper than purchasing store-bought items and allowed them to "exercise individual taste and style."[114] Because stores like Kingsway also published descriptive weekly announcements about new stock in the local press, those with access to newspapers could get an idea of what was in the store without actually setting foot in it.

Fixed pricing, written product information, and price tags may have intimidated customers who could not read, and many people preferred bargaining in outdoor markets, where retailers sold many of the same goods. Credit customers who worked in the market often resold directly from the UAC itself, a practice that was beneficial for those who desired certain items but were not eligible for store credit. Kingsway tended to accommodate only wealthier patrons, and those it deemed "regular" customers; Van der Staaij-Ghartey notes that the only reason Accra department stores gave her credit was because she was married to a European from another well-known firm.[115] By contrast, in the city's open market a customer who could not pay in full could haggle over prices and negotiate credit options and terms. In the 1958 *Accra Survey*, Ione Acquah argued that many customers favored markets over retail stores operated by firms: "The majority of [consumers] prefer the personal touch of the petty trader to the impersonal, and, not infrequently, rude behavior of the shop assistant; they like to haggle over price . . . the traders are more easily accessible and they often allow, in contrast to the shops, time to pay."[116]

Cases of remaking and reselling of goods illustrate that divisions between Kingsway and local markets were blurred, and my own interviews confirm this. Former UAC manager Michael N. Ankumah remembers touring rural areas in the late 1960s to sell shares and educate people about shareholding. He vividly recalls one old man who fell asleep during the presentation and woke up to say, "UAC shirts, it would be a very good shirt. I'll buy one."[117] While the prospective buyer had misunderstood (Ankumah was selling stocks, not shirts), it is clear from this encounter that customers in the rural areas were familiar with UAC products and with people transporting and reselling goods from cities. Instead of accepting Kingsway as the "general standard of shopkeeping," which was the intention of the UAC's directors, local retailers and consumers integrated the store into their own practices of buying and selling, consequently shaping Kingsway's participation in the local economy.[118]

Department stores have existed in major West African cities since the mid-twentieth century. The legacy of colonial capitalism, struggles for political independence, and increased urbanization fueled the multiple economic and political motivations behind the building of the Kingsway store in Accra. For the UAC, agreeing to invest in the £500,000 department store was a public relations strategy and an attempt to legitimize the company's activities in a future independent Ghana. In addition, it was a means for the UAC to shed its past as an old colonial merchant firm and align itself with larger retail developments happening around the world. Kwame Nkrumah's intervention was also a major factor in the construction of Kingsway. While local authorities were divided on whether a large-scale retail development should be part of an expanding postcolonial city, Nkrumah supported Kingsway as an addition to a long list of large-scale development projects he envisioned as key to the building of a new modern nation.

Meanwhile, beneath the new store's sleek exterior, various social and cultural conflicts emerged on the selling floor. The presence of white-collar working women, young managers supervising older employees, and shoplifting European housewives challenged preexisting local and colonial notions of authority based on gender, age, and race. In addition, fixed-price labels, written product information, and the practice of self-service catered to literate, more educated consumers. Consequently, the new Kingsway became a space for elite and emerging middle-class Ghanaians to distinguish themselves from the lower classes and participate in a shared sociability. In-store events like beauty contests and fashion shows, and Kingsway's sit-down restaurant, provided additional opportunities to be seen, to mingle, to share news, and to gossip—all activities that could work to affirm one's class standing. To some extent the new Kingsway exacerbated social inequalities and illuminated the limitations of large-scale development projects intended by the Nkrumah government to benefit all Ghanaians.

By the mid-1960s the identity of Kingsway as a "premier shopping destination" began to fade. On his 1967 West Africa tour, the UAC's chairman lamented, "It was very disappointing to visit Kingsway Accra. It is so empty of merchandise, and much of the merchandise in it is dull and shabby."[119] Kingsway's shift from an elegant, well-stocked store to one of barren shelves was due in part to two larger changes in the country's political and economic climate: the first was Nkrumah's articulation of a Pan-Africanist, anticolonial, and socialist vision for Ghana's future that emphasized the leading role of the state sector in development; the second was his establishment of various policies and regulations in hopes of doing so.[120] Nkrumah believed that decentering both foreign and domestic private capital, was necessary to fight the "evils of neo-colonialism." As part of his plan he implemented the country's first austerity budget in July 1961, and introduced a series of import license restrictions, which made it difficult for foreign firms to import goods. He also established the Industrial Development Corporation, which favored the local manufacturing of previously imported—and increasingly essential—commodities such as soap, tobacco, shoes, and furniture.[121] The creation of state-owned industries, Nkrumah argued, would diversify Ghana's economy, making the country less reliant on the production and export of cocoa for government revenue and foreign exchange. Ultimately, he hoped these developments would also help move Ghana from a producer-based economy to an industrial-based one.

Another factor contributing to the decline of Kingsway was Nkrumah's establishment of the state-owned Ghana National Trading Corporation (GNTC). Initially formed in April 1961 through the purchase of a small foreign firm called Commonwealth Trust Limited, Nkrumah expanded GNTC operations one year later by acquiring a second, more prominent, foreign business, A. G. Leventis & Company, that had been well known and successful on the coast since the 1930s.[122] Referred to by the press as Ghana's "state shopping project," the GNTC's distribution structure was modeled on that of the UAC.[123] Its mission was quite different, however; the GNTC's focus was to reclaim the country's import-export business from foreigners and to reinvest the commercial profits into improving Ghana's infrastructure (roads, hospitals, schools, and universities). Nkrumah appointed Patrick H. Fitz-Gerald, who had recently retired as the UAC's Ghana general manager, to head the new company. Similar to the UAC's establishment of Kingsway, the corporation opened a chain of department stores, with its flagship store Ghana House located in central Accra. Additionally, it operated district branches and retail stores throughout the country.[124] By 1965, the GNTC's operations had surpassed those of the UAC. Whereas the UAC operated 112 wholesale and retail shops, the GNTC operated 210, though neither of these numbers accounted for nearly twenty-one thousand credit customers who held passbooks with both the GNTC and the UAC at this time.[125] While Nkrumah established various state-owned industries and a number of regulatory market policies in hopes of improving the lives of Ghanaians, little did he know that over the next few years they would lead to unimaginable mismanagement of the country's economy and to his own political demise.

4 "Shop Window on the World"
Ghana's First International Trade Fair and the Politics of Wealth and Accumulation

Come businessmen of the world. Let us work together for our mutual benefit and in the true spirit of free enterprise.

—*Business Weekly*, January 30, 1967

On February 1, 1967, thirty countries—from Africa, the Americas, Asia, Europe, and the Middle East—inaugurated Ghana's first International Trade Fair. Situated about six miles from Accra's city center, in an area behind the Kpeshie Lagoon near Labadi Beach, the newly constructed fair site attracted over 950,000 visitors—two and a half times the population of Accra. In addition to paying guests, attendees included the Asantehene, the *amanhene* (paramount chiefs from each region of Ghana), foreign ministers of state, and representatives from Ghanaian-owned companies and large multinational firms. According to Ghana's *Business Weekly*, the fair's theme, "Developing Africa," was meant to showcase what African countries had to offer the world, including advances in manufacturing, industry, science, and technology. The nineteen-day event was also intended to be a "shop window on the world," displaying new consumer products from around the globe for customers both inside and outside Africa.[1] The fair was a media spectacle, and local news correspondents published detailed daily reports on all aspects of it. Likewise, a team of *Daily Graphic* photographers captured images of visitors, exhibitors, and goods that appeared next to headlines and articles each day.

The execution and timing of the international event was in part the result of major changes in the country both politically and economically. On February 24, 1966, a joint coup d'état led by members of Ghana's armed services and police service overthrew Kwame Nkrumah's Convention People's Party (CPP) government while he was on a diplomatic mission to Beijing.[2] The National Liberation Council (NLC), which would be the first of many military regimes to rule Ghana, imagined itself as a "transitional government" empowered by the people and charged with revitalizing the Ghanaian economy. This role required rescuing Ghana from Nkrumah's socialism and what had become his authoritarian leadership style, and making way for a new civilian government based on democratic principles. Within days of the coup the regime announced its plans to embrace a free market economy, encourage private business, and adopt the policies of the International Monetary Fund (IMF) and the World Bank, as well as the conditions attached to the foreign aid that came with it.[3] In his speech at the trade fair's opening, Lieutenant General Joseph Arthur Ankrah, the NLC's first chairman, positioned the international event as an opportunity to regain the confidence of businessmen at home and abroad and inaugurated the fair as an "economic revival."[4] The event, in other words, was built upon a faith in the free market, and thus symbolic of a larger post-Nkrumah refashioning project meant to recast the country's political and economic allegiances.

Efforts to construct a new image for Ghana on an international stage were also embedded in local politics. Here we will see the emergence of another group of people who until the coup had been relegated to a mostly symbolic status: the chiefs or traditional rulers. The mass publicity surrounding chiefly presence at the fair worked to reestablish state support of traditional chieftaincy—the precolonial institution of governance with executive, legislative, and judicial powers. This group of men was historically a linchpin in the daily functioning of Ghana, but had been marginalized by British colonial powers and later muted by Nkrumah's establishment of various state-owned enterprises. While I agree with political historians who have described these efforts as the NLC's desire to return to "a reformed past," I argue that we must also consider deeper economic motivations. The NLC's attempts to reinstate chieftaincy had important implications for the future of Ghana's economy.[5] Chiefs had become a part of the established business class, and disapproved of attempts on the part of the CPP to centralize and control individual accumulation. Under the guise of free market capitalism, the NLC was attempting to not only reorder political and economic authority but also to redefine the very meaning of *consumption*. That process, as we'll see, was rooted in long-standing debates about the nature and meaning of wealth. By presenting a democratization of goods or the idea that equal access to a wide and limitless array of commodities was an inalienable right, the regime also sought to gain legitimacy among the Ghanaian public, whose consumer aspirations had been stifled under Nkrumah during the years of the First Republic (1960–66).

This chapter therefore uses Ghana's first International Trade Fair as a lens to understand how the politics of wealth and accumulation was negotiated in the post-Nkrumah period. I argue that struggles over access to goods and consumer practices constituted key terrains on which these contests were waged. Criticisms about the extravagant spending habits of CPP officials, as well as the economic immorality of women and youth during the Nkrumah period, were rooted in older beliefs about the ethics of accumulation and individual rights to attainment. Such attitudes also reveal how gender and generational hierarchies persisted in shaping consumer ideologies. The NLC's realignment with Western economies must therefore be situated in relation to, and in conversation with, ongoing local conflicts over the nature of wealth and its limitations.[6] As we saw with the case of foreign firms in chapter 1, these ideologies affected how consumer markets functioned. By recovering some of the controversies surrounding accumulation during the 1960s, this chapter expands on accounts of how African consumption was shaped by the social and cultural logics of exchange.[7] Instead of focusing on how these logics affected consumer preferences and the meaning of particular goods, however, I use them to understand how and why the category of consumer itself remained a contested one.

REVIVAL VIA OVERTHROW

For many Ghanaians, independence symbolized a chance to improve their material lives and provided hope for a more equitable distribution of the country's resources; Nkrumah's promises for a better future seemed within reach. But what soon became clear was that the moment of independence was actually the peak of the country's economic prosperity. By the mid-1960s, a drastic drop in the world market price of cocoa—the state's main source of revenue—and excessive government spending on large-scale development projects slowed economic growth. To curtail economic decline, Nkrumah introduced a series of import license regulations, commodity price controls, and austerity measures.[8] Such restrictions were also intended to eliminate foreign domination of Ghana's economy, a key aspect of Nkrumah's continued fight against neocolonialism. These policies greatly affected how foreign firms operated; conducting business in Ghana increasingly depended on securing one of the limited number of import licenses and contracts from the government. Intended to halt inflation and decrease import dependence, these restrictions instead created periodic shortages of everything from sugar to building materials. An official government commission of inquiry found that lining up outside the Ghana National Trading Corporation (GNTC) became a "condition of purchase" for even the most essential commodities, including food items. What consumers resented most, however, was that after hours of waiting in the sun and rain, storekeepers forced them to pay inflated prices and often decided on a whim that "goods were finished" for the rest of the day (even though stock was available).[9]

Moreover, competition over contracts and licenses bred corruption at all levels of distribution, from the unloading dock at the port to the upper echelons of government.[10] As a former Union Trading Company (UTC) manager recalled in detail, "The battle for contracts took on the most incredible forms. Salesmen employed every means imaginable to pull ministers, state secretaries and senior officials onto their side . . . buyers' delegations were invited to Europe. To get anywhere near winning a contract required ideas and fantasy." As both local and foreign businessmen offered large amounts of money to sweeten deals and found other creative ways to win contracts, the value of the bribes skyrocketed: from 5 percent, to 10, 12, and then 15 percent and, in one of the last large deals, 25 percent (US$6.5 million).[11] Winning government favor through backdoor deals and gift-giving became a requirement to conducting business in Ghana.

Coupled with Nkrumah's restrictive import policies, this mismanagement dealt a severe blow to what consumers had come to expect from their modernizing country. Appointed by Nkrumah to investigate shortages, the Abraham Commission held that the immediate causes "were first and foremost the non-issuing of import licenses in a rational manner."[12] Investigators further blamed shortages on the practice of hoarding by firms and local retailers as well as the inability, logistically, of the state-run GNTC to distribute large quantities of goods efficiently.[13] Ghana's manufacturing and export industries also suffered. As shortages of required materials and spare parts reached dire levels, production came to a halt.[14] When these shortages were combined with increasing levels of unemployment and poor housing, many Ghanaians grew disillusioned with the outcomes of independence and with Nkrumah's leadership.[15]

The lavish lifestyles of various CPP ministers and senior officials further fueled public resentment. As Emmanuel Akyeampong has argued, "in the midst of economic austerity, and in spite of the socialist platform adopted in 1961, CPP government officials lived lives of personal ostentation."[16] They spent their leisure time socializing in plush state-owned hotels and in the old social clubs previously frequented by British colonial officers. This group of men initiated a new elite culture, characterized by the accumulation of houses, cars, and young girlfriends, as well as the consumption of expensive imported items. Takyiwaa Manuh argues that it was during the Nkrumah period that the "sugar daddy syndrome" emerged; young women were lavished with gifts, found jobs, and had apartments rented for them by older CPP men.[17] In a 1961 confidential report to the secretary of state for commonwealth relations and the British prime minister, the high commissioner in Ghana wrote that local newspapers attacked the party's propaganda secretary and minister of the interior, Krobo Edusei, in particular, for "his champagne parties and his joy riding" and noted "veiled references to the *droit de seigneur* he and his friends are said to exercise over Ghana Airway hostesses."[18]

As basic items like sugar, milk, and rice disappeared from store shelves and market stalls, resentment and frustration grew with each report highlighting the extravagant consumption habits of Nkrumah and the CPP, as well as the young women benefiting from their patronage. Anger intensified among ordinary Ghanaians, as well as the traditional elite and the country's middle class, about social and moral decline in general and the dangers of consumerism in particular.[19] The pitfalls of conspicuous consumption were captured in an article published in the *Ghanaian Times* by popular journalist and feminist Mabel Dove: "Kwame Nkrumah, his gang, and his followers, taught people that the best type of citizen in the community was the man who lives in luxurious surroundings, owned long expensive cars, whose palaces or flats were so furnished that the visitor feared to walk on the soft carpet or sit on the comfortable chair."[20] Such attitudes reveal a striking, and pervasive, shift in the country's view on wealth. Consumption on display could no longer be celebrated and positioned as a symbol of the new nation's prosperity, as it had been in the years leading up to and immediately following independence. As we have seen, Nkrumah and the CPP, as well as many upper- and middle-class shoppers, had hoped that the construction of new consumer spaces, and the goods sold therein, would help shed the country's image as a colonial dependency and challenge notions of African inferiority. But as prices increased and shortages persisted, lavish purchases—especially those of the country's political elite—made glaringly evident the widening gap between the powerful and the poor. More important, it revealed the inability of Nkrumah's administration to ensure the nation's future prosperity. As a result, the 1966 coup that overthrew Nkrumah was not met with any widespread popular resistance. Within days, groups of citizens tore down Nkrumah's statues and the military renamed the many roads, circles, buildings, and universities previously named in his honor. The former president left China to Conakry, Guinea, where he remained in exile, never to return to Ghana.

The NLC's ability to appropriate the public's discontent leading up to the coup and exploit stories about CPP ministers' luxurious lifestyles directly following it further played a role in gaining public support. After the coup, the NLC used press coverage describing the extravagant spending habits of CPP leaders as evidence of the nation's moral degeneration under Nkrumah. While officials like Kwaku Boateng (minister of the interior) and Atta Mensah (secretary to the Ministry of Communications and Works) were singled out, the most infamous spender was Edusei, who owned a number of ostentatious houses, including one built by an Italian architect, and who even slept on a "£3,600 gold-plated bed."[21] Nkrumah himself also came under fire; "the self-styled redeemer," *Time* magazine reported, "nearly bankrupted his country by building palatial hotels, modernistic palaces and a cozy hideaway for his favorite mistress."[22] Although political elites were the initial targets of the press, their families and relations also shouldered some blame. Newspaper articles reported the relentless giving of jewelry, gifts, and pocket money on the part of CPP ministers—especially to their wives and girlfriends, and reports read like retail store stock lists, itemizing each gift and detailing size, color, quantity, and price. After the coup, several prominent CPP leaders and ministers were arrested, put on trial and, like their former leader, driven into exile.

The NLC's claims that Nkrumah and the CPP had morally corrupted Ghanaian society were inseparable from the economic motives behind the coup. Almost immediately the new military government positioned free market capitalism as the key to Ghana's economic recovery; it also appointed an official government commission of inquiry, headed by Annie Ruth Jiagge, to probe the legality of CPP ministers' acquired properties and assets. While the amount of wealth plundered was not as excessive as originally believed, the publicity surrounding the Jiagge Commission and its very public investigations affirmed the sentiment expressed by coup supporters. In a radio speech just weeks after taking control, Ankrah outlined the NLC's economic policy, announcing that private business would make up the largest sector of the economy (in terms of the number of persons engaged and gross output); he assured the public that no private enterprise would be forced to accept government participation, and that a new Salaries Review Commission would be appointed to address the rise in cost of living and ensure a more equitable distribution of resources.[23] Additionally, he promised that shortages in essential commodities would be eliminated and import controls eventually abolished. It was unclear, however, how the NLC's insistence on a free market would safeguard equal distribution.

Ghana's first International Trade Fair acted as a visual representation of the NLC's post-Nkrumah reconstruction strategy and served as political and cultural capital to gain legitimacy both within the country and around the world. The fair projected a new relation between state and society through the exhibition of goods and the various ceremonies used to solidify geopolitical allegiances—a process historian Andrew Apter has defined as the "political economy of cultural production."[24] Aided by national and international press coverage, the NLC also used the fair to publicly condemn CPP leadership and the corruption that they argued had flourished under the regime's socialist agenda.[25] In addition, by presenting the fair as a "shop window on the world"—a global marketplace of abundance and unlimited possibility for all consumers—the NLC challenged the CPP's monopolization of wealth and its exclusive right to consume, which many believed occurred at the county's expense.

GEOPOLITICS AND ECONOMIC REALIGNMENT

Plans for the fair were plagued by both national and international financial concerns. Originally intended to open in 1965, the fair was postponed by Nkrumah in order to complete a number of additional large construction projects,[26] including a revolving restaurant modeled after the one at the top of the famous London Post Office Tower and a huge boating lake in the shape of the African continent. Besides the fair's centerpiece, an ultramodern three-story circular building with elevated footways leading up to it, none of Nkrumah's other projects were brought to fruition (fig. 4.1). According to the international press, delays also resulted from lack of interest on the part of foreign governments and businesses and Nkrumah's imposition of heavy import controls the year before.[27] After the coup, British and US advisers disapproved of the NLC's plans to continue with the fair, citing Ghana's "chaotic economic situation and crushing burden of debt" as evidence that the new regime was unfit to host.[28] In addition, new IMF-imposed austerity measures fueled negative attitudes toward the fair—especially those of Western governments who saw the event as especially inappropriate for a country that had fallen into heavy debt.

Despite widespread criticism, the NLC officially opened the fair on February 1, 1967. The number of rented spaces and firms representing foreign industry indicated a large international interest. Described by *Business Weekly*

FIGURE 4.1. Ghana's first International Trade Fair, original brochure cover, February 1965. Reproduced with kind permission of Unilever from the original at the Unilever Archives, UAC/2/1/B/7/2/4/5.

as the "first of its kind ever staged by Ghana or any similar ex-colonial country," it was estimated that about two thousand firms and organizations representing both governments and private industry set up information booths, instructive films, interactive demonstrations, and open-air displays and exhibited everything from washing powder to mining and road-building machinery.[29] Divided into three sections—foreign governments, multinational firms, and made-in-Ghana goods—the 108-acre trade fair site housed six permanent pavilion spaces built by the Ghanaian government.[30] Designed by Polish architects working for the Ghana National Construction Corporation under Nkrumah, the steel, concrete, and glass buildings were described by the British High Commission as "elegant, but extravagant."[31] Seven other pavilions were built by participating governments, with the British, US, and West German pavilions noted as among the largest. Private multinational firms, including Shell Oil and the United Africa Company, also constructed their own buildings.[32] The large white circular building in the middle of the fair site was reserved for African participants and manufacturers of Ghanaian goods.

Attracting new trade partners and restoring the confidence of old ones was a major goal of the fair. Prior to the event the NLC sent promotional brochures and other materials to foreign governments and businesses to encourage participation. Even the official application form contained an outline of the regime's economic policies and several photographs and images of large development projects and industrial sites, including the Volta Dam, Tema Harbor, and the Volta Aluminum Company's aluminum smelter, as evidence of Ghana's potential.[33] During the show, the NLC held five seminars to publicize investment possibilities and incentives and to announce new development projects and opportunities. Each seminar was opened by a member of the NLC and was followed by a discussion session led by senior civil servants who were responsible for formulating and administering plans.[34] Geared toward businessmen—Ghanaians, visitors, and expatriates alike—the participatory focus of the seminars was intended to create an image of the new government as open to the concerns of both the local business class and foreigners.

Beyond building new business relations and revitalizing old ones, the fair was also a marketplace to sell consumer goods. While companies took orders for larger items such as heavy machinery and office supplies, products available for direct sale included books, shoes, foodstuffs, glassware, brassware, suitcases, toys, and cosmetics. The selling of services by banks, shipping companies, and airlines was also a part of the fair. The crowd was a mixture of ordinary customers and retailers who hoped to test and buy new consumer products, and business owners who required larger mechanized equipment. The British high commissioner estimated that total orders placed at the fair amounted to about £7.5 million, which did not include all the items that people bought and took home the same day.[35] Newspapers reported that countries like Czechoslovakia and Italy had sold out of all samples by the second week. Practically all the goods on show at the US pavilion, worth more than $600,000, sold as well. "The success of the fair was staggering," an officer from the US Department of Commerce told the *New York Times*, noting that it was "definitely beyond [my] expectations."[36] While profit on sales was definitely a major objective for participating businesses, commodities on display were also imbued with their own signs and symbols.

For ordinary visitors the fair was a combination of product display, spectacle, and entertainment. The Kumasi and Accra Breweries sponsored beer gardens, and the Tema Chocolate Factory sponsored a tram to transport visitors around the entire trade fair site; beyond that, the Volta Aluminum Company used its stand as a depot to bus visitors to its factory in Tema, about a one-hour drive east, for tours. Other popular attractions included fashion shows, live pop music performances, and free vaccinations against smallpox and measles by the US Agency for International Development at the US pavilion; a model railway exhibited by the Japanese; the Photo Me

International instant passport photo booth at the British pavilion, and the "ultramodern kitchen and bathroom" put on display by the GNTC.[37] Following years of consumer disappointment, the encounter with an abundance of new products from around the world was figured by local journalists as a magical experience. "To the average Ghanaian," one *Daily Graphic* writer noted, it was a "return journey to Alice's Wonderland."[38] But such a comparison also suggests the sad reality for a number of visitors: many of the fantastic items showcased were too expensive, and thus out of reach.

Nevertheless, the variety of goods displayed and the introduction of new products represented the emancipatory potential of free market capitalism. This connection between free choice as consumers and political freedom and democracy was not unique to Ghana; it was a link made frequently in the context of international trade fairs and exhibitions during the Cold War.[39] In the 1950s and 1960s, trade exhibitions became sites of "cultural diplomacy" on the African continent and beyond, and ultimately were major arenas for the battle between capitalism and communism.[40] Probably the best known example of this is the 1959 "kitchen debate" at the American National Exhibition in Moscow, where Vice President Richard Nixon argued to General Secretary Nikita Khrushchev that a consumer-based economy gave American housewives freedom from domestic drudgery and opportunities for leisure, individuality, and a higher standard of living. In Ghana, the trade fair's changing roster of participants—those who signed on before and after the coup—also illustrates this point. For example, the US government, which had initially declined to participate under Nkrumah, joined the list of exhibitors after he was overthrown. To further demonstrate its support, the United States rented 26,000 square feet of space to construct a large geodesic dome as its main exhibition pavilion.

Additionally, the NLC kept communist countries from participating in the show.[41] Such a move required a remaking of the Chinese pavilion. Under Nkrumah, Ghana had established formal diplomatic ties to the People's Republic of China (PRC), and from 1960 to 1966 the PRC administered a "flourishing embassy" and a technical assistance program in Accra. After the coup the PRC was forced to withdraw its embassy when the NLC deported about two hundred Chinese aid workers and embassy staff.[42] In order to retain Chinese presence at the fair without fear of being accused of communist sympathies, the NLC solicited support from Taiwan, the Republic of China, to replace PRC participation. Observers described the nationalist Chinese pavilion as "intricate and attractive," with "foodstuffs, textiles, glassware, brassware, household fittings and equipment."[43] The NLC canceled the Soviet Union's exhibition plans altogether, and this shift caught the attention and approval of the US government, which had been made very nervous by Nkrumah's visits to Moscow and his invitations to members of the Eastern Bloc to visit Accra. These last-minute changes to the Chinese pavilion and the elimination of Soviet participation were a way for the NLC to prove its allegiance to capitalist rather than communist nations.

Twenty-three countries participated in National Days, elaborate public ceremonies that signified new geopolitical alliances. These formal celebrations provided each host country with the opportunity to showcase its commercial and industrial achievements and its trade relationship with Ghana. Since the number of participating countries outnumbered the days of the fair, every day became a National Day, with two ceremonies on each day to ensure that each country had its turn. The ceremonies were carefully orchestrated, and each began with the playing of the respective country's national anthem and the raising of its flag. This enactment was followed with a short speech given by either a minister or the ambassador from the participating country and was concluded with a response from an officiating member of the NLC and the raising of the Ghanaian flag to Ghana's national anthem. The sight of two country flags flying side by side, accompanied by song, moved international diplomacy into the realm of public spectacle. The ceremonies not only represented the promise of new global partnerships but also capitalist solidarity.

In addition to solidifying bonds with new countries, National Days provided an opportunity for Ghana's former adversaries to renounce past conflicts. For example, on its National Day, Ivory Coast pledged its allegiance to the NLC and announced future policies based on friendship and unity. The country's first president, Félix Houphouët-Boigny, a staunch advocate for capitalism and for maintaining a close relationship with France (Ivory Coast's former colonial ruler) had been one of Nkrumah's major rivals. Rumor has it that after an intense shouting match over Africa's future, the two presidents had made a ten-year bet on whose country—Ghana or Ivory Coast—would be "more advanced." Given that each man advocated an opposing economic ideology, the bet was in part the result of a disagreement between which system—socialism or capitalism—was best for the continent.

The participation of the Nigerian government and eighteen Nigerian companies under the theme "Nigeria Looks Ahead" signified the country's desire to construct a new relationship with Ghana. While showcasing products from Nigeria's own growing industries—canned food, marble, plastic products, and handicrafts—the nation's presence at the fair also advocated for stronger financial ties between the two countries and the benefits of intra-African trade. After experiencing its own military coup—one that overthrew the country's first president, Nnamadi Azikiwe—in January 1966, Nigeria's new leaders proposed the establishment of a common market and a customs-free West African trade zone. For the NLC, National Days provided opportunities to mend broken ties and regain the confidence of neighboring West African leaders.

At the time, the military takeover of Ghana's government was one of six on the continent in four months.[44] The *New York Times* reported that "the script varied little in style from the military takeovers in the Congo, Dahomey, Central African Republic, Upper Volta, and Nigeria. Yet in terms of impact, Ghana's was by far the most important event." For the United States, the NLC government represented a major turn in a Cold War conflict that had been waged between capitalist and socialist governments on African soil. National Days, a British trade fair adviser noted, attracted much attention in the press and in radio and television programming—not only in Ghana but in the other participating countries.[45] In this context, public ceremonies at the fair not only allowed the NLC to establish, repair, and strengthen Ghana's political and economic relations around the world but also allowed the regime to publicly reintroduce itself to the international community as a kinder and gentler military government, one that valued cooperation with the West.

Yet Cold War tensions and renewed alliances were not the only geopolitical narratives represented at the fair; constant comparisons to the US pavilion on the part of the British High Commission suggest a sense of anxiety about growing Americanization. At Ghana's trade fair, British efforts to compete with Americans by creating "bigger and better" displays demonstrated a continued uneasiness about the spread of American influence—especially into Britain's former colony.[46] The US exhibition space was a mix of American-made products and pro-US propaganda. US global cultural hegemony had been a cause for concern in European societies since the First World War, and the "invasion" of American-made products and the US marketing industry's ability to popularize new categories of goods—instant coffee, breakfast cereal, and blue jeans—had been cause for alarm.[47] Although US-Ghana relations had become rocky under Nkrumah, the 1966 coup changed the terms of American involvement in the country. It was reported that over seventy American companies, including Westinghouse Electric (New York City), Lucky Heart Cosmetics (Memphis, Tennessee), Happ (Greeneville, Michigan), Emerson (Jersey City), and Hasco Jewelry (Brooklyn) exhibited at the fair. A market development officer for the US Department of Commerce noted that showcased products were selected specially for "their suitability in West Africa," as if to establish the United States as having some sort of superior understanding of African needs.[48] Published statements such as these, as well as the ability of the United States to quickly rescind its refusal to participate and organize a pavilion of its own, did not go unnoticed by British officials.

British reporting on American participation in the fair captured fears that US firms might imagine Ghana as their next new big sales territory and export a more persuasive "American way of life." This anxiety may have been the motivation for constructing what was later described by the British high commissioner as a somewhat over-the-top British pavilion. Under the theme "Britain and Ghana Partners in Progress," the 37,760-square-foot British pavilion was the largest of all the government-sponsored pavilions. The building was a prefabricated Coseley building designed by the UK Central Office of Information. Made of gleaming white fiberglass panels, it lit up at night, and inside was a large map of Africa indicating the emergent states of the British Commonwealth with colorful transparencies of British-funded development projects. In addition to the 140 British manufacturers who displayed their goods in the British pavilion, there was also a massive twenty-five-ton excavator fitted as a mobile crane with red, white, and blue flashing lights; the highest exhibit at the entire fair, it attracted much attention. Also garnering a large crowd were the occasional appearances of five pipers of the King's Own Scottish Boarders, who were flown in for the event. In the end, the commissioner admitted that the British pavilion "was an impressive building though perhaps a little over elaborate and over expensive for the purpose."[49]

Ultimately, the NLC happily exploited Cold War and other geopolitical tensions in hopes of attracting new sources of international support and financing. Yet the regime also treated the fair as an opportunity to gain political legitimacy among the Ghanaian public. The fair's focus on building the private sector appealed to the local business class, a group whose interests had been marginalized by Nkrumah's plans of nationalizing the economy.[50] Among ordinary Ghanaians, the benefits of pro-Western realignment, which symbolized a democratization of goods, was also alluring. For visitors, the assortment and availability of goods on display sent a clear message: Nkrumah and the CPP were no longer the only ones who could enjoy the comforts, conveniences, and luxury of commodities from around the world.

MANAGING INDIVIDUAL WEALTH AND ACCUMULATION

To conceive of Ghana's trade fair as operating primarily in the realm of international politics or as a space to work out geopolitical rivalries masks its momentous significance within local politics. In a confidential letter to the secretary of state for the commonwealth evaluating the success of the fair, the British high commissioner reported, "Internally, it was a great morale booster for the people of Ghana; and for the National Liberation Council, perhaps their most significant success since the revolution a year before, demonstrating as it did, the stability and popularity of the new regime. It provided also evidence both of the significant progress made in combating the economic difficulties caused by bad administration in the past."[51] Marked by the attendance of almost one million visitors over the span of nineteen days, the fair was heralded by outside observers as a sign of widespread NLC support. Yet to attribute the success of the event to the NLC's popularity overlooks the fair's place within ongoing social debates, particularly concerning the relationship between the postcolonial nation-state and the accumulation of wealth. Under the guise of free market ideologies, the NLC promoted a definition of accumulation that acknowledged and supported an individual's right to attainment. Consumer goods on display—presented as within reach of all Ghanaians, even if in aspirational terms—affirmed this commitment. The right to accumulate, however, was not unlimited. As we shall see, consumption within certain groups, especially women and youth, was still considered in need of regulation.

To fully appreciate how the fair was rooted in accumulation ideology, we must look back to older conceptions of wealth and the state. Focusing mainly on Asante, T. C. McCaskie has argued that the legitimacy of state power in precolonial Ghana rested on the ability of its leader, the Asantehene, to ensure "the nation's moral and practical well-being, its past and its future, its increase."[52] To assert and maintain its authority the state also created mechanisms to control the individual accumulation of wealth. Throughout the nineteenth century, chiefs bestowed those that distinguished themselves in areas of business and enterprise with the special title *abirempon* (big men). Although conspicuous consumption and public display were key characteristics of *abirempon* status, their wealth was still considered social, not individual. "To be an *abirempon*," McCaskie argues, "was all at once to preside over society and to be responsible for its maintenance and continuity."[53] Additionally, after death an *abirempon*'s wealth reverted to the state and was redistributed.[54] Thus, in principle, the relationship between state and society operated within a consensual framework, one that upheld above all the value of collective prosperity.

According to his critics, Nkrumah's administration had monopolized access to wealth at the expense of society's well-being. In other words, it had breached the social contract. It is no surprise, then, that many Ghanaians celebrated Nkrumah's downfall and welcomed the arrival of the soldiers. While on the surface his socialism promised collective prosperity, the behavior of Nkrumah's administration proved otherwise. Most of all, his economic vision offended Ghana's established business class, which vehemently opposed his efforts to nationalize business and industry. Representing a new model of *abirempon*, this group had developed in the early twentieth century alongside expanding economic opportunities. While they enacted older *abirempon* characteristics like generosity and reciprocity, these men rejected state interference in the accumulation and disposal of capital.[55] In fact, the group was instrumental in garnering support for the 1948 boycott detailed in this book's introduction. With the withdrawal of the British government and the diminishing power of foreign firms after independence, the *abirempon* directed their criticisms toward Nkrumah. By affirming their commitment to private enterprise through the international trade fair, the NLC challenged the conception of the Ghanaian state as the primary instrument for the regulation and distribution of wealth.

By attempting to reestablish the importance of older forms of authority, the NLC called into question the hegemonic power of the state to fully control the economy. Nowhere was this message clearer than in the International Trade Fair's opening ceremony and the mass publicity surrounding the vaunted place granted to local chiefs. In a letter to the Commonwealth Office, the British high commissioner reported, "The opening ceremony was attended by all the members of the [National Liberation] Council (the first time they had all appeared together on one platform in public, out of doors), the Paramount chiefs of all the regions of Ghana, senior officials of the Government, the diplomatic corps, exhibitors at the Fair and important foreign commercial visitors. The presence of the greatest gathering in many years of the Chiefs and their retinues, of the Army and the Police in their ceremonial uniforms, made the occasion very colourful."[56]

Nkrumah saw the chiefs as an obstacle to constructing a modern nation-state and derided chiefly power as "antique," "feudalistic," and "unprogressive."[57] By asking chiefs to participate alongside government officials and business representatives, the NLC used the opening ceremony to counter these claims. So, too, did press coverage. Photographs and reports of Nana Osei Agyman Prempeh II, the Asantehene, riding shoulder-high in his palanquin to the fair site with his huge entourage—linguists, priests, musicians, soldiers, and various subchiefs—made the newspapers and headlines. There were also detailed articles of Nana Kofi Awuah II, the Dominasehene, receiving a smallpox vaccination at the US pavilion, as well as images of General Ankrah smiling and embracing Tumu Koro, the president of the Upper Region House of Chiefs and Nana Ofori Atta II, the Okyenhene, at the opening ceremony. Together these reports and images challenged notions that traditional chiefly authority was in any way at odds with "progress" and the modern nation.

Political historians have argued that publicly recognizing the institution of chieftaincy was part of the NLC's attempt to secure a degree of legitimacy among the people, as chiefs were still respected in rural and some urban areas.[58] Yet I argue that it also reimagined a particular relation between wealth and the state. Even before independence, CPP members had seen chiefs as competition for not only political but also economic authority. Chiefly power was central to accumulation ideology in precolonial Ghana; in addition to bestowing titles, chiefs controlled access to resources, labor, and land. Whereas chiefs as traditional officeholders had previously been considered obstacles to the aspirations of the business class, McCaskie argues that by the 1930s they had become part of it.[59] Therefore, by marginalizing chieftaincy after independence through legislation and later nationalization, Nkrumah was empowering the nation-state to command wealth. Thus, Ghana's International Trade Fair represented a battle between different accumulation ideologies. At stake were the individual's right to accumulate and distribute wealth and the role of the nation-state in mediating this process.

This contest was not limited to the economic realm, however. As demonstrated in the historical figure of the *abirempon*, the legitimacy of wealth always entailed social obligations. Nkrumah and the CPP were not the only ones to be accused of economic immorality; Ghanaian women and youth were also targeted, but for different reasons. The belief that individual accumulation without moral responsibility was a form of "economic wickedness" endured throughout the twentieth century, but its boundaries were not always clear.[60] Thus, accumulation ideology—the system of thought about the meaning and uses of wealth—was never applied universally by those in power. One major reason was that its articulation intersected with other identities, including gender and age. The discourses surrounding the improper consumer practices of young men and women reveal how the accumulation of wealth and its limitations were being negotiated more broadly. It also demonstrates how the democratization of goods presented at the fair was still regulated by certain social norms and hierarchies that limited access.

DISCIPLINING WOMEN AND YOUTH

Ghana's economic stability went hand in hand with what the NLC described as a need for "social reconstruction."[61] According to Colonel A. A. Afrifa, the NLC's second chairman, Nkrumah's socialist programs had undermined "the authority of parents, teachers and elders" by seducing youth "to look upon the state as a better substitute for the parent."[62] These anxieties were not new; social changes associated with increased urbanization and wage labor during the colonial period had drawn attention to the behavior of youth. In particular, cities became vibrant spaces of youth culture and resistance. Young men and women used various elements of their changing worlds—consumer goods, forms of education, avenues of work, leisure activities, and places for socializing (bars, social clubs, dance clubs)—to challenge not only colonial power but also traditional authority.[63] After independence the presence of the younger generation in the public sphere became hypervisible. Youth programs like the Young Pioneers and the Ghanaian Builders Brigade offered new opportunities for social mobility, as well as alternative paths to respectability and adulthood for young men and women alike.[64] They also provided young men and women with opportunities for economic autonomy outside the authority of chiefs, parents, and elders. Among Nkrumah's critics, programs directed at empowering youth were considered disruptive to older social structures, particularly in relation to the gender and generational hierarchies on which they rested.

While concerns over the economic autonomy of women—especially those who were unmarried—had surfaced throughout the colonial period, Nkrumah legislation and rhetoric made debates over gender roles a national issue.[65] Women's increased visibility in national politics and in the country's workforce was a key point of contention. After independence, Nkrumah made special provisions for the election of women to the National Assembly and removed discriminatory practices in education and the civil service. During his term, education rates for women rose, more women entered universities, and several took on new professions previously closed to them. Although Nkrumah's efforts increased women's presence in politics and wage employment, opportunities remained limited, primarily benefiting upper- and middle-class women and CPP members.[66] Nevertheless, the increased social status of a few ignited anxiety regarding the many.

Social commentaries from the mid- to late 1960s echoed concerns over perceived changes in generational and gender relations while stressing the importance of increased discipline and the reeducation of youth as possible solutions. A 1968 article titled "Maintaining Authority in the Home" argued that while parents should never use excessive force or the "iron hand," they should uphold the virtues of obedience in the home and instill this value in their children. According to the anonymous author, parents must urge children to respect and understand authority; anything less would be a sign of parental weakness.[67] Additionally, in a speech given at Nkonya Secondary School, economics lecturer and NLC supporter Jones Ofori-Atta urged students and all youth to unite and save Ghana "from drowning in a moral cesspool." As a strong opponent of Nkrumah's economic policies, Ofori-Atta argued that the stability of Ghana required a new deal based on "moral re-armament."[68] The correlation made between the economy and morality is striking; it suggests that economic recovery required ethical behavior among youth. "Rearmament," a military-derived term in support of the military government, was the only way to undo what Ofori-Atta believed was a type of social chaos created by the CPP.

Some writers also called directly for government intervention in promoting social discipline. For example, the president of the Eastern Region of Chiefs, Nana Annorkwei II, argued that "the indecent behavior of students in the schools and colleges" was brought on by the old regime.[69] He encouraged the NLC and organizations like the Christian Council of Ghana to enforce moral education programs in schools and universities.

Another prominent voice in the attack on Nkrumah was Emma Jiagge, who became the national organizer of the women's section of the Centre for Civic Education under the NLC.[70] In a 1968 article she argued that, more than ever, Ghana needed "an organization which would help restore traditional discipline." In particular, she blamed Nkrumah's regime for the degeneration of Ghanaian womanhood and called for the participation of more women's groups to "curb the evils" that had arisen over the previous decade.[71] Implicit within Jiagge's accusations was also a concern over the "sugar daddy" and "gold digger" relation between older (presumably married) men and young, single women. To critics, this exchange was a major sign of the economic immorality of both the CPP and the young women who benefited from these relationships.

Public criticisms of moral decline were thus inextricably linked to shifting notions about the boundaries of accumulation. Many discussions about the immorality and indiscipline of youth, for instance, were articulated through debates about their consumption practices. A popular comic strip published in the *Evening News* illustrates this point; first appearing in 1968, the aptly named *Kofi Brokeman* series followed the life of its eponymous young bachelor, who was cash poor but passed himself off as a "big man" through flashy cars and clothes. Used mostly in situations to impress and lure young attractive women, Kofi's displays of wealth were never his own. The fancy furnishings and nice suits were either loaned to him on credit or borrowed from others.[72] While Kofi is the one guilty of deception, it is the young women's behavior that is represented as most despicable. Throughout the series they are seduced by Kofi's material goods and consider them to be more valuable than his personal character. "Hello Mr. Richman Kofi you're my king of the world," one of the women declares as she stands close with her arms around him. Together, the women in the comic also conspire to trick Kofi into buying them gifts. As one of the women instructs her friend, "You'll need a wig, ready-made dresses, shoes, underwears [*sic*], dumas, lace material, nightgown [*sic*], lavender and a host of beauty creams . . . and don't forget to ask for two pairs of shoes you know we wear the same size."[73] In another strip, one of the women brags to her friend about Kofi that "the boy is too good, look at what he gave out for pocket money yesterday." She goes on to explain, "This is evidence of a good catch," as she is pictured laughing and throwing money in the air.[74] The series portrays the danger of material goods as artificial expressions of social status, and condemns material greed, but it presents young women as most susceptible to these dangerous phenomena.

So how did notions about youth, women, and accumulation play out at the Ghana International Trade Fair? For the most part, public discourse about the economic immorality of young men and women was made known in their conspicuous absence from the fair. Unlike Nkrumah, who had positioned the younger generation as central to the development of the new nation, the NLC marginalized the role of young people. After the coup, the NLC targeted leaders of Nkrumah's youth programs, like the Builders Brigade, for corruption and abuse.[75] In addition, the stereotyped image of the CPP's rank and file as young, reckless hooligans or "verandah boys" was served up as an example of the dangers associated with involving youth in politics. (The term *verandah boy* was initially used widely to describe groups of disaffiliated youngsters involved in petty theft or other activities deemed criminal during the Second World War, but by the 1950s the term was applied to anyone considered to be a troublemaker, agitator, or rebel.)[76] In the eyes of critics, the behavior of young people was part of the problem that the NLC was meant to fix. It is not surprising, then, that beyond demands for their obedience and discipline, youth were excluded from the narrative of Ghana's economic reconstruction.

But it is the limited representation of women that most reveals how efforts to discipline youth were connected to broader attempts to control accumulation. These limitations were not always only about how many possessions one owned; they were also about access to economic power. Speeches, photographs, and ceremonies featured in both the national and international press depicted the trade fair as a male-only event. While women were among the thousands of visitors and served as official pavilion guides hosting visiting dignitaries, the list of exhibitors included only one female business owner; Kate Ohene, described as a "modest and frank Akwapim housewife," represented the extent of women's participation. [77] Through her inclusion, marked as unusual by observers who described her as "the one-and-only," Ohene represents a larger marginalization of women from the realm of active and valuable businesspeople.[78] This image was further reinforced in business literature that circulated during the period. For example, while the 1967 *Handbook of Commerce and Industry* celebrated the trade fair as a sign of economic progress, female-dominated marketplaces like Makola were listed in the handbook as "tourist attractions" rather than functioning spaces of commercial exchange.[79]

The fair attempted to reassert a gendered division of labor that relegated women's proper consumption and accumulation to the private sphere. Through Ohene's incorporation as the sole businesswoman, she was elevated as an example of traditional, respectable femininity. This representation was reinforced nine months later at the smaller, less well-known Ideal Home Exhibition. The weeklong event held at the Accra Community Centre sought not only to assist in the growth of Ghanaian industry, similar to the trade fair, but also to promote the "improvement of the Ghanaian home." In this sense, the Ideal Home Exhibition was an extension of the International Trade Fair; the two events even shared some of the same exhibitors. But unlike the trade fair, the latter exhibition was geared toward women. Through press coverage, advertisements, and published images the event glorified the ideal Ghanaian housewife.[80] For instance, the Tema-based Ghana Pioneer Aluminum Factory advertised that its brand of cooking utensils, pots, and frying pans formed an "important section of a home" where the "hungry husband" could be satisfied after a "day's hard work."[81] Likewise, the Ghana Pioneer Plastic Company linked its line of products with ideals of housewifery, emphasizing a woman's role as a knowledgeable and effective household manager; according to the company, items like storage containers were essential for the housewife who knew the importance of household budgeting and understood the value of money.

The ideal home was one that was run economically, and in turn a thrifty household contributed to improving the country's economy. But the ideal home was also a place carrying a disciplined form of domesticity characterized by a neat division of labor and the enactments of gender roles that assumed the subordination of wives under their husbands. In opposition to the circulating image of the "gold-digging" young woman who benefited from her "sugar daddy" and, in the process, drained the national economy, the ideal housewife consumed in ways that were neither immoral nor self-centered.[82] Instead, her role as a good mother, housekeeper, and cook contributed to creating the modern, stable family environment that was necessary, according to the NLC and its supporters, to rebuild Ghana. The assertion of an ideal wife and mother worked to reconfigure the nature of women's economic contributions in a changing Ghana; it glorified one particular type of contribution—that of housewife—over all other contributions. Labor conducted outside the home and within the marketplace, although the norm for many women in Ghana, put them in a precarious position, especially in relation to the state.[83] The enterprising credit customers and ambitious young Kingsway saleswomen discussed in earlier chapters were curiously absent from this national narrative. While many of these women undoubtedly attended the fair, their contributions were rendered largely invisible.

Public attitudes about the indiscipline of young men and women manifested within criticisms about their consumption practices. While young men's spending habits and conspicuous consumption were often the butt of jokes, as illustrated by the *Kofi Brokeman* comic strip, the practices of young single women were deemed most repulsive. The image of the respectable middle-class married housewife should be understood not only as an attempt to forward a particular gendered relationship that elevated male authority but also as an effort to control boundaries of accumulation. By leaving out the very important role of women as workers, entrepreneurs, and businesspeople, the International Trade Fair reinforced a gendered and class-based vision of the national economy. This narrative, coupled with the NLC's free market policies, constructed a tight connection between government and business bureaucracies—a relationship that, feminist scholars have argued, concentrated political and economic power in the hands of a male elite.[84] In many ways the fair provided a platform for the NLC to align itself with what R. W. Connell has described as "transnational business masculinity." Feminist studies on global restructuring have termed similar forms of global relations dominated by men as "techno-muscular capitalism." Connected to the gender politics of neoliberalism and the power of the contemporary global political economy to produce, reassert, and maintain a hegemonic form of masculinity, aspects of this particular formation of patriarchy unfolded at Ghana's first International Trade Fair.[85] While more research is needed on how this type of power played out among the various groups of elite men involved, the unification at the fair of chiefs, local and foreign businessmen and politicians, and the military—even if only symbolic—articulated a new type of economic power, one that marginalized the contributions and labors of many groups of women.

Appealing to both international and local audiences, Ghana's first International Trade Fair was part of the larger post-Nkrumah reconstruction project.

The NLC used the fair not only to regain the support of foreign governments and attract investors, exploiting Cold War tensions, but also to win favor with the Ghanaian public and its established business class. Under the guise of free market capitalism, the NLC was also seeking to redraw the boundaries of consumption. By presenting a democratization of goods, the new regime challenged Nkrumah and the CPP's monopolization of wealth and the policies that had bestowed upon the former regime exclusive rights. The benefits of realignment with Western economies and governments were elevated through consumer models that connected capitalism to promises of stability and abundance.

Notions about consumption were rooted in the societal ethics of accumulation. Negating the extravagant spending habits of the CPP, and attempting to resurrect chieftaincy and promote the ideal of wife and mother, were ways in which ideas about wealth and accumulation were being renegotiated in the postindependence period. So, too, were widespread criticisms about the improper consumption practices of youth and the "sugar-daddy" phenomenon that vilified young women as "gold diggers"—economic parasites. Thus, accusations about Ghana's moral decline cannot be separated from economic concerns.

Ghana's first International Trade Fair and the events surrounding it were inseparable from debates over accumulation and the role of the modern state. While in hindsight scholars have identified more continuities than changes in the political and economic structures of the CPP and the military regimes that followed it, the 1966 coup did reveal a moment at which many Ghanaians reevaluated the relationship between the postcolonial state and society. At the time, even the famous feminist journalist Mabel Dove went so far as to label the coup a "healing tonic" for the nation's sickness and misery under Nkrumah.[86]

At the closing ceremony, Michael Akuoko Otu, the air vice marshal of the Ghana Armed Forces and chairman of the Trade Fair Committee, announced that the next Ghana International Trade Fair would take place in 1969, but these plans never came to fruition. As chapter 5 will demonstrate, increased militarization of the economy in the 1970s would lead to stronger government efforts to redefine and control consumer practices. Within conditions of extreme scarcity, a new military state brought to power by a second coup would police the boundaries of accumulation, this time relying on physical force and intimidation.

5 "Power to the People"

Militarization of the Market and the War against Profiteers

After three and a half years of military rule, the National Liberation Council (NLC) made good on its initial promise to transfer power back to a civilian government.[1] In August 1969, the NLC held a general election, and Kofi Abrefa Busia took office as Ghana's second elected prime minister. Less than three years later, the military intervened again; on January 13, 1972, while Busia was undergoing medical treatment in London, Ghana's army took control of the government, installing Colonel Ignatius Kutu Acheampong as the new leader. The military officers who staged the coup d'état justified their intervention by accusing Busia and his Progress Party government of corruption and economic mismanagement. In rhetoric similar to that of the 1966 coup, the 1972 military government couched its legitimacy in the notion of reform, aptly naming itself the National Redemption Council (NRC).

When the NRC took control, the Ghanaian economy was in crisis. Under Busia's government the world market price of cocoa had plummeted, and the country had fallen into a severe balance-of-payment deficit. As a result, Ghana became heavily indebted to a number of foreign firms and governments. To create income to satisfy the country's creditors, Busia had implemented an austerity budget in 1971 that not only cut wages and abolished a number of allowances for government employees and army servicemen but also eliminated social services such as the free medical care system introduced by former prime minister Kwame Nkrumah.[2] Busia also devalued the Ghana cedi and banned a wide range of imports, causing major shortages in food and essential items and an increase in what was defined as black market trading. Not only had cuts in government spending proven inadequate in easing Ghana's economic troubles, but by reducing services, government employee wages, and expenditure on the armed forces, Busia and the Progress Party also offended many previous supporters who had voted them into office.

As a result of these austerity measures, large sectors of the public—including trade unionists, civil servants, and police and military officers—welcomed the 1972 coup. As in the time of the NLC-led coup that had overthrown Nkrumah, citizens had grown fed up with poor economic conditions and chronic commodity shortages. From the very beginning, Acheampong announced plans to reverse many of Busia's policies, vowing first and foremost "to control rather than be controlled by the economy."[3] Using nationalist rhetoric similar to Nkrumah's, minus the socialist slant, Acheampong emphasized the need for state intervention in the economy and policies that emphasized national self-reliance. Once in power, the NRC restored benefits to public servants and took over the majority of shares of foreign-owned enterprises. The regime also implemented the Investment Policy Decree of 1975, which limited foreign holdings in large-scale Ghanaian industries.[4]

In addition, Acheampong initiated programs to encourage rural and agricultural development as well as domestic food production. Operation Feed Yourself, launched in 1972, aimed at cutting back the country's growing reliance on imports and thus eliminating heavy expenditures of foreign exchange (the value of the cedi on the world market). By producing locally, Acheampong hoped that Ghana would be able to establish more stable and equitable relations within the global market. While Operation Feed Yourself yielded some impressive results in its early years in the areas of maize and rice cultivation, the program's progress was short-lived. Food shortages and rising prices continued, and by 1974 the Ghanaian economy had fallen to its lowest point since independence. Acheampong's refusal to repay several outstanding foreign debts exacerbated problems by damaging international business relationships and sources of credit and financing, including those in Europe and the United States.[5]

While Acheampong recognized that Busia's economic strategies and the country's lack of foreign exchange led to high prices and commodity shortages, he also identified an enemy closer to home: local retailers. Specifically, he accused retailers of hoarding, profiteering, and smuggling and of diverting scarce goods to the black market to avoid government-imposed pricing meant to curb inflation. The NRC addressed these problems by intervening systematically in consumer markets; domestic measures included increased surveillance of ports and borders, strict enforcement of government price controls, and tighter control of distribution through the state-owned Ghana National Trading Corporation (GNTC). The military government criminalized those buying and selling outside state-regulated guidelines and punished retailers accused of "unlawful" selling. At the same time, Acheampong attempted to garner support from the public for his policies; through press and radio messages he announced plans to appoint groups of civilian price inspectors to watch over local marketplaces and wholesale and retail stores in their communities. He also encouraged all citizens to report unlawful trading activities to government authorities. Using overtly militaristic language, Acheampong declared what he described as an "economic war."

By 1975 the regime had tightened its hold on the market. Acheampong reorganized the NRC by dismissing the remaining civilian members and creating a new ruling body called the Supreme Military Council (SMC).[6] Made up of commanders from various branches of the armed services, the SMC gained complete control of the economy as well as all public institutions and state-owned corporations. Empowered by Acheampong to take control of commodity distribution, these high-ranking military officials quickly made sure to supply themselves and their beneficiaries first. The regime established a chit system whereby regional offices issued official notes or vouchers to customers for scarce goods; each chit specified the name of a specific item and the quantity allowed for purchase. The NRC required agents from all trading firms to report the arrival of stocks to their respective regional offices before selling, and it was from this information that chits could be allocated. Yet not all people were considered eligible to receive these valuable pieces of paper. The SMC granted the privilege sparingly: members of the military, police, and civil service were given priority; others were required to line up in front of retail stores for leftover goods after chit allocations had been fulfilled. Such a system intended to better control the release of goods from factories and warehouses increasingly concentrated power in the hands of the military. Chits for essential commodities were bought and sold and became a business for profit. In response to restrictive government policies, retailers created what scholars have described as a "beat-the-system" arrangement.[7] When soldiers stepped up disciplinary measures by more forcefully patrolling markets and stores and seizing goods, retailers retaliated by withholding commodities from the market altogether. As one former United Africa Company manager recalls, selling went "underground."[8] As a strategy to escape the watchful eye of the soldiers, people sold goods out of their private homes or at secret meeting spots.

This chapter explores how militarization and increased market surveillance altered Ghanaians' relationship with goods and the ways in which they practiced consumption. It shifts attention away from the popularly studied coastal cities and onto the experiences of those living in the nation's interior. Far away from the administrative capital in Accra, the Brong-Ahafo region became a hotbed of tension and violence between the military, the police, and local residents, all of whom fought over what goods were accessible and how they should be sold. Brong-Ahafo's proximity to the Ivory Coast border and the presence of one of the most heavy-handed army battalions in Ghana made market transactions for these residents riskier than for those living in other, more densely populated, coastal cities. Soldiers and police were not the only regulating market force at work, however; ordinary residents, including civil servants, teachers, and farmers, also participated in Acheampong's "economic war." In Brong-Ahafo, one of the primary ways residents did so was through letter writing. Addressed to regional commissioners and district administrators, letters complained about high prices and shortages and provided information regarding specific retailers and stores. These letters thus became tools to seek revenge and settle old scores, but at the same time, they also expressed larger concerns about an increasingly coercive military government, political corruption, and economic exclusion.

The events that unfolded in Brong-Ahafo were not entirely exclusive to the region; they reflected decades of Ghana's reliance on an export-driven economy, colonial legacies of distribution and market controls, interference from foreign firms, and the limits posed by postcolonial development projects. Even so, historians have taken a backseat in analyzing the events of the 1970s as part of larger, ongoing conflicts and tensions surrounding the market.[9] Instead, scholarship for the period has been dominated by political scientists, economists, and development scholars and overshadowed by grand narratives of economic decline and failure.[10] Yet my analysis of oral histories and letters demonstrates a rich history of social and political engagement with the military state that challenges understandings of this decade as a time marked by "a paralysis of political life."[11] By focusing on consumer politics, this chapter examines how larger economic processes controlled by the military played out in individual lives and communities. More specifically, it reveals what anthropologist Brenda Chalfin has called "the affective and embodied dimensions of state authority," and what I describe as the intimate effects of scarcity and economic uncertainty.[12] As goods became more difficult to attain and definitions of what constituted proper selling more rigid, suspicion, fear, and anger disrupted market practices and the relationships in which they were embedded.

BRONG-AHAFO, BORDER PATROLS, AND *KALABULE*

By the time Acheampong rose to power, Brong-Ahafo was one of nine administrative regions that made up Ghana.[13] Further split into several districts that were overseen by district administrators, each of these regions was headed by a regional commissioner whose office was located at the regional capital. Under British rule, the Brong and Ahafo (Akan-speaking) chiefdoms formed part of the northwestern Ashanti region. In 1946, a separatist movement led by Brong and Ahafo chiefs formed due to ongoing conflicts with Kumasi (the capital of the Ashanti confederacy) over the control of land and cocoa. After years of conflict the movement was successful, and in 1959 Kwame Nkrumah and the Convention People's Party (CPP) government established the Brong-Ahafo region.[14] As a major timber, cocoa, and food-producing area, the region, which lies in a forest zone, became central to larger national debates concerning rural development.[15] Civilian and military regimes that ruled Ghana after independence had their own ideas of how to support the country's rural communities, with the aim of increasing both agricultural output and cocoa revenues. Under Nkrumah, the CPP government began channeling funds into Brong-Ahafo for the construction of local government buildings and schools and for social and welfare services. Other development projects included Sunyani Airport, the Bui Hydroelectric Dam, and the construction of new army barracks.[16]

In the late 1960s Busia, whose hometown of Wenchi is in Brong-Ahafo, initiated a program titled Rural Development in Action.[17] While criticized for showing favoritism toward his home region, Busia's emphasis on services like clean water, electricity, and roads was designed more as a strategy to stem urban migration than to help local farmers. He hoped that infrastructure developments would maintain more stable rural communities and reduce the number of people moving to Ghana's urban centers.[18] By 1970 the population of Brong-Ahafo had grown, but in comparison to other regions it was still relatively low.[19] At the time Ghana's total population had reached around nine million people; out of that number, Sunyani, the regional capital and largest town in Brong-Ahafo, had a population of 23,780, which was a fraction of the populations in other cities like Accra (564,194), Kumasi (260,286), and Tamale (83,653). Aside from Sunyani, other large Brong-Ahafo towns were Berekum (14,296), Techimann (12,068), and Wenchi (13,836).[20]

In addition to being the focus of rural development initiatives, the Brong-Ahafo region has a legacy of large military and police presence. Because it shares a border with Ivory Coast, interference from border guards and customs agents in everyday commercial life has been a regular occurrence since long before the region was officially named. Although the NRC government and later the SMC government implemented some of the country's harshest economic regulatory measures, they were not the first. In the early twentieth century the British colonial administration created the Gold Coast Customs Preventative Service to stop the smuggling of cocoa and other commodities by Gold Coasters and foreigners, particularly in border areas like Brong-Ahafo and Trans-Volta.[21] During the colonial era, Brong-Ahafo towns along the Ivory Coast border like Pamu and Dormaa Ahenkro were among those under heaviest surveillance as police, and later groups of soldiers, patrolled for smugglers and regularly organized roadblocks and conducted vehicle searches.[22]

After the NRC seized power in 1972, state involvement and surveillance in border regions intensified, and under Acheampong border patrols became the fourth wing of the armed forces.[23] While the government acknowledged that border guards had in the past engaged in smuggling of their own, the solution was to "instill military discipline" by requiring training at the military academy. In Brong-Ahafo, a number of older guards were dismissed and replaced with younger ones; injecting "new blood into the organization" would improve conditions—or so the government thought.[24] While soldiers were supposed to prevent smuggling, poor working conditions and pay encouraged many to use their positions to build up lucrative operations by collecting bribes and conducting business *with* smugglers. In Brong-Ahafo the incorporation of all border guards into the army swelled the military presence in the region, which was already home to the infamous Third Battalion, stationed at Liberation Barracks on the outskirts of the region's capital and known for being young, energetic, and destructive.[25]

Aside from government policies aimed at controlling market prices, shifting definitions about what constituted proper selling also affected changes in retailing. In border regions like Brong-Ahafo, however, smuggling was the major concern, and it took on three different forms. First, people carried Ghanaian-grown products—mainly cocoa and rice—across borders to take advantage of a producer price that was often five times higher than that paid in Ghana. Second, people transported and sold scarce goods—soap, sugar, sardines, and cooking utensils—across borders to maximize profits and avoid price controls.[26] Third, retailers brought goods, which were scarce—canned fish, French chewing gum, and bread—into Ghana to sell on the Ghanaian black market.[27] The flow of goods across borders fluctuated based on the enforcement of price controls and market availability. Instead of implementing economic solutions, like raising the price paid for local produce or easing price restrictions, the NRC began to intensify market surveillance and defined nearly all types of cross-border selling as smuggling.

According to the NRC, smuggling often went hand in hand with hoarding and profiteering, all considered forms of what the regime described as "economic sabotage." Together these practices came to encompass a whole set of market activities, some that had previously been understood as legitimate. The regime detailed and condemned many of these actions in the Price Control Decree of 1972.[28] Reminiscent of colonial market controls imposed during the Second World War and under Nkrumah, section 6 of the decree assigned maximum selling prices on several imported essential items such as soap, sardines, tomato paste, and condensed milk, as well as constructed definitions of terms like *hoarding* and *profiteering*, both of which were punishable through jail time, fines, and the forfeit of goods.[29]

The NRC defined *profiteering* as the sale of any item above the government-controlled price. It defined *hoarding* in four different ways: (1) when any person kept or obtained goods of any one kind in quantities unreasonably in excess of his immediate requirements; (2) when any person kept or obtained goods in a manner likely to create or contribute to a shortage of those goods as regarded their availability to the public; (3) when any person who normally carried on the business of selling goods refused without reasonable excuse to sell any goods in his possession to a person who reasonably required them and offered to buy them; and (4) when any person who normally carried on the business of selling goods refused without reasonable excuse to sell goods except upon condition that other goods were bought therewith (evocative of the age-old, and despised, practice of conditional sales).[30] Phrases like "unreasonable excess," "reasonable excuse," and "likely to create shortage," however, left a substantial amount of room for military and police interpretation. Such broad definitions also led to selective enforcement.

The state and the public often used the terms *smuggling*, *hoarding*, and *profiteering* interchangeably, and the term *smuggling* was not exclusively used in the context of carrying goods across national borders. In a letter to the regional commissioner in Sunyani, for example, a resident from Bechem used the term *smuggling* to describe how retailers from his community diverted supplies to other cities within Ghana; he complained that Bechem retailers "smuggled" goods to more populated cities like Kumasi and Wenchi for higher profits.[31] The letter writer's use of the term implies that he was simultaneously accusing Bechem traders of hoarding (keeping goods from the public) and profiteering (taking the goods out of Bechem in hopes of maximizing profits). This overlap could be the reason that Ghanaians I interviewed often describe all three practices under one umbrella term, *kalabule*, a word assumed to derive from the Hausa expression *kara bude*, meaning "Keep it quiet" or "Hide it."[32] One GNTC stocktaker also describes its meaning as "Don't open."[33] By enacting the 1972 Price Control Decree, the NRC government criminalized anyone engaged in *kalabule* and further cast them as "enemies of the state."

THE POLITICS OF ENFORCEMENT

After the 1972 coup, the enforcement of price controls and antihoarding laws by soldiers and police made it clear that the military government took seriously its role as a market regulator. As was the case with almost all preceding governments, the NRC took over the national press and used it to gain support for its policies and strengthen its image as "enforcer."[34] Newspapers featured headlines and published dozens of articles about retailers apprehended for selling above authorized prices: one trader from Yamfo was sentenced to three months of hard labor for selling a bottle of TCP antiseptic for GH₵1.60 instead of GH₵0.98; a twenty-three-year-old trader from Techiman who sold two cakes of Sunlight soap for GH₵0.70 instead of GH₵0.34 was sentenced to six months in jail; two storekeepers were fined a total of GH₵60.00 and sentenced to three months for selling above controlled prices; and one trader was fined GH₵125.00 and sentenced to four months imprisonment for the same crime, as well as banned from future trading.[35]

Retailers were not the only ones targeted; the military also punished those who provided services. Local newspapers similarly published stories about butchers, bakers, bar owners, and even newspaper boys who "cheated" customers.[36] In one case, soldiers accused tro-tro and taxi drivers in Japekrom of profiteering.[37] Drivers claimed that because the price of gasoline had risen, they were forced to also raise passenger fares. Unwilling to make exceptions, the military disregarded their excuses and humiliated two drivers and truck park overseers by forcing them to publicly perform an hour-long military drill in the middle of the parking lot. As the presiding magistrate at Techiman District Court argued, the punishments for these practices were intended to serve as deterrents for others "anxious to make illegal profits."[38] Through the press, retailers and consumers were being placed on opposing sides of Acheampong's "economic war."

But the lines between the two groups were not as rigid as the NRC had made them out to be, and the enforcement of laws was highly selective. Wealthier retailers had the resources to either pay off or create alliances with the police, soldiers, border guards, and other state officials. In letters sent to the regional commissioner from Brong-Ahafo residents noted that bribing, splitting profits, and providing goods to authorities for turning a blind eye to these larger retailers' illicit activities was common. As an anonymous letter from Wenchi signed "Patriotic Citizen" reported, "The Police are the first offenders, because nobody in his right senses can understand why they stand aloof in the face of this high incidence of profiteering. . . . They have been bribed into silence . . . [and are] supplied with, free of charge, cartons of milk, sugar, mackerel, soap, etc. when the consignment of essential commodities arrive at their border post at Wenchi. It's a pity they have sold their souls for packets of sugar!"[39] The letter turns the SMC's economic rhetoric on itself; by identifying the inability of police to enforce market regulations and accusing them of selling their souls for packets of sugar, the writer calls into question the legitimacy of the state and its efforts to stabilize the market. Privileged access to essential commodities had silenced the police force and undermined its efforts to enforce the law.

Those who had some connection to soldiers or the police, such as family members, wives, and girlfriends, also received protection. In a letter titled "Enemies of the Revolution," Joseph Brown from Atebubu wrote, "the Police Force which I consider to be dead are the best friends of these enemies. Some of their wives are even in the petty trading business."[40] Similarly, Docas Boateng described how Japekrom policemen allowed their wives, some who had never traded before the coup, to smuggle scarce goods across the Ivorian border for profit. She also reported police themselves transporting bags of cocoa across the border to sell for "plenty money." She instructed the regional commissioner: "[send] men whom you trust to go to the villages you will [be] surprise[d] to see police carrying cocoa." Emphasizing the irony of the situation, she then asked him if the police were there "to check the smugglers or are they the smugglers?"[41] These accusations illustrate that all—even those entrusted to enforce market regulations—were suspect.

But to what extent did these stories and reports deter Brong-Ahafo retailers? Residents with whom I spoke in both interviews and informal conversations told stories about jail sentencing, fines, and beatings. In one of the most extreme cases, Nana Anwasi Agyemang, then a young clerk for the GNTC in Sunyani (fig. 5.1), remembers, pointing at a window, that "they say a certain man sold some exercise books to somebody in front of here. They just lay him [down on the ground], give him about twenty-four lashes for selling exercise books. He was severely beaten."[42] This type of violence was also inflicted on paying customers. Agyemang remembers that soldiers insisted on escorting him and other GNTC employees on sales trips to neighboring towns and villages. While there to enforce price controls and fair allocations,

FIGURE 5.1. Ghana National Trading Corporation staff, Nsawam, March 28, 1968. Photo courtesy of Nana Anwasi Agyemang (aka Joseph Kwasi Onwonah).

soldiers acted abusive toward customers whom they were supposedly there to serve. As Salamatu Idrisu Samu—whose father was a Wenchi storekeeper and who sold items herself—remembers, "You had to line up to get goods and [at] that time if you want to buy a full piece of cloth they would beat you . . . so only two people can buy a piece of cloth to share."[43] Consumers who ignored limits on goods or simply attempted to buy according to older standards were also subject to the soldiers' violence.

Fear of soldiers' brutality and public humiliation acted as powerful deterrents, altering selling practices and driving some retailers out of business. As Nana Ameyaw, a former Berekum storeowner, explains, "When people came to buy, you were afraid to sell even though you had some in stock . . . [the military] patrolled the markets and arrested those who sold above control prices."[44] Soldiers also made periodic surprise visits to shops to check stocks and prices.[45] Ameyaw recalls being forced to sit in his store during usual business hours, even when shelves were empty, as a precautionary measure to prevent him from selling behind the soldiers' backs. When he could no longer take the pressures of shopkeeping, he finally quit.[46]

Yet even with the ominous presence of soldiers, people continued to buy and sell things both legally and illegally. Wenchi farmer Alhaji Abdul Momin Musah remembers that increased military presence led to the creation of new selling strategies: "During the days of Acheampong, items like cloth, if you want to buy, they would not show the whole cloth to you, they will only show to you a piece of cloth tied on a broom; then after bargaining, payment is made [and] the cloth is given out secretly. I mean, they would not show you the whole cloth if you are interested. It would only be shown [with] the broom."[47] Musah's story reveals how worry, fear, and uncertainty motivated new ways of selling and added an element of secrecy to market transactions: samples of cloth tied to broom handles leaning against a wall near a seller's home was coded market language among residents of Wenchi. The creation of such a strategy also demonstrates the savviness of some sellers and the limits of the state's coercive power. Salamatu Idrisu Samu recalls avoiding the gaze of soldiers by concealing goods under her clothing and buying from wholesalers outside Wenchi. She recalls that, in those days, "I went to Kumasi to buy things and brought them to Wenchi. If we go there on our way [back], because it is considered smuggling, we hid those items like thread for sewing, threads for hair, cloth, and other things."[48] While she admits to having been caught once and accused of smuggling, she argues that it was the soldier's behavior that forced her do so. Trading was the primary means she had of making money to feed her children and pay school fees.

Retailers were not the only ones targeted for surveillance; soldiers and police also monitored individual shoppers. As Nana Ameyaw explains, "Even when you had finished buying, they could ask to look through your shopping, ask where you bought [certain goods] from, and follow you to the store to query the storekeeper."[49] Ameyaw's explanation reveals that retailers exercised caution in selling goods, and customers took care when buying. According to authorities these searches, sometimes conducted at random, were meant to prevent hoarding. Any person in possession of goods beyond the level needed for "immediate consumption" or daily use could be considered guilty of hoarding and punished. Fear of being watched, followed, and interrogated by soldiers and police undoubtedly produced feelings of nervousness and anxiety, and consumption became a liability as soon as a customer stepped into a shop; hopes of returning home unnoticed and untouched was the goal.

But efforts to control consumption went beyond pestering and harassment; Acheampong created formal mechanisms to check consumer activity. The idea of consumers as potential hoarders was at the core of new coordinated military actions like Operation Bring Out. Starting sometime in 1972, the Third Battalion began conducting house-to-house searches for goods they believed had been unlawfully hoarded.[50] While they targeted the homes and businesses of known retailers, they also searched the homes of ordinary citizens. As Nana Ameyaw remembers, "A combined team of police and soldiers went from house to house, searching through every person's room. You opened all your trunks, lockers, or wardrobes for them to look through . . . and when they finished, they marked your house with the date of the exercise."[51] After confiscating goods, the military was responsible for breaking large amounts into smaller quantities and selling them to the public at government-controlled prices; all proceeds were to be handed over to the government. As Gwendolyn Mikell has noted, in border areas such as Brong-Ahafo military officers became the major suppliers of scarce imported commodities.[52] In other words, the military acted as a retail sales force, distributing and selling goods on behalf of the state.

The justifications for these home searches were based on the belief that market shortages were caused by retailers, sometimes disguised as ordinary consumers, who hoarded goods in high demand and reaped profits by charging outrageous prices. While government reports reveal that these searches were conducted on scheduled days and in an official and organized manner, residents remember them as frequent and disruptive. The soldiers were "going house to house searching all the time," Agyemang remembers, and they often conducted searches on a whim.[53] Such intrusions, we can assume, produced a whole range of warning signals and signs used by residents to notify one another about potential raids.

The ambiguous meaning attached to the term *hoarding* and the power of soldiers to determine whether a person was guilty of it contributed to widespread suspicion. As Berekum storeowner Ameyaw remembers, soldiers "took up a case against you if you held more than three or four pieces of cloth."[54] Another resident from Sunyani recalls, "When they come and see one carton of sardine in your house you are making hoarding . . . one carton of milk, its over . . . even empty bottle beer [*sic*] . . . I was having about five cartons of sardine . . . I threw it in the bush because when they get you they will beat you."[55] Depending on a soldier's discretion, possession of more than one of any item could be considered hoarding and cause for action. The authority of the military to decide if a person possessed, or intended to use, commodities such as cloth, milk, and beer lawfully is what drove many, like the Sunyani residents above, to discard items for fear of being beaten or detained. Through such measures, the military state was attempting to redefine accumulation ideology. While Ghanaians have always placed limitations and boundaries on individual accumulation, and thus on consumption, as we have seen, soldiers during the 1970s resorted to doing so by physical force.

Military missions like Operation Bring Out illustrate the state's power in defining the limits of legitimate consumption during this period. Private homes and businesses became spaces of public surveillance where the government attempted to regulate when and how its citizens bought and sold the everyday items of life. The possibility of home searches changed the way ordinary residents in Brong-Ahafo interacted with and thought about goods. If an individual's personal belongings—even those locked away in trunks and wardrobes—could be searched and scrutinized, how did that surveillance change people's views on commodities and consumption? Longtime Sunyani resident Agyemang describes some of the attitudes residents held after hoarding raids started: "You should lessen your things, small items, you shouldn't keep more. When you keep more, that means you are hoarding. But when they say hoarding, what is hoarding? If you are in your house having about twenty half-pieces of cloth, is this hoarding? But at that time they would arrest you, if you are lucky they will just put you in court and sentence you . . . that court, too, is a military tribunal."[56] Agyemang's experiences were in part the result of new reconfigurations of accumulation shaped by fear of being caught or having too much. Despite the scarcity of certain commodities, being in possession of any item, regardless of the amount, could be a potential offense against the state. Even though some residents believed that Operation Bring Out and military definitions of hoarding were arbitrary, this belief did not stop them from exercising extreme caution in obtaining goods or even living without certain items they had enjoyed before.

Salamatu Idrisu Samu remembers people being forced to hide personal items, including wedding gifts, from fear of confiscation: "If you are even married, the cloths that people give to you, they [soldiers] would search and say that you are hoarding goods so they would take those cloths away. So even some people would take their things and hide [them] in the bush."[57] She also remembers that this did not ensure safety, as thieves were known to follow in the soldiers' wake and steal hidden goods. And when soldiers caught on to this practice they would force people to lead them to their hiding places, especially if a home search was unsuccessful in uncovering "hoarded goods."[58] While the public did not sit back and condone such activity, fear of violence or legal punishment prevented some residents from speaking out. As we will see, the government also used public searches to win support from frustrated consumers and place blame for economic problems on those who engaged in *kalabule* rather than on state mismanagement.

"ENEMIES OF THE REVOLUTION"

The Acheampong regime positioned hoarding, profiteering, and smuggling as national problems and encouraged all citizens to join the fight against them. While the military kept a broad and watchful eye, enforcing a general vigilance against retailers large and small, evidence suggests they also followed leads from citizens who in phone calls and letters identified potential culprits. In one case, one S. Frafra from Adjaponkrom wrote a letter on behalf of the town's farmers explaining how Adjaponkrom's storekeeper, Opanyin Kwabena Baah, hoarded goods and retailed them at "cut-throat prices."[59] In a fit of patriotism, he further argued that Opanyin Baah's practices discredited the present government and asked that the regional commissioner intervene as soon as possible. In another case, Peter K. Opuku from Wenchi described a supposed cigarette hoarder, Salifu Dagomba, as an "enemy of the revolution" and urged the regional commissioner to "act immediately."[60] Whether or not the accusations against Baah or Dagomba were true, the letters reveal how residents used the language of the state, broadcast on the radio and through the press, to prompt government action on their behalf.

Dozens of these types of letters eventually made their way to the Brong-Ahafo regional archive. Some are surprisingly detailed, containing everything from a storekeeper's prices to the instructions on how to locate a specific individual—including road names and landmarks. A letter from an Nkoranza resident is worth quoting in its entirety:

> Dear Sir,
>
> I am very happy to write you this letter. If you receive this letter try your best to come. We have four shops here, they are cheating us.
>
> The first storekeeper her name is Akosua Fabea. When coming from Bonsu it is on your right hand side. She sells one Sunlight [bar of soap] for 45p. [Sometimes] she don't want to give you some at all.
>
> Another man, who is called Kofi Munufie he is a wicked man. He sells one Geisha [bar of soap] for 50p . . . He sells one bottle of beer for 90p, instead of 70p and he sells Lux [soap] 45p, milk 20p, sugar 3 [cubes] for 5p. Try to look over all the four stores, their house numbers are D.57, D.17, D.47, D.42.
>
> Another man [is] also smuggling gun powder. His name is Kwesi, house number D.59. Sometimes he sends it to these houses D.58, D.14. If you come and don't find it in D.59, go to these two. If you receive this letter, try to come in time otherwise he will go to another town and sell some more.
>
> I end here with much greeting to you.
>
> Your friend,
> Yaw Sarfo[61]

Sarfo's letter shows how conscious residents were of government price controls, and it evokes the language of the state, citing maximum retail prices for essential commodities. Regional and district administrators posted price lists around towns and near shops to prevent price inflation, and residents used these to prove and strengthen their cases against the accused. Similar letters suggest that complaints against retailers represented more than desires to adhere to national laws and policies, however; accusations may have also taken on personal dimensions. Scarcity and increased surveillance had the potential to heighten old conflicts between residents and create new scapegoats out of desperation. Life in smaller Brong-Ahafo towns was more intimate than in large cities like Accra or Kumasi, and accusing one's neighbor of *kalabule* could have larger implications in a community. A police arrest could wipe out the competition (to the benefit of a struggling businessperson) or be used to settle small-town political disputes over land, government office, or allocation of government funds.

Independent storekeepers and retailers were not the only ones accused of illegal activities; Brong-Ahafo residents also reported employees working for state-run commercial firms like the GNTC. In 1973, Kwame Armah wrote a letter to both the regional office at Sunyani and the district office at Wenchi, which reported that a manager for the GNTC in Wenchi sold only to his favorite customers and denied having goods in stock. Armah explained that when customers entered the store, they were met with excuses like "the goods are for some special people from Accra," "they are not for sale," or "there is none."[62] Addressing these accusations, the Wenchi district administrator penned a response letter that defended the GNTC manager and reported that there was no evidence of such practices, claiming that the accusations from the general public and market women were "based on hearsay."[63] He explained that when new goods arrived in Wenchi, the GNTC manager set some aside for workers to buy after working hours, and it was this practice that may have caused confusion among store customers. Since workers at the Wenchi district office most likely received portions of new consignments and benefited from this practice, the district administrator's explanation may have been an effort to cover up or turn a blind eye to the situation.

In another letter, a man living in Kyeraa reported that the GNTC storekeeper in his town also hoarded goods: "Only yesterday about twenty cartons of Geisha [soap] were brought from Sunyani to be sold to the public, but after the [storekeeper] sold five [he] told the public that everything was finished."[64] He further described how the storekeeper took to selling goods in the middle of the night and worked with market women; the women transported the goods to surrounding towns, sold them at prices above those dictated by the government, and split the profits with the storekeeper. Compared to the GNTC store in Wenchi, the one in Kyeraa catered to a much smaller community. The Kyeraa storekeeper thus found it in his best interests to align himself with the market women in the town. The fact that the storekeeper conducted sales in the middle of the night also demonstrates the level of secrecy that retailers resorted to as a means of avoiding the soldiers' wrath.

While some letters were anonymous, several were not, and letter writers themselves were equally as vulnerable as the people they accused. For this reason, pleas for government protection accompanied the reporting of illegal retailing activities.[65] In one such case, Mallam Alhassan Siddi from Yeji pleaded for military intervention: "The Police Sergeant at the Yeji police station . . . is doing all under his power to create troubles for me; this action is carried out for the simple reason that I have reported profiteering at GNTC and reported the police as a whole . . . they are trying to sabotage the economic war waged by the N.R.C. I should therefore be grateful if you would come to my aid as soon as possible before I find myself in hot water."[66] Problems usually occurred when someone reported that certain soldiers or police officers were themselves involved in the hoarding or profiteering they were supposed to be protecting the country from. In many cases, these accusations were correct. As Gwendolyn Mikell argues, corruption was widespread, especially among the military and police, whose functions in controlling "contraband" gave them opportunities to confiscate goods for their own use.[67]

That said, Nana Anwasi Agyemang, who was employed as a salesman at the GNTC, argued that distributing and selling goods had become so dangerous that he required protection from the military and police. In an interview, he explains that it was necessary to use military escorts: "I used to go with [the soldiers] to sell goods to the rural areas . . . to watch me, to protect me . . . you won't go without the soldiers."[68] He recalls that the public took their frustrations out on GNTC salesmen, and that the soldiers were there to enforce order, since customers also fought among themselves.[69] According to Agyemang, the soldiers not only protected him but also, to some extent, acted as witnesses who shielded him from accusations that he was unfairly distributing goods or keeping any goods for himself. While he supported the use of soldiers as escorts and stated that they were necessary to keep angry crowds in check, he also condemns them, believing that many of them used excessive force. He sadly recounts stories of customers being beaten and the brutality inflicted by certain soldiers.

Agyemang escaped soldiers' beatings; he admits, "I was lucky then." But not everyone was as fortunate and, whether to avoid punishment or potential danger, many went into hiding and even left Brong-Ahafo.[70] Nana Ameyaw admits, "I ran from Berekum to hide here at Kyeraa. I was a prominent businessman at Berekum, but I had to run back to my hometown."[71] He left because operating his retail business in Berekum had become too risky. To escape potential harm, he abandoned his store, gave up retailing, and sought protection back home.

Agyemang explains that people ran away to larger towns and sometimes left their families behind during this period: "You will leave your house and go and leave your wife and children . . . usually people used to go to Accra. [In] Accra they don't know you, so when you go there you are free, but [in] Sunyani, here, they know your house, where you stay, so that was the problem we were facing."[72] Although people who fled to their hometowns sought protection through close friends and relatives, people who left for Accra sought anonymity in the crowded city. Although suspicions surrounding consumption habits and *kalabule* practices ran high in all parts of Ghana, former Brong-Ahafo business and storeowners claimed that they suffered the most from these practices because of the Third Battalion's close proximity.

LETTER WRITING AND PRICE INSPECTIONS

Regardless of state efforts to control distribution and prices, shortages in Brong-Ahafo continued, and reports described retailers selling goods on the black market above, and sometimes for nearly double, the government-imposed prices. Table 5.1 shows controlled prices versus market prices in 1976 as reported by the Wenchi district office.

As a result of certain retailers' blatant disregard for price controls, Acheampong initiated a plan to reintroduce price inspection—a move that further pitted retailers against consumers.[73] He published advertisements in daily newspapers and made announcements on the radio recruiting ordinary civilians to work as price inspectors.[74] In a 1977 speech at the annual Nnayem Festival at Odumasi-Krobo in the Eastern Region, he enhanced his campaign by vehemently encouraging all Ghanaian citizens to join in what he described as the "war" against hoarding and profiteering. The *Daily Graphic* published Acheampong's call for public action on its front page under the headline "Power to the People: War against Profiteers."[75] Those who engaged in *kalabule* were not only "enemies of the state" but had become "enemies of the people."

Over the next year, dozens of price inspector applications flooded the regional office in Sunyani; applicants included teachers, civil servants, craftsmen, farmers, and members of youth organizations. In their applications,

TABLE 5.1. Controlled prices versus market prices in 1976, as reported by the Wenchi district office

Item	Control price	Present market price
Milk	0.22	0.40
Pilchard (sardines)	0.26	0.50
Packet of sugar	1.50	3.50
Omo, satchet	0.10	0.20
Omo, large size	0.65	1.20
Lux soap	0.30	0.40
Guardian soap	0.16	0.35
Key soap bar	0.95	1.50
Embassy cigarettes (pack of 20 sticks)	0.80	1.00

Source: J. T. Quarshie, superintendent of special branch, to regional commissioner, Sunyani, and the director of special branch, Accra, February 18, 1976, BRG 1/1/52, PRAAD-S.

candidates described practices of hoarding and profiteering in their own towns and then explained how they could contribute to the enforcement of price controls and the antihoarding campaigns. Some candidates used the language of patriotism and responsibility to the nation to bolster their applications. Charles Owusu Boateng from Wenchi wrote that he was "a full-blooded Ghanaian of twenty-six years old from the Ashanti region" and that he would like to help the SMC government "track down unpatriotic and wicked Ghanaians."[76] E. M. Kuma-Amoako argued that his town of Kwame-Danso had become a den of "unpatriotic criminals" who "cheat the fellow people of their own country," adding, "It is time I come to join the crusade to fight the elements who are setting our Revolution anticlockwise."[77] Both applicants used the language of the nation to forward their claims. While Boateng used his "Ghanaianness" and Akan identity to establish eligibility, Kuma-Amoako evoked the language of criminalization and the destruction of the greater good.

Other applicants focused on obtaining official price inspector licenses or identity cards. A group of four civil servants from Kintampo argued that government-issued identity cards would give them the "legal backing" to fight any practices that fell under *kalabule* "without fear."[78] Others claimed that they needed identity cards to be taken seriously by retailers and police.[79] Joseph Domoah, a teacher from Yeji, claimed that while participating in helping the government check prices, he had "become a big enemy of the storekeepers." As a result, he argued that he needed an identity card to legitimize his authority and to distinguish himself from everyday snitches.[80]

While price inspector applicants hoped to work *with* military and police, others believed that identity cards would grant them the power to make arrests themselves.[81] Members from the P&T Employees Credit Union even applied for a license to conduct their own house-to-house searches in Sunyani. Union representatives stated, "We are anxious to expose these traders since they refuse to heed to the Head of State warning to refrain from their unpatriotic attitude. . . . We have no alternative but to resort to this action to enable us [to] enjoy the fruits of our labour."[82]

As the letters from angry residents illustrate, retailers outwardly defied government price controls. Although being arrested or fined was always a risk, some retailers continued to conduct business on their own terms.[83] As one angry Atebubu resident wrote, "It has come to the notice that traders in Atebubu town have established a new system of trading," implying that local traders had invented new strategies to exchange goods in spite of government regulations.[84] There were numerous reasons applicants volunteered and pledged their support to the government's price control campaign: some were clearly fed up with paying inflated prices and wanted to increase the legitimacy of their reports; others may have seen the position as a means to steady employment or fast cash. Wilson Owusu Badu, a former choir director, wrote, "I am jobless [and] . . . I would be mighty grateful if you would help rescue me from my employment state by recommending me for such an appointment."[85] In another case, W. A. Kusi asked if he could collect commission on every person he caught.[86] In actuality, Kusi's proposition was not unreasonable, owing to the fact that he probably saw soldiers and police profiting both financially and materially from their interactions with retailers. His letter suggested that he only wanted to be included in their plans.

In the end, the regional commissioner at Sunyani refused to provide civilians with identity cards or provide wages for the work and stated that the "misapplying of such certificates could only be imagined." He notified all district administrators that "the idea of Volunteer Price Inspectors is that workers and the public at large should volunteer to expose all cases of profiteering to the appropriate agencies for action."[87] The Trade Union Congress in Sunyani would henceforth nominate all volunteers; all other applications should cease.

Some of these applications were surely a means to exact revenge on enemies, or just to flex one's muscles; yet their fervency represents the desire on behalf of some Ghanaians to participate in a political process that would ensure fair and equal access to goods. Volunteering to participate in state-sponsored campaigns against hoarding and profiteering expressed people's frustration with their lack of economic power and their inability to obtain goods. Although the "enemies" were no longer expatriate firms or the colonial government, the desire for economic autonomy was still central to the individual consumer's struggle.

When Acheampong came to power in 1972, his revolutionary rhetoric, coupled with the idea of economic empowerment, appealed to audiences who had grown more and more frustrated with the outcomes of Ghanaian independence. Angry consumers pledged their support to Acheampong's campaigns against hoarding and profiteering with the hope of reducing inflated prices and persistent commodity shortages. Desires for a more equitable and predictable commodity distribution system also drew supporters. Just a few months after the coup, however, people grew increasingly disillusioned with Acheampong and the NRC. Soldiers and police, whose official jobs were to ensure that retailers distributed goods fairly and sold to customers at the appropriate prices, used their authority to instead secure goods for themselves. As corruption in retail and distribution continued, virtually all forms of accumulation fell under suspicion. By the late 1970s virtually all citizens—from those in the market to those employed by government ministries—were implicated in practicing some form of *kalabule*. Yet Acheampong targeted the activities of retailers the most, and called on all Ghanaian citizens to help supervise the market and wage a "war against profiteers." Some brave Brong-Ahafo letter writers pointed out that his policies were misdirected, as these efforts should have instead been applied to the police and soldiers who he entrusted to enforce his laws.

In the midst of this growing discontent Lieutenant-General F. W. K. Akuffo staged a coup on July 5, 1978, and forced Acheampong to resign and to retire from the military. Akuffo's government became known as the Supreme Military Council II and was tasked with guiding Ghana back to civilian rule. But it was doomed from the beginning, as the military had already lost any form of legitimacy among the people; in less than a year Akuffo and his council were overthrown by junior military officers in a bloody coup that led to his assassination. The June 4th Revolution of 1979 staged by the Armed Forces Revolutionary Council would give way to even more oppressive market controls implemented by yet another military government, the Provisional National Defense Council and its leader, Flight Lieutenant Jerry John Rawlings. Rawlings's aims to once and for all end political corruption and *kalabule* practices were harsher and more destructive than those of any previous regime. But the revolution marked only the beginning of what would be some of the harshest and most oppressive economic conditions in Ghana's history.

Afterword

From Structural Adjustment to Shopping Malls

> *In almost every aspect of life, 1983 marked an historic low. In the cities the daily petrol queues from 3:00 a.m. dominated the life of many. Matches and toilet paper could not be bought for any money and people trekked on foot from store to store in search of a few kilos of rice or maize or a half-litre of palm oil. Groups of middle-class businessmen and professionals would sometimes group together and take a truck into the rural areas to try and buy yams, cassava or plantain. Even then they would have to travel from one village to another as the farmers themselves barely had enough to eat, let alone sell. As inflation briefly soared to more than 100 per cent, civil servants, used to sending home money and other presents to support the family in the village, now suffered the indignity of having to beg parcels of food from aged parents in the rural areas.*
>
> —Kevin Shillington, *Ghana and the Rawlings Factor*

PRESIDENT JERRY JOHN RAWLINGS's efforts to clean up hoarding and profiteering proved even more severe than those of his predecessor, Ignatius Kutu Acheampong. Groups of armed soldiers ransacked shops and select businesses throughout Accra, regarding the destruction of retail spaces and the confiscation of goods as a justifiable "redistribution of wealth."[1] Lebanese businessmen and African women were particularly singled out. The most infamous event occurred in Accra on August 18, 1979, when Rawlings ordered the bulldozing of Makola No. 1, the leading market for food, textiles, and manufactured items in the country. The market was controlled by women, and the incident led to the arrest and public beating of numerous female retailers by soldiers.[2] While Rawlings and the Armed Forces Revolutionary Council considered themselves to be a transitional government that would return Ghana to civilian rule for a short period, Rawlings would nonetheless seize power again on December 31, 1981.[3]

Under Rawlings and the Provisional National Defense Council (PNDC), domestic measures to control the market became increasingly destructive and violent. Police and military, as well as semiofficial militias, stepped up measures to enforce price controls, confiscate goods, patrol markets, and vigorously punish "offenders." The Rawlings government also threatened that traders caught hoarding goods would be "taken away to be shot by firing squads."[4] By 1981, Makola No. 2 and the main markets in Kumasi, Korforidua, and Sekondi had also been destroyed. Even upscale department stores like Kingsway could not obtain basic goods, and were so desperate to fill their shelves that they resorted to selling produce like cocoyam and plantain, cheap items typically bought at outdoor markets and from farmers. Lining up to buy vegetables and necessities like soap, sometimes for hours, became a way of life. Coping with scarcity and strict market regulations necessitated a total reallocation of time and energy.[5] Shopping became an entire day's work, and whole households were often expected to wait in lines to buy even a cube of sugar.

Market Encounters concludes with Rawlings's ascendance to power, but does so for conceptual rather than political reasons. It was also during this period that a new regulating force within the Ghanaian economy was introduced: structural adjustment. As captured in the Shillington epigraph above, for many Ghanaians 1983 marked a "historic low," but that was the result of a number of other factors that had shocked the country in the preceding years.[6] When the PNDC took office, the economy was already in a state of disarray. By the 1980s severe shortages and inflation worsened. As the quality of life diminished, an estimated two million Ghanaians left the country; some went to Nigeria, and several thousand—especially professionals, including doctors, lawyers, and academics—left for Europe and North America. As Kwamina Panford has demonstrated, the years leading up to the revolution "witnessed one of the most massive brain drains in Ghana."[7] Local hospitals, secondary schools, and universities suffered.

Additionally, the effects of a severe drought in the countryside between 1981 and 1983, and a series of bush fires, destroyed valuable agricultural land that halted the production of local food and exportable crops like cocoa.[8] At the same time, the return of around 1.2 million Ghanaians (roughly one-twelfth of the nation's total population) who were expelled from Nigeria in January–February 1983 intensified the strain on the country's already limited resources. The Rawlings government, by then under extreme financial pressure, responded by forming the National Emergency Relief Committee to deal with the influx of its citizens and began appealing to international agencies and the United Nations for food and medical aid.[9] Ironically, returnees were first housed in transit camps at Ghana's International Trade Fair Site in Accra, a space that just two decades earlier had showcased promises of free market capitalism as an avenue to wealth and abundance.

As a result of these dire conditions, 1983 marked the year that Rawlings and the PNDC initiated negotiations with the International Monetary Fund (IMF) and the World Bank to bail the country out of bankruptcy. That May the government took the drastic step of devaluing the cedi. One month later, the Secretary for Finance and Economic Planning, Kwesi Botchway, announced the toughest austerity budget of any government since independence. Prices on daily items soared, rising 100–300 percent, and government subsidies were slashed to reduce the budget deficit. Import surcharges were also imposed on all but the most basic essentials; the price of meat rose from twenty cedis per kilo to eighty-three cedis, while the price of a bottle of beer doubled to twenty cedis and a pack of cigarettes to forty cedis.[10] Strict austerity measures and the adoption of the four-year Economic Recovery Programme (EAP) were preconditions for a US$300 million loan from the IMF.[11] While the initiation of the EAP was intended to restore economic productivity, encourage saving and investments, reduce Ghana's international debt, and increase the availability of essential consumer goods, it instead forced a large majority of Ghanaians into extreme poverty.[12]

The damage caused by international financial institutions and neoliberal economic policies have been covered extensively, as have the negative effects of structural adjustment programs (SAPs) under the guidance of the World Bank and the IMF.[13] "Structuralists" considered a deregulated or liberalized economy as a necessary and sufficient condition for Ghana's economic recovery and growth.[14] Adjustment programs like the EAP focused on scaling back the public sector, eliminating social services, and removing any obstacles that distorted the free market. As Lynne Brydon has pointed out, the countries of the "so-called 'South'" have adopted these measures with varying degrees of "desperation, enthusiasm or success."[15] While the PNDC and its successor government, the National Democratic Congress, were not the first Ghanaian regimes to implement World Bank and IMF policies, they held one of the longest relationships ever with both institutions—not only in Ghana but in all of Africa. By accepting the terms and conditions set out by these agencies, Rawlings would receive millions of dollars in financial assistance and transform Ghana into what donors celebrated as their "SAP darling."[16]

It is easy to see the events of the 1980s as an illustration of Rawlings's mismanagement or international institutions' tendency to condescend to African nations, assuming that Western economic wisdom knows how to better meet the needs of people living in those countries than do the people themselves. Yet my research on consumer politics in Ghana reveals how we might understand these conditions as part of a longer history of intervention and reform that shaped Africa's place in the world.[17] Since the colonial period, Ghana's economy has been marked by (often dramatic) ebbs and flows, from periods of relative abundance to severe scarcity. As Deborah Pellow and Naomi Chazan have convincingly argued, Ghana's leaders "have been acutely aware of their country's dependence and of the limitations this condition imposed on the types of relations Ghana could conduct with other states."[18] *Market Encounters* demonstrates that this understanding also holds true for retailers and ordinary consumers. Their strategies to make a cedi and to build a life for themselves reveal the perpetual intersection of social worlds and economic processes and show how access to goods historically depends on the construction and maintenance of social relationships. Yet tracking such continuities over the twentieth century offers more than just an illustration of how contemporary economic conditions are products of a colonial legacy; a focus on African consumer history uncovers the ways in which Ghanaian men and women have managed persistent mechanisms of market control and shaped the terms of engagement within a larger capitalist system. By framing consumer culture as always and inherently political, and as a product of various social struggles and historical conflicts, we can better understand how seemingly straightforward economic figures and facts manifested themselves within people's personal lives and relationships.

This book has argued that the expansion of consumer capitalism in West Africa must be understood through the shifting relationships between foreign companies, colonial and postcolonial governments, and groups of African retailers and consumers. The primary objective of my research has been to expand histories of consumerism to accommodate the ways in which African men and women have encountered and experienced the global market. Categories like *consumer, consumerism*, and *consumer culture* cannot be universally applied. African consumer practices were produced by and through a multitude of social relations framed by specific histories of colonial domination, struggles for independence, postcolonial nation building, extreme scarcity, and military violence. Consumer history from an African-centered perspective further expands understandings of consumerism to include the importance of distribution. For example, the culture of reselling, the role of thousands of commercial intermediaries, and various policies and programs designed to make distribution systems "fair" are central to the ways that goods reached people in both the cities and the countryside. Thus, business and supply networks that linked people throughout Ghana, the United Kingdom, and Continental Europe had an economic as well as a social history that cannot be separated from consumer culture. Through these historical links we are also able to identify how ideas about race, gender, and other power relations were constructed within commercial networks that span the globe and are embedded in the terms and conditions that shaped African participation. *Market Encounters* therefore helps us better understand contemporary economic issues—including foreign aid and investment, elite-centered development, economic marginalization and exclusion, and the uneven circulation of global capital.

A history of Ghanaian consumer politics, for instance, can elucidate the larger issues surrounding consumer-centered development projects in Ghana today—namely, the planning, construction, and promotion of places like Accra Mall, "the mall with it all." In 2007, I was in Ghana to witness the country's fiftieth anniversary as an independent nation. Throughout the year, the government hosted several "Ghana @ 50" events including cultural exhibitions and performances, the eleventh International Trade Fair (dubbed the Golden Jubilee Fair), and the ninth Summit of the Assembly of the African Union in Accra, which brought together various African heads of state. In connection with these celebrations was also the opening of what developers described as Ghana's first "world class shopping centre"—the long-awaited Accra Mall.[19] Located north of the capital's original city center, the mall is situated at the intersection of Tetteh Quarshie Interchange and Spintex Road, just off the Tema Motorway. It is surrounded by middle- and upper-class residential areas and is a short distance from several upscale tourist hotels and Kotoka International Airport.

Through local newspapers, radio, and television commercials, developers promoted the mall as a safe and congenial shopping environment as well as a site of entertainment and leisure.[20] On opening day Joseph Owusu-Akyaw, a founding partner and the mall's main spokesperson, delivered an inaugural address to a large audience, including then president John Agyekum Kuffor.[21] In it he proclaimed that Accra Mall would not only serve as a national symbol of modernization and progress but would also raise the standard of living, act as a major tourist destination, and help boost foreign investment. Additionally, he claimed that the mall would cater to the upper and growing middle-income groups, foster the development of "middle-class taste," and encourage Ghanaians to shop in more "formalised shopping facilities."[22]

Throughout 2007, I followed local press coverage and publicity for the mall and had numerous conversations with Accra residents about visiting it. Some went to the mall out of curiosity or as something fun to do with friends, but most still did their shopping in and around their own neighborhoods or at one of Accra's twenty-eight large open-air markets, often complaining that the mall's location was inconvenient.[23] Others I spoke with revealed intentions to buy items at stores like Shoprite and resell them for small profits. While weekly Shoprite circulars clearly stated, "We reserve the right to limit quantities" and "No traders," the women I spoke with listed goods ranging from glassware to sweets in their potential resale plans.[24] In those weeks preceding Ghana's fiftieth anniversary celebrations, I was struck by the almost identical connections between the publicity surrounding the opening of the mall and the opening of Kingsway Department Store in 1957; Owusu-Akyaw's claims that Accra Mall would provide Ghanaians with their "first local modern shopping experience" echoed those made by Kwame Nkrumah fifty years earlier. Nkrumah had also positioned Kingsway as a symbol of national development, promising Ghanaian consumers "*the* modern shopping experience."

Today large-scale urban retail developments still function as symbols of propelling Ghana into the modern era. Ghanaian ministers and businessmen, foreign and local alike, use ideologies of consumerism to attract foreign investment and to gain political and financial support from the upper and middle classes. Though contemporary developers claimed that the construction of Accra Mall would increasingly attract Ghanaian consumers to more formalized shopping facilities, they failed to recognize that these establishments already exist and had for decades. Not only is this development discourse strategic, it is also dangerous. Promises of modernization and "progress" mask the realities of most people's everyday lives. The majority of Ghanaians, and many other consumers living in poorer countries, do not shop at "formalized shopping centers"—not because they don't exist but because of local and global economic constraints; family obligations, the hardships of daily life, and the lack of quick and reliable public transportation leave no time for travel or leisurely shopping trips.

The connection between the openings of the Kingsway Department Store and Accra Mall, fifty years apart, bring the need for a deeper sense of Ghanaian consumer history into sharp focus. To more fully understand how contemporary commercial developments shape discourses about Ghana today we need a more nuanced approach that accounts for its past.[25] Using consumer politics as an analytical lens allows us to peel back complex layers of meaning behind more recent manifestations of consumer culture, moving beyond discourses that are too often framed in terms of an African government's frivolous spending and mismanagement of economic resources. Only with such nuance can we hold productive conversations about Ghanaian consumerism that accounts for its rich and interconnected history, as well as its economic, political, and social future.

Notes

INTRODUCTION: CONSUMING HISTORIES AND CREATING ECONOMIES

1. The Old Polo Grounds occupy the same location in Accra where Kwame Nkrumah, Ghana's first prime minister and president, gave his famous midnight independence speech on March 6, 1957. It is now the site of the Kwame Nkrumah Mausoleum and Memorial Park.

2. About 69,000 men served in the Gold Coast Regiment of the Royal West African Frontier Force during World War II. Most served in East Africa and about 30,000 served in Burma. Discrepancies in the allocation of food, clothing, and pay between European and African units during the war were another key issue. Adrienne M. Israel, "Ex-Servicemen at the Crossroads: Protest and Politics in Post-War Ghana," *Journal of Modern African Studies* 30, no. 2 (1992): 359–68.

3. European firms were not the only ones affected; protesters also targeted Lebanese, Syrian, and, to a lesser extent, South Asian businesses. Aiken Watson, *Report of the Commission of Enquiry into the Disturbances in the Gold Coast* (Accra: Government Printing Department, 1948).

4. Dennis Austin, *Politics in Ghana, 1946–1960* (Oxford: Oxford University Press, 1964); Maxwell Owusu, *Uses and Abuses of Political Power: A Case Study of Continuity and Change in the Politics of Ghana* (Chicago: University of Chicago Press, 1970).

5. Eric Sachs, *Report of the Commission of Enquiry into the Representations made by W. E. Conway, A. D. W. Allen, A. G. Leventis, and A. G. Leventis and Co. Repudiating Allegations in the Report of the Commission of Enquiry into the Conduct and Management of the Supplies and Customs Departments* (Accra: Government Printing Department, 1948), 19.

6. Member firms included the United Africa Company, G. B. Ollivant, G. Gottschalk, John Holt, the Compagnie Française de l'Afrique Occidentale, the Société Commerciale de l'Ouest African, Paterson and Zonchonis, the Union Trading Company, the Swiss African Trading Company, and the Commonwealth Trust. Richard Rathbone, "Businessmen in Politics: Party Struggle, 1945–57," *Journal of Development Studies* 9, no. 3 (1973): 391–401; D. K. Fieldhouse, *Merchant Capital and Economic Decolonization: The United Africa Company 1929–1994* (Oxford: Clarendon, 1994); Sarah Stockwell, *The Business of Decolonization: British Business Strategies in the Gold Coast* (Oxford: Clarendon, 2000).

7. Watson, *Report of the Commission of Enquiry*, 36.

8. These hold ups or producer strikes prohibited the sale of cocoa to European firms. Polly Hill, *The Migrant Cocoa-Farmers of Southern Ghana: A Study in Rural Capitalism* (Cambridge: Cambridge University Press, 1963); Gareth Austin, "Capitalists and Chiefs in the Cocoa Hold-Ups in South Asante, 1927–1939," *International Journal of African Historical Studies* 21, no. 1 (1988): 63–95; A. G. Hopkins, "Economic Aspects of Political Movements in Nigeria and the Gold Coast, 1918–1939," *Journal of African History* 7, no. 1 (1966): 133–52; Gwendolyn Mikell, *Cocoa and Chaos in Ghana* (New York: Paragon House, 1989); Cyrelene Amoah-Boampong, "Defying Merchant Capital in the Gold Coast," *History in Action* 4, no. 1 (2014): 1–9.

9. Watson, *Report of the Commission of Enquiry*, 34–36. See also "The Boycott of 1948," *The Ghanaian*, December 1963, 10, 15.

10. The agreement that firms would reduce their profits on imported goods was reached after meetings between representatives of the local chamber of commerce, the colonial government, and the Joint Provincial Council of Chiefs (which supported Nii Bonne's campaign).

11. Watson, *Report of the Commission of Enquiry*, 12.

12. In 1874 Britain claimed the coastal zone and its interior as a crown colony and defeated and annexed Asante after a series of wars between 1824 and 1901. The British Gold Coast Administration comprised three territories referred to as Ashanti, the Colony, and the Northern Territories.

13. Statement by Emil Leoliger, assistant to Mr. Knittel, former general manager, UTC Accra, n.d., UTC 4856: Riots 1948, BMA; statement by Mr. H. Lutzelschwab, agent, Korforidua, n.d., UTC 5014: Riots Gold Coast, 1948, BMA.

14. John Holt estimated the cost from damages to the UTC to be around £300,000, to G. B. Ollivant around £100,000, and to the UAC around £750,000. Figures taken from Stockwell, *The Business of Decolonization*, 72. A note on currency: until 1958 Ghana's currency was the British West African pound, with shillings and pennies as major units. The British West African pound exchanged at par with UK pound sterling.

15. The topic of British business and decolonization in West Africa has been well-researched, particularly for Ghana and Nigeria. Important examples include Fieldhouse, *Merchant Capital and Economic Decolonization*; Stockwell, *The Business of Decolonization*; Robert Tignor, *Capitalism and Nationalism at the End of Empire: State and Business in Decolonizing Egypt, Nigeria, and Kenya, 1945–1963* (Princeton, NJ: Princeton University Press, 1998); Stephanie Decker, "Corporate Legitimacy and Advertising: British Companies and the Rhetoric of Development in West Africa, 1950–1970," *Business History Review* 81 (2007): 59–86; Axel Harneit-Sievers, "African Business, 'Economic Nationalism,' and British Colonial Policy: Southern Nigeria, 1935–1954," *African Economic History* 23 (1995): 79–128.

16. "The Boycott of 1948," *The Ghanaian*, December 1963, 31.

17. Statement by Mr. E. Glattfelder, former agent at Winneba, n.d., UTC 5014: Riots Gold Coast 1948, BMA.

18. Statement by Walter Schmid on behalf of B. A. Okudjetoe, UTC storekeeper at Adidome, March 16, 1948, UTC 4856: Riots Gold Coast 1948, BMA; P. H. Fitz-Gerald to all stations and London office, UAC of Ghana Ltd. General Manager's Circulars, item 138, UAC/2/20/3/3/3, UARM.

19. Frederick Pedler to Edward Russell Baines, July 19, 1948, Mss. Afr. S.1814, box 21, RHL.

20. Dmitri van den Bersselaar, "'Doorway to Success?': Reconstructing African Careers in European Business from Company House Magazines and Oral History Interviews," *History in Africa* 38 (2011): 257–94, esp. 262.

21. W. E. Conway, *Report of the Commission of Enquiry into the Distribution and Prices of Essential Imported Goods* (Accra: Government Printing Department, 1943), 2.

22. Ibid., 3.

23. Ibid.

24. Ibid., 2.

25. To some extent this perspective also reproduces a world systems/core–periphery approach to how global economies function. Shaping my study are several important works on African economies, globalization, and transnationalism that have challenged this restrictive model. See especially James Ferguson, *Global Shadows: Africa in the Neoliberal World Order* (Durham, NC: Duke University Press, 2006); Frederick Cooper, *Africa in the World: Capitalism, Empire, Nation-State* (Cambridge, MA: Harvard University Press, 2014); Ato Quayson, *Oxford Street, Accra: City Life and the Itineraries of Transnationalism* (Durham, NC: Duke University Press, 2014); Charles Piot, *Remotely Global: Village Modernity in West Africa* (Chicago: University of Chicago Press, 1999); and Jeremy Prestholdt, *Domesticating the World: African Consumerism and the Genealogies of Globalization* (Berkeley: University of California Press, 2008).

26. Particularly useful to articulating these points are Sara S. Berry, *No Condition Is Permanent: The Social Dynamics of Agrarianism Change in Sub-Saharan Africa* (Madison: University of Wisconsin Press, 1993); Thomas McCaskie, "Accumulation, Wealth and Belief in Asante History II: The Twentieth Century," *African* 56, no. 1 (1986): 3–38; and Jane Guyer, *Money Matters: Instability, Values, and Social Payments in the Modern History of West African Communities* (Portsmouth, NH: Heinemann, 1995).

27. Brenda Chalfin, *Neoliberal Frontiers: An Ethnography of Sovereignty in West Africa* (Chicago: University of Chicago Press, 2010), 15.

28. Ericka Beckman, *Capital Fictions: The Literature of Latin America's Export Age* (Minneapolis: University of Minnesota Press, 2012), 14.

29. For an excellent overview of consumption studies scholarship, see Frank Trentmann, "Introduction," in *The Making of the Consumer: Knowledge, Power and Identity in the Modern World* (Oxford: Berg, 2006), 1–27.

30. Erika Rappaport, Sandra Trudgen Dawson, and Mark J. Crowley, "Introduction," in *Consuming Behaviours: Identity, Politics, and Pleasure in Twentieth-Century Britain*, ed. Erika Rappaport, Sandra Trudgen Dawson, and Mark J. Crowley (London: Bloomsbury, 2015), 3.

31. Trentmann, "Introduction," 14.

32. One major exception was the manufacturing and bottling of beer by Overseas Brewery Limited. The firm opened its Accra factory in 1931. Gold Coast Government, *The Gold Coast Handbook* (London: Baylis, 1937), 74.

33. Port facilities were first located in Axim, Cape Coast, Keta, Saltpond, and Sekondi. After 1928, Accra and Takoradi handled most of the country's import-export trade. Kwamina Dickson, *A Historical Geography of Ghana* (Cambridge: Cambridge University Press, 1971).

34. While focusing on nineteenth-century Nigeria, the pioneering research on commercial intermediaries by Kenneth Onwuka Dike has been particularly useful. See Kenneth Onwuka Dike, *Trade and Politics in the Niger Delta, 1830–1885: An Introduction to the Economic and Political History of Nigeria* (Oxford: Clarendon, 1956).

35. United Africa Company, "Merchandise Trading in British West Africa," *Statistical and Economic Review* 6 (1950): 1–41, esp. 16–17.

36. Ibid., 17.

37. Deborah Quartey, interview with the author, Tema, June 19, 2007.

38. Akuse agent to head office, March 15, 1932, UTC 4480: Akuse Correspondence, BMA.

39. Christian Spoerri, "Forty Years of Service for the BHG," 1961, UTC 4968, BMA.

40. "Report of Mr. D. D. Pitcher's Visit to the Gold Coast, January 1 to April 4, 1929," Visit Reports, box 32, UAC/20/5/1/1, UARM, p. 49; Nkawkaw agent to headquarters, February 4, 1933, document 16, UTC 4435: Nkoko Correspondence, BMA; telegram, April 24, 1930, UTC 4410: West Africa, General Agent, BMA; Nkawkaw agent to headquarters, December 10, 1929, UTC 4435: Nkoko Correspondence, BMA.

41. "Report of Mr. D. D. Pitcher's Visit to the Gold Coast," p. 50.

42. P. T. Bauer, *A Study of Competition, Oligopoly and Monopoly in a Changing Economy* (Cambridge: Cambridge University Press, 1954).

43. Scholarship on the history of advertising is vast; foundational literature includes Jackson Lears, *Fables of Abundance: A Cultural History of Advertising in America* (New York: Basic Books, 1995); and Roland Marchand, *Advertising the American Dream: Making Way for Modernity, 1920–1940* (Berkley: University of California Press, 1986). A survey of advertising in the UAC's corporate archive reveals that there is no sustained discussion of advertising or its value in promoting the sale of merchandise until the mid-1950s.

44. A. C. C. Baxter, London, to general manager, Accra, "UAC London Conference—Merchandise," Ghana (Accra) General Manager's Private Files, file 30, September 13, 1955, UAC/2/20/3/2, UARM.

45. Ironically, Africans featured largely as objects in advertisements meant to entice European shoppers to buy products produced in Britain's empire. Anandi Ramamurthy, *Imperial Persuaders: Images of Africa and Asia in British Advertising* (Manchester, England: Manchester University Press, 2003).

46. These strategies were used by the UAC's in-house advertising company, West African Publicity, to promote goods in the Gold Coast, Nigeria, and Gambia. Only later did the company engage in print advertising, and newspaper advertisements were not as successful as hoped due to limited readership. See Dmitri van den Bersselaar, *The King of Drinks: Schnapps Gin from Modernity to Tradition* (Boston: Brill, 2007), 120.

47. Decker, "Corporate Legitimacy and Advertising;" Stephanie Decker, "Building Up Goodwill: British Business, Development, and Economic Nationalism," PhD diss., University of Liverpool, 2006; Bianca Murillo, "'The Devil We Know': Gold Coast Consumers, Local Employees, and the United Africa Company, 1940–60," *Enterprise and Society* 12, no. 2 (2011): 317–55.

48. E. Gyimah-Boadi and Richard Jefferies, "The Political Economy of Reform," in *Economic Reforms in Ghana: The Miracle and The Mirage*, ed. Ernest Aryeetey, Jane Harrigan, and Machiko Nissanke (Trenton, NJ: Africa World Press, 2000), 32–48.

49. Willie A. Abraham, *Report of the Commission of Enquiry into Trade Malpractices in Ghana* (Accra: State Publishing Corporation, 1965), 28–29.

50. A Correspondent, "Who Creates the 'Shortages'? The 'Dubious Customer,'" *Daily Graphic*, September 12, 1966.

51. The hated practice of conditional sales embedded in West African economies also complicates the notion of choice. This term *conditional sales* was coined by

British colonial administrators to describe a particular practice by which purchasers are compelled to buy something they do not require in order to obtain some essential item they do. Firms had long applied pressure on African sellers to buy aged or unwanted stocks in order to gain access to other fast-moving lines. The practice was not limited to the Gold Coast; a 1948 commission of inquiry in Nigeria, for instance, recorded cases where consumers were forced to buy unnecessary items including embroidered table runners, pipe racks, mustard, satin ribbons, and table tennis sets in order to purchase essential goods like kerosene, soap, gasoline, and sugar. P. W. Adshead, *Report of the Commission of Enquiry into Conditional Sales* (Lagos: Government Printer, 1948). Conditional or forced selling undertaken by firms is evident; see "Report of Mr. D. D. Pitcher's Visit, Gold Coast Business," December 1936, Visit Reports, UAC/2/20/5/1/2, UARM; *Issues to Retail Stores*, ca. 1945, UAC of Ghana Ltd. General Manager's Circulars, item 64, UAC/2/20/3/3/3, UARM.

52. Sherene Seikaly, *Men of Capital: Scarcity and Economy in Mandate Palestine* (Stanford, CA: Stanford University Press, 2016).

53. Some examples in the field include Neil McKendrick, John Brewer, and J. H. Plumb, *The Birth of a Consumer Society: The Commercialization of Eighteenth-Century England* (London: HarperCollins, 1984); Richard Wightman Fox and T. J. Jackson Lears, eds., *The Culture of Consumption: Critical Essays in American History 1880–1980* (New York: Pantheon, 1983); Lizabeth Cohen, *A Consumer's Republic: The Politics of Mass Consumption in Postwar America* (New York: Vintage, 2004); and T. H. Breen, *The Marketplace of Revolution: How Consumer Politics Shaped American Independence* (Oxford: Oxford University Press).

54. Jean Comaroff and John Comaroff, *Of Revelation and Revolution: Christianity, Colonialism and Consciousness in South Africa*, vol. 1 (Chicago: University of Chicago Press, 1991), 18.

55. Although these understandings have been rigorously critiqued and challenged, taints of modernization and world systems theories still make their way into contemporary scholarship. The designations of *global* and *local* to frame consumer behaviors in places considered the "non-West" also perpetuate this view. For a key example, see Peter N. Stearns, *Consumerism in World History: The Global Transformation of Desire* (London: Routledge, 2001). For a brilliant collection that provides an overview of this literature and challenges it by showing how global commodity and cultural flows shaped multiple geopolitical locations, see The Modern Girl around the World Research Group: Alys Eve Weinbaum, Lynn M. Thomas, Priti Ramamurthy, Uta G. Poinger, Madeline Yue Dong, and Tani E. Barlow, *The Modern Girl around the World: Consumption, Modernity, and Globalization* (Durham, NC: Duke University Press, 2008).

56. Some examples include Kwame Arhin, *West African Traders in Ghana* (London: Longman, 1979); Kwame Daaku, *Trade and Politics on the Gold Coast, 1600–1720: A Study of the African Reaction to European Trade* (London: Clarendon, 1970); Raymond Dumett, "African Merchants of the Gold Coast, 1860–1905: Dynamics of Indigenous Entrepreneurship," *Comparative Studies in Society and History* 25, no. 4 (1983): 661–93; Ray Kea, *Settlements, Trade, and Politics in the Seventeenth-Century Gold Coast* (Baltimore: Johns Hopkins University Press, 1982); Edward Reynolds, *Trade and Economic Change on the Gold Coast, 1807–1874* (London: Longman, 1974); and Margaret Priestley, *West Africa Trade and Coast Society: A Family Study* (London: Oxford University Press, 1969).

57. For an excellent analysis of this transformation within the political economy of the Atlantic market in people, see Stephanie E. Smallwood, *Saltwater Slavery: A Middle Passage from Africa to American Diaspora* (Cambridge, MA: Harvard University Press, 2007), esp. chap. 2.

58. Walter Rodney, *How Europe Underdeveloped Africa* (Washington, DC: Howard University Press, 1974), 135.

59. A. G. Hopkins makes this distinction in "African Economic History: The First Twenty-Five Years," *Journal of African History* 30, no. 1 (1989): 157–63.

60. Stanley B. Alpern, "What Africans Got for Their Slaves: A Master List of European Trade Goods," *History in Africa* 22 (1995): 5–43.

61. Robin Law, ed. *From Slave Trade to "Legitimate" Commerce: The Commercial Transition in Nineteenth-Century West Africa* (Cambridge: Cambridge University Press, 1995).

62. Stockwell, *The Business of Decolonization;* Decker, "Corporate Legitimacy and Advertising."

63. Jean Allman and Victoria Tashjian, *"I Will Not Eat Stone": A Woman's History of Colonial Asante* (Portsmouth, NH: Heinemann, 2000); Gareth Austin, *Labour, Land, and Capital in Ghana: From Slavery to Free Labour in Asante, 1807–1956* (Rochester: University Press, 2005); Hill, *The Migrant Cocoa-Farmers in Southern Ghana*; Mikell, *Cocoa and Chaos*; Ivor Wilks, *Forests of Gold: Essays on the Akan and the Kingdom of Asante* (Athens: Ohio University Press, 1993).

64. Gold Coast Government, *Blue Book for 1914* (Accra: Government Printer, 1915).

65. Violent competition over land and direct restrictions on African profits from farming, which were evident in places like Zimbabwe and Kenya, did not exist in the Gold Coast.

66. Thomas E. Kyei, *Our Days Dwindle: Memories of My Childhood Days in Asante*, ed. Jean Allman (Portsmouth, NH: Heinemann, 2001), 29.

67. Jeff Crisp, *The Story of an African Working Class: Ghanaian Miners' Struggles, 1870–1980* (London: Zed, 1984); Raymond E. Dumett, *El Dorado in West Africa: The Gold-Mining Frontier, African Labor, and Colonial Capitalism, 1875–1900* (Athens: Ohio University Press, 1998); Richard Jefferies, *Class, Power and Ideology in Ghana: The Railwaymen of Sekondi* (Cambridge: Cambridge University Press, 1978).

68. For pioneering scholarship in this field, see Claire Robertson, *Sharing the Same Bowl: A Socioeconomic History of Women and Class in Accra* (Bloomington: Indiana University Press, 1984); Christine Obbo, *African Women: Their Struggle for Economic Independence* (London: Zed, 1980); Christine Oppong, ed., *Female and Male in West Africa* (London: Allen and Unwin, 1983); and Allman and Victoria, *"I Will Not Eat Stone."* Early literature on urban and middle-class professional women has also guided my thinking on women's financial autonomy and strategies. See especially Carmel Dinan, "Sugar Daddies and Gold-Diggers: The White Collar Single Women in Accra," in *Female and Male in West Africa*, ed. Christine Oppong (London: Allen and Unwin, 1983), 344–66; Christine Oppong, *Middle Class African Marriage: A Family Study of Ghanaian Senior Servants* (London: Allen and Unwin, 1981); Eugenia Date-Bah, "Male and Female Factory Workers in Accra," in *Female and Male in West Africa*, ed. Christine Oppong (London: Allen and Unwin, 1983), 266–74; and Deborah Pellow, *Women in Accra: Options for Autonomy* (Algonac, MI: Reference Publications, 1977).

69. Gracia Clark, *Onions Are My Husband: Survival and Accumulation by West African Market Women* (Chicago: University of Chicago Press, 1994), 33.

70. Timothy Burke, *Lifebuoy Men, Lux Women: Commodification, Consumption, and Cleanliness in Modern Zimbabwe* (Durham, NC: Duke University Press, 1996). Other important works on consumer history include Prestholdt, *Domesticating the World*; Van den Bersselaar, *The King of Drinks*; and Anne Kelk Mager, *Beer, Sociability, and Masculinity in South Africa* (Bloomington: Indiana University Press, 2010).

71. Prestholdt, *Domesticating the World*, 4.

72. Outside the field of history, important work on Ghanaian consumers includes Brenda Chalfin, "Cars, the Customs Service, and Sumptuary Rule in Neoliberal Ghana," *Society for Comparative Studies in Society and History* 50 (2008): 424–53; Brenda Chalfin, *Shea Butter Republic: State Power, Global Markets, and the Making of an Indigenous Commodity* (New York: Routledge, 2004); Akosua Keseboa Darkwah, "Going Global: Ghanaian Female Transnational Traders in an Era of Globalization," PhD diss., University of Wisconsin, 2002; Birgit Meyer, "Christian Mind and Worldly Matters: Religion, Materiality in the Nineteenth-Century Gold Coast," in *Modernization on a Shoestring: Dimensions of Globalization, Consumption, and Development in Africa and Beyond*, ed. Richard Fardon, W. M. J. van Binsbergen, and R. A. van Dijk (Leiden: EIDOS, 1999), 155–77; Birgit Meyer, "Commodities and the Power of Prayer: Pentecostalist Attitudes towards Consumption in Contemporary Ghana," in *Globalization and Identity: Dialectics of Flow and Closure*, ed. Birgit Meyer and Peter Geschiere (Oxford: Wiley-Blackwell, 1999), 151–76. See also research in the field of Performance Studies by David Afriyie Donkor, *Spiders of the Market: Ghanaian Trickster Performance in a Web of Neoliberalism* (Bloomington: Indiana University Press, 2016).

73. The study of African popular culture and leisure has also provided an important foundation for understanding how African audiences and publics used specific cultural forms, including fashion, art, film, and music, as sources of empowerment, expression, consciousness, and social conflict and change. For Ghana, important works include Nate Plageman, *Highlife Saturday Night: Popular Music and Social Change in Urban Ghana* (Bloomington: Indiana University Press, 2012); Catherine Cole, *Ghana's Concert Party Theatre* (Bloomington: Indiana University Press, 2001); and Stephanie Newell, *Ghanaian Popular Fiction: "Thrilling Discoveries in Conjugal Life" and Other Tales* (Athens: Ohio University Press, 2000).

74. As other scholars have argued, this perspective ignores the significance of consumption in premodern, colonial, fascist, and socialist societies. For an overview of this literature, see Trentmann, "Introduction."

75. For examples on how consumer politics has previously been studied, see Cohen, *A Consumer's Republic*; and Breen, *The Marketplace of Revolution*.

76. Tony Ballantyne and Antoinette Burton, *Moving Subjects: Gender, Mobility, and Intimacy in the Age of Global Empire* (Champaign: University of Illinois Press, 2009), 2.

77. See Alusine Jalloh, *African Entrepreneurship: Muslim Fula Merchants in Sierra Leone* (Athens: Ohio University Press, 1999); Ghislaine Lydon, *On Trans-Saharan Trails: Islamic Law, Trade Networks, and Cross-Cultural Exchange in Nineteenth-Century Western Africa* (Cambridge: Cambridge University Press, 2012); Sarah Abrevaya Stein, *Plumes: Ostrich Feathers, Jews, and the Lost World of Global Commerce* (New Haven, CT: Yale University Press, 2010); Janet MacGaffey and Rémy Bazenguissa-Ganga,

Congo–Paris: Transnational Traders on the Margins of the Law (Bloomington: Indiana University Press, 2000); and Paul Stoller, *Money Has No Smell: The Africanization of New York City* (Chicago: University of Chicago Press, 2002).

78. For an overview of important literature on the gendering of the global economy, see Carla Freeman, "Is Local: Global as Feminine: Masculine? Rethinking the Gender of Globalization," *Signs* 26, no. 4 (2001): 1007–37; and Modern Girl around the World Research Group, *The Modern Girl Around the World*. New scholarship on racial formations in colonial and postcolonial Ghana addresses such questions, as well; see Jemima Pierre, *The Predicament of Blackness: Postcolonial Ghana and the Politics of Race* (Chicago: University of Chicago Press, 2013); and Carina E. Ray, *Crossing the Color Line: Race, Sex, and the Contested Politics of Colonialism in Ghana* (Athens: Ohio University Press, 2015).

79. Anna L. Tsing, *Friction: An Ethnography of Global Connection* (Princeton, NJ: Princeton University Press, 2005), 12.

80. The bulk of my archival research was conducted in the corporate records belonging to the UAC and the UTC. While I consulted documents housed in the Accra, Cape Coast, and Sunyani depositories of Ghana's Public Records and Archives Administration Department, as well as those available at the National Archives of the United Kingdom, I found that state archives revealed very little about the world of consumption and particularly lacked information regarding the decades following independence. Most government files were limited to specific price control decrees and official commissions of inquiry into customs, import licensing, and trade malpractices.

81. M. C. Powell, "A Study of the Behavior and Personality of Clerks and Other Literate Employees in the Office of a European Firm Trading in Ghana, 1954–58," unpublished manuscript, Mss. Afr. S.1433, RHL.

82. On Lebanese and Syrian business communities in Ghana, see Emmanuel Akyeampong, "Memories of Place and Belonging: Identity, Citizenship, and the Lebanese in Ghana," *Ghana Studies* 7 (2004): 25–42; Emmanuel Akyeampong, "Race, Identity and Citizenship in Black Africa: The Case of the Lebanese in Ghana," *Africa* 76, no. 3 (2006): 297–323; Isaac Xerxes Malki, "Productive Aliens: Economic Planning and the Lebanese in Ghana, c. 1930–1972," *Mashriq and Mahjar* 1, no. 1 (2013): 85–114.

83. This method reflects a broader shift over the past two decades from looking at the "archive as source" to the "archive as subject." See Achille Mbembe, "The Power of the Archive and its Limits," in *Reconfiguring the Archive*, ed. Carolyn Hamilton et al. (Dordrecht: Kluwer Academic, 2002), 19–27; Antoinette Burton, "Introduction: Archive Fever, Archive Stories," in *Archive Stories: Facts, Fiction, and the Writing of History*, ed. Antoinette Burton (Durham, NC: Duke University Press, 2006), 1–24; Ann Laura Stoler, *Along the Archival Grain: Epistemic Anxieties and Colonial Common Sense* (Princeton , NJ: Princeton University Press, 2010).

84. The problems and limitations associated with the use of oral sources have been debated at length by professional historians of Africa since the 1950s and will not be rehashed here. For an excellent summary of these debates, see Luise White, Stephan F. Miescher, and David William Cohen, eds., *African Words, African Voices: Critical Practices in Oral History* (Bloomington: Indiana University Press, 2001).

85. As historian Alusine Jalloh argues, the collection and recording of oral testimony from African businesspeople to understand the global economic past is a matter of great importance and urgency. Alusine Jalloh, "Reconstructing Modern African Busi-

ness History," in *Africanizing Knowledge: African Studies Across Disciplines*, ed. Toyin Falola and Christian Jennings (New Brunswick, NJ: Transaction, 2002): 149–61.

86. David William Cohen, Stephan F. Miescher, and Luise White, "Introduction: Voices, Words, and African History," in *African Words, African Voices: Critical Practices in Oral History*, ed. Luise White, Stephan F. Miescher, and David William Cohen (Bloomington: Indiana University Press, 2001), 19; emphasis in the original.

87. Formal employment included those who received monthly pay, some of whom were also eligible for company benefits.

88. For an exception, see Van den Bersselaar, "'Doorway to Success?'"

CHAPTER 1: A DOOR "WIDE OPEN"

1. E. D. Morel, "Africa to the Fore," *African Mail*, April 30, 1915, 301. Established in 1901, the *African Mail* was founded as "an independent organ representing the commercial, industrial and political interests of West Africa." Its editor, Edmund D. Morel, is best known for establishing the Congo Reform Association and becoming one of King Leopold II's harshest critics. Less is known about his commercial career. In 1890 Morel began working as a clerk for Elder Dempster and Company, a large shipping firm that managed a substantial part of West Africa's import-export trade. Politically he was also part of a small group that self-identified as the Third Party, along with wealthy businessman John Holt and the infamous travel writer/ethnographer Mary Kingsley. Early on, the group, also known as the Liverpool Sect, advocated for the development of a "true colonial conscience in Britain" primarily through the increased study of West Africa and its "traditions" and encouraged development through "free trade." The *African Mail* was thus a Third Party mouthpiece, combining business interests with ethnographic inquiry. The journal was previously known as the *West African Mail* (1903–6), and before that *West Africa* (1901–2). While readership comprised mostly US, British, and European audiences, excerpts from the publication were included in West African newspapers geared toward African elites. See Kenneth Dike Nworah, "The Liverpool 'Sect' and British West African Policy," *African Affairs* 70, no. 281 (1971): 349–64; Anandi Ramamurthy, *Imperial Persuaders: Images of Africa and Asia in British Advertising* (Manchester, England: Manchester University Press 2003), 63–76; and Stephanie Newell, "An Introduction to the Writings of J. G. Mullen, An African Clerk, in the *Gold Coast Leader*, 1916–19," *Africa* 70, no. 3 (2008): 384–400, esp. 384.

2. Most economic histories of colonial trading companies, including Fieldhouse's, are focused at the institutional level. D. K. Fieldhouse, *Merchant Capital and Economic Decolonization: The United Africa Company 1929–1994* (Oxford: Clarendon, 1994).

3. This chapter draws on research from the UAC and UTC corporate archives, as well as memoirs and oral histories of former employees. While I focus mainly on correspondence and letters from 1910 to 1940, I also analyze official reports and documents from later periods. Major issues and concerns that firms address in hindsight, specifically discussions about "how times have changed," were particularly useful.

4. My analysis here builds on historical conceptualizations of Africa and theories of "otherness" and difference. See V. Y. Mudimbe, *The Invention of Africa* (Bloomington:

Indiana University Press, 1988); and Achille Mbembe, *On the Postcolony* (Berkeley: University of California Press, 2001), 2.

5. Frederick Cooper, "Africa and the World Economy." *African Studies Review* 24, no. 2/3 (1981): 38.

6. A. G. Hopkins, *An Economic History of West Africa* (London: Longman, 1973), 92–94.

7. Carina E. Ray, *Crossing the Color Line: Race, Sex, and the Contested Politics of Colonialism in Ghana* (Athens: Ohio University Press, 2015), 34–39; Margaret Priestley, *West Africa Trade and Coast Society: A Family Study* (London: Oxford University Press, 1969), 106–113.

8. Raymond E. Dumett, "John Sarbah, the Elder, and African Entrepreneurship in the Gold Coast in the Late Nineteenth Century," *Journal of African History* 14, no. 4 (1973): 653–79; John Emanuel Ocansey, *African Trading, or, The Trials of William Narh Ocansey of Addah, West Coast of Africa, River Volta*, 3rd ed. (Accra: Ghana Academy of Arts and Sciences, 1989).

9. In 1807 it became illegal for British subjects to engage in the slave trade, and in 1833 the institution of slavery was abolished in all of Britain's imperial possessions. In spite of these measures, we know that a number of enslaved Africans crossed the Atlantic Ocean well after those dates. As scholars have debated, the 1860s through 1880s were the more active decades of reduction and suppression.

10. Hopkins, *An Economic History of West Africa*, 148–66; see also A. Adu Boahen, *African Perspectives on Colonialism* (Baltimore: Johns Hopkins University Press, 1987), esp. chap. 2.

11. Hopkins, *An Economic History of West Africa*, 150. The African Steam Ship Company was formed in England in 1851 and began regular service to the West Coast the following year.

12. Ibid., 153.

13. The imposition of colonial caravan tolls in 1898 and a general policing of trade routes also contributed to this shift. Kwame Arhin, *West African Traders in Ghana* in the Nineteenth and Twentieth Centuries (London: Longman, 1979), 70–71.

14. Kwamina B. Dickenson, *A Historical Geography of Ghana* (Cambridge: Cambridge University Press, 1971), 356.

15. Via telegraph, stock and price information could be more easily sent between general managers and district agents. H. Lauren van der Laan, "Modern Inland Transport and the European Trading Firms in Colonial West Africa," *Cahiers d'Études Africaines* 21, no. 84 (1981): 547–75.

16. Elizabeth Wrangham, "An African Road Revolution: The Gold Coast in the Period of the Great War," *Journal of Imperial and Commonwealth History* 32, no. 1 (2004): 1–18. See also Jennifer A. Hart, *Ghana on the Go: African Mobility in the Age of Motor Transportation* (Bloomington: Indiana University Press, 2016).

17. Wrangham, "An African Road Revolution," 9. The UTC claimed that it introduced the first motor vehicle in 1904. See "The Story of the Basel Trading Company, 1859–1935," supplement, *West African Review*, November 1935.

18. Letter from the Chief of Beyin requesting that a UTC store be opened in his district, May 31, 1926, UTC 4442: Sekondi Correspondence, BMA.

19. Timothy Burke, *Lifebuoy Men, Lux Women: Commodification, Consumption, and Cleanliness in Modern Zimbabwe* (Durham, NC: Duke University Press, 1996), 84.

20. Richard Rathbone, "World War I and Africa: Introduction," *Journal of African History* 19, no. 1 (1978): 3.

21. Daniel Mark Stephen, "'The White Man's Grave:' British West Africa and the British Exhibition of 1924–1925," *Journal of British Studies*, 48, no. 1 (2009): 102–128, E. D. Morel, "The Coming Trade Boom," *African Mail*, November 13, 1914, 61.

22. Ramamurthy, *Imperial Persuaders*; Stephan Constantine, "'Bringing the Empire Alive' The Empire Marketing Board and Imperial Propaganda, 1926–1933," in *Imperialism and Popular Culture*, ed. John M. Mackenzie (Manchester, England: Manchester University Press, 1986), 192–231 Erika Rappaport, Sandra Trudgen Dawson, and Mark J. Crowley, eds., *Consuming Behaviours: Identity, Politics, and Pleasure in Twentieth-Century Britain* (London: Bloomsbury, 2015).

23. B. R. Tomlinson, "The British Economy and the Empire, 1900–1939," in *A Companion to Early Twentieth Century Britain*, ed. Chris Wrigley (Oxford: Blackwell, 2003), 198–211; Frank Trentmann, *Free Trade Nation: Commerce, Consumption, and Civil Society in Modern Britain* (Oxford: Oxford University Press, 2009).

24. Kofi Takyi Asante, "Collusion, Collaboration (Cooperation) and Conflict: How African Merchants Shaped the Formation of the Colonial State in the Gold Coast, 1850–1950,"Paper presented at the *3rd Annual Symposium of Graduate Students in African Studies*, Bloomington, Indiana University, March 2013; Kofi Takyi Asante, "Purchased Allies or 'Thorns in the Side of the Government'? African Merchants and Colonial State Formation in the Nineteenth Century Gold Coast," PhD diss., Northwestern University, 2016.

25. Lebanon formed part of the Ottoman Empire until 1918, when the empire was dismembered following the defeat of Austria, Germany, and Turkey in the First World War. Andrew Arson, *Interlopers of Empire: The Lebanese Diaspora in Colonial French West Africa* (Oxford: Oxford University Press, 2014).

26. Emmanuel K. Akyeampong, "Race, Identity, and Citizenship in Black Africa: The Case of the Lebanese in Ghana," *Africa* 76, no. 3 (2006): 297–323.

27. For an excellent overview of the CFAO, see Catherine Coquery-Vidrovitch, "L'Impact des Interests Coloniaux: S. C. O. A. et C. F. A. O. dans l'Ouest Africain, 1910–1965," *Journal of African History* 16, no. 4 (1975): 595–621.

28. Timothy Burke, "Fork Up a Smile: Marketing, Colonial Knowledge and the Female Subject in Zimbabwe," *Gender and History* 8, no. 3 (1996): 440–56.

29. "Report of Mr. D. D. Pitcher's Visit to the Gold Coast, January 1 to April 4, 1929," Visit Reports, box 32, UAC/20/5/1/1, UARM, p. 1.

30. GBO began as a Manchester-based concern established in 1858. In 1934, it became financially associated with the UAC, but it continued to compete with the actual UAC until the 1960s; there was, in other words, "regulated" internal competition. The SAT entered the Gold Coast in 1922, specifically as a cocoa-buying firm with headquarters in Kumasi, and the UAC bought out the SAT in 1936. See Rhoda Howard, *Colonialism and Underdevelopment in Ghana* (New York: Africana, 1978), 100–101.

31. Although the UAC's main buying organizations were in London and Manchester, by the 1950s it operated buying departments in Bombay, Brussels, Hamburg, Milan, New York, and Osaka. Buyers specialized in particular types of manufactured goods, and were divided into sections: provisions (including drinks and tobacco), drugs and perfumery, and hardware and haberdashery. A separate department dealt with technical goods, which were mainly supplied through the specialized companies and the motor division. In Manchester the textile buying department bought textiles and dealt

with textile printing and processing. Orders for the Gold Coast were initiated either by the buying departments in the United Kingdom or by sales managers at the main office in Accra.

32. Juliet Oppong-Boateng, "Economic Enterprises of the Basel Mission Society in the Gold Coast: A Study of the Basel Mission Trading Company from 1959 to 1917," MPhil thesis, Institute of African Studies, University of Ghana, 2014.

33. Similarly, the British government confiscated the assets of the BMS and deported its missionaries. At the time, the BMS had been transformed into an organized church consisting of about 196 congregations. Margaret Gannon, "The Basle Mission Trading Company and British Colonial Policy in the Gold Coast, 1918–1928," *Journal of African History* 24, no. 4 (1983): 503–15; Peter Schweizer, *Survivors on the Gold Coast: The Basel Missionaries in Colonial Ghana*, 2nd ed. (Accra: Smartline, 2000).

34. See Burke, *Lifebuoy Men, Lux Women*; and Jean Comaroff and John Comaroff, *Of Revelation and Revolution: Christianity, Colonialism and Consciousness in South Africa*, vol. 1 (Chicago: University of Chicago Press, 1991).

35. Here I draw on sources from a number of firms, including the UAC, the UTC, GBO, and John Holt, as well as Allister Macmillan, *The Red Book of West Africa: Historical and Descriptive, Commercial and Industrial Facts, Figures and Resources* (London: Cass, 1969).

36. As road construction continued, the company subsequently opened district branches farther north. By 1951 the UAC upgraded Akim Oda, Dunkwa, and Swedru to full districts. "Report of Mr. D. D. Pitcher's Visit, Gold Coast Business," December 1936, Visit Reports, UAC/2/20/5/1/2, UARM, p. 7.

37. United Africa Company, "Merchandise Trading in British West Africa," *Statistical and Economic Review* 6 (1950): 11–17.

38. An important exception was the SAT, which operated out of Kumasi.

39. Stephanie Decker, "Postcolonial Transitions in Africa: Decolonization in West Africa and Present Day South Africa," *Journal of Management Studies* 47. No. 5 (2010): 791–813, see 798 .

40. UTC's Nsawam agent reported better sales at competitors' stores that displayed items behind glass. G. Hoffman, Nsawam agent to head office, Basel, July 20, 1934, UTC 4485: Dunkwa, Abangoase, Tamale u.a. Correspondence, BMA.

41. Basel Trading Company Ltd., Akuse to Basler Handels-Gesellschaft A.G. board of directors, Basel, September 1, 1933, UTC 4480: Akuse Correspondence, BMA.

42. Margaret Priestley, *West Africa Trade and Coast Society*, 5.

43. Circular no. 54, February 19, 1931, UTC 4480: Akuse Correspondence, BMA.

44. London office to general West African branches and district managers, "European Staff in West Africa," October 12, 1947, UAC/1/2/3/7/9, UARM.

45. Burke, *Lifebuoy Men, Lux Women*, 84.

46. Macmillan, *The Red Book of West Africa*, 172.

47. A similar argument has been made with regard to missionaries in South Africa. See Comaroff and Comaroff, *Of Revelation and Revolution*, 43–48.

48. Fieldhouse, *Merchant Capital and Economic Decolonization*, 124.

49. Ibid.

50. G. Hoffman, Nsawam agent to head office, Basel, July 20, 1934; Nkoko agent to head office, March 3, 1934, UTC 4435: Nkoko Correspondence, BMA.

51. *Circular Letter Ref. Merchandise No. 483: Merchandise Sales*, October 27, 1954, UAC file 32, UARM, p. 17.

52. E. D. Morel, "The Coming Trade Boom," *African Mail*, November 13, 1914, 61.

53. General business report on Saltpond, April 12, 1923, UTC 4436: Saltpond Correspondence, BMA.

54. Frederick Pedler, *The Lion and the Unicorn in Africa: United Africa Company, 1787–1931* (London: Heinemann, 1974), 203.

55. "The Story of the Basel Trading Company," 3.

56. "Histories of the UTC, ca. 1958," UTC 4452, BMA. P. D. Curtin, "'The White Man's Grave': Image and Reality, 1780–1850," *Journal of British Studies* 1, no. 1 (1961): 94–110.

57. The "white man's grave" was originally applied by the British to Sierra Leone and was extended over all of West Africa during the nineteenth century. As Purnima Bose argues, these narratives of death and disease worked to disavow, in part, the violence of colonialism by transferring it onto the colonial subjects and creating a native pathology that essentialized subjects as inherently prone to irrational violence. *Organizing Empire: Individualism, Collective Agency, and India* (Durham, NC: Duke University Press, 2003), esp. chap. 4.

58. The extent to which these claims were exaggerated is unclear. Many times descriptions of exhaustion and sickness accompanied desperate requests for leave and pleas to return home. As H. D. Wentworth acknowledged, "constant change in overseas personnel . . . will always be a feature of West African trade as long as the climate is bad and hazardous." H. D. Wentworth (OBL) to M. Preiswerk, London, April 30, 1945, Overseas Buyers Ltd. Dr. M.P., New York, Dossier 6, 1940–45, UTC 4190, BMA; review of staff letters and responses, Dr. M.P., New York, Dossier 2, 1940–45, UTC 4194, BMA.

59. Instruction of the Mission Trade Company in Basel for the factory's agents on the Gold Coast, May 26, 1909, file 7, Sources of the Basel Mission Trading Company, Q-6, BMA.

60. "Report of Mr. D. D. Pitcher's Visit, Gold Coast Business," p. 14.

61. Akuse agent to head office, August 17, 1932, UTC 4480: Akuse Correspondence, BMA.

62. Board of directors to Sekondi agent regarding report by acting general manager W. H. Rawtron, June 27, 1939, G. B. Ollivant Division, file 39, UAC/2/10/1/12, UARM.

63. For historical literature on colonial medicine, pathologizing Africans, and the construction of empire, see Megan Vaughan, *Curing Their Ills: Colonial Power and African Illness* (Stanford, CA: Stanford University Press, 1991); Jock McCulloch, *Colonial Psychiatry and "The African Mind"* (Cambridge: Cambridge University Press, 1995); and Matthew Heaton, *Black Skin, White Coats: Nigerian Psychiatrists, Decolonization, and the Globalization of Psychiatry* (Athens: Ohio University Press, 2013).

64. *Instructions for European Shopkeepers*, March 1939, UTC 4198, BMA. The cover reads, "Instructions for European storekeepers: this instruction is for European employees that run retail sales at the Gold Coast or in Nigeria. The content of this booklet is strictly confidential in the presence of a third party."

65. Arthur Wettstein, "Union Trading Company in Ghana, Some Reminiscences of a Former Employee," unpublished manuscript, sent via e-mail to the author, July 10, 2010.

66. For an excellent analysis on the threat of interracial couples to colonial race relations, see Carina Ray, *Crossing the Color Line: Race, Sex, and the Contested Politics of Colonialism in Ghana* (Athens: Ohio University Press, 2015).

67. In 1957, when he married Mercy Adwoa Kwadua Kwafo, Roth recounted, "I was was probably the first expatriate within the UAC Group of Companies in the Gold Coast who was going to marry a local girl and keep his job." Hans Rudolf Roth, *Because of Kwadua: Autobiography of Hans Rudolf Roth* (Accra: Afram, 2008), 124. Also see Hans Buser, *In Ghana at Independence: Stories of a Swiss Salesman* (Basel: Basler Afrika Bibliographien, 2010), 33, for examples of how firms enforced these rules through bribing watchman and stewards and examining staff's laundry.

68. Wettstein, "Union Trading Company in Ghana."

69. UTC board of directors to Nkoko agent, April 15, 1933, UTC 4435: Nkoko Correspondence, BMA.

70. *Instructions for European Storekeepers.*

71. Agents' circular no. 18, December 12, 1931, UTC 4410: West Africa, General Agent, 1931–35, BMA. As distinct from independence from colonial rule, the meaning here is self-sufficiency.

72. Stephan F. Miescher, *Making Men in Ghana* (Bloomington: Indiana University Press, 2005), 5.

73. Saltpond agent to board of directors, October 21, 1927, UTC 4437: Saltpond Correspondence, BMA; Tamale agent to head office, May 24, 1934, UTC 4485: Dunkwa, Abangoase, Tamale u.a. Correspondence, BMA; board of directors to Korforidua agent, April 20, 1954, UTC 4494, BMA.

74. For a general picture of Kwawu trading history, see Peter C. Garlick, "The Development of Kwawu Business Enterprise in Ghana Since 1874—An Essay in Recent Oral Tradition," *Journal of African History* 8, no. 3 (1967): 463–80.

75. Saltpond agent to Basel, general report, December 5, 1924, UTC 4436: Saltpond Correspondence, BMA.

76. Saltpond agent to Basel, general report, October 21, 1927, UTC 4437: Saltpond Correspondence, BMA. Earlier reports by the Basel Mission Trading Company characterized coastal Africans as "vain and self-important"; Confidential Notification on Trade and Industry of the Basel Mission (small booklet), 1884, Sources of the Basel Mission Trading Company, file 5, Q-6, BMA.

77. Kumasi agent to Basel, June 11, 1913, UTC 4412: West Africa, General Agent, BMA.

78. Saltpond agent to Basel, December 5, 1924.

79. A. R. I. Mellor (London) to West African general managers, August 6, 1937, UAC/1/10/3/3/4, UARM.

80. A. R. I. Mellor to West African general managers, July 22, 1943, UAC/1/10/3/3/7, UARM.

81. "Report of Mr. D. D. Pitcher's Visit, Gold Coast Business," p. 1-4.

82. Nkawkaw agent to Mr. Binhammer, Korforidua, July 27, 1928, UTC 4449: Korforidua Correspondence, BMA.

83. Ann Laura Stoler, *Carnal Knowledge and Imperial Power: Race and the Intimate in Colonial Rule.* (Berkeley: University of California Press, 2002).

84. Nkawkaw agent to Mr. Binhammer, Korforidua, July 27, 1928; G. Hoffman, Nsawam agent to head office, Basel, July 20, 1934.

85. UTC headquarters to Nkawkaw agent, January 23, 1932, UTC 4435, BMA.

86. Ibid.

87. W. E. Conway, *Report of the Commission of Enquiry into the Distribution and Prices of Essential Imported Goods* (Accra: Government Printing Department, 1943), 2.

88. Hans Boehi, Kumasi to Mr. Wintz, Accra general agent, re: African buyers, January 27, 1930, UTC 4409: Agent Conference, BMA.

89. Nkawkaw agent to Mr. Wintz, Accra general agent, re: passbooks, ca. 1930, UTC 4409: Agent Conference, BMA; emphasis in the original.

90. Hans Boehi, Kumasi to Mr. Wintz, Accra general agent, January 27, 1930.

91. "Report of Mr. D. D. Pitcher's Visit to the Gold Coast," p. 27.

92. Akuse agent to head office, July 7, 1932, UTC 4480: Akuse Correspondence, BMA.

93. Akuse agent to board of directors, Basel, April 12, 1934, UTC 4481: Akuse Correspondence, BMA; Hohoe agent to board of directors, Basel, August 26, 1936, UTC 4479: Hohoe Correspondence, BMA.

94. Akuse agent to head office, August 17, 1932, UTC 4480: Akuse Correspondence, BMA.

95. Christian Spoerri, "Forty Years of Service for the BHG," 1961, UTC 4968, BMA.

96. A. Custer to head office, October 24, 1940, UTC 4163, BMA.

97. Board of directors to Hohoe agent, September 16, 1938, UTC 4479: Hohoe Correspondence, BMA.

98. This absence changed as my research moved closer to the 1940s and 1950s, when Africans began to fill managerial positions.

99. UTC headquarters to Cape Coast agent, UTC 4483, BMA.

100. Correspondence between UTC board of directors and Nkawkaw agent, December 8, 1933, January 2, 1934, January 31, 1934, and March 3, 1934, UTC 4435: Nkoko Correspondence, BMA.

101. William Atta Krofah, interview with the author, Accra, March 26, 2007.

102. Achille Mbembe, *On the Postcolony* (Berkeley: University of California Press, 2001), 107.

103. Kwesi Akumenya Cato, interview with the author, Accra, September 13, 2007.

104. Purnima Bose and Laura E. Lyons propose the theory of "corporation fetishism" to describe the way present-day corporations have the power to transform, enhance, or devastate communities through decisions and policies. See Purnima Bose and Laura E. Lyons, *Cultural Critique and the Global Corporation* (Bloomington: Indiana University Press, 2010).

105. Jutus Nii Kpakpo Allotey, interview with the author, Accra, June 8, 2007.

106. Sadiku Musah, interview with the author, Accra, April 7, 2007; William Atta Krofah, interview with the author, Accra, July 9, 2007.

107. Krofah interview, July 9, 2007.

108. Important works include John Comaroff and Jean Comaroff, eds., *Modernity and Its Malcontents: Ritual and Power in Postcolonial Africa* (Chicago: University of Chicago Press, 1993); Peter Geschiere, *The Modernity of Witchcraft: Politics and the Occult in Postcolonial Africa* (Charlottesville: University of Virginia Press, 1997); and Henrietta L. Moore and Todd Sanders, eds., *Magical Interpretations: Material Realities: Modernity, Witchcraft and the Occult in Postcolonial Africa* (London: Routledge, 2001).

109. See Bianca Murillo, "'The Devil We Know': Gold Coast Consumers, Local Employees, and the United Africa Company, 1940–60," *Enterprise and Society* 12, no. 2 (2011): 317–55.

110. Edward Akurang Dankwa, interview with the author, Accra, March 5, 2007.

111. *Adufudee pa* was also applied to the UAC's practice of undercutting other firms in price.

112. Basel Trading Company Ltd., Akuse to Basler Handels-Gesellschaft A.G. board of directors, Basel, July 7, 1932, UTC4480, BMA.

113. For an excellent discussion on rumor and gossip as history, see Luise White, *Speaking with Vampires: Rumor and History in Colonial Africa* (Berkeley: University of California Press, 2000).

114. Emmanuel Akyeampong, "Sexuality and Prostitution among the Akan of the Gold Coast c. 1650–1950," *Past and Present* 156 (1997): 144–73, esp. 162.

115. Frances Sam, "Why I Prefer British Goods," in "Credit Customer's Legacy," *Unicorn* 2, no. 10 (1956): 10–11.

116. Karl Marx, *Capital: A Critique of Political Economy*, vol. 1, trans. B. Fowkes (Harmondsworth: Penguin, 1977), esp. chap. 1.

117. In Ghana, spiritual powers and the use of juju have historically been linked to success in both business and politics. Peter C. Garlick, *The Ghanaian Entrepreneur: Studies in Trading in Ghana* (Accra: University of Ghana, 1962), 195–57.

118. Nana Opare Ameyaw, interview with the author, Kyeraa, July 20, 2007.

119. Ibid.; Nana Oworae, interview with the author, Kyeraa, July 20, 2007.

120. Burke, *Lifebuoy Men, Lux Women*, 6–8

121. *Pep Talk for New Arrivals*, Mss. Afr. S.1814, F.P.49/40c, RHL.

122. Sarah Stockwell, *The Business of Decolonization: British Business Strategies in the Gold Coast* (Oxford: Clarendon, 2000); Decker, "Building up Goodwill."

123. Works focused specifically on Ghana include: Stockwell, *The Business of Decolonization*; Decker, "Building up Goodwill"; Fieldhouse, *Merchant Capital and Economic Decolonization*.

CHAPTER 2: "WE CANNOT AFFORD TO BE FOOLED"

1. J. Lenggenhager to head office, Basel, October 3, 1941, UTC 4484: Cape Coast Correspondence, BMA.

2. Benjamin N. Lawrance, Emily Lynn Osborn, and Richard L. Roberts, "Introduction: African Intermediaries and the 'Bargain' of Collaboration," in *Intermediaries, Interpreters, and Clerks: African Employees in the Making of Colonial Africa*, ed. Benjamin N. Lawrance, Emily Lynn Osborn, and Richard L. Roberts (Madison: University of Wisconsin Press, 2006), 4.

3. Ibid., 29.

4. Moses Ochonu, *Colonialism by Proxy: Hausa Imperial Agents and Middle Belt Consciousness in Nigeria* (Bloomington: Indiana University Press, 2014), 13, calls this group "African subcolonials."

5. Additionally, scholars have studied the mediating roles of Africans as police, soldiers, and workers in the railway and mining industries. See Michelle Moyd, *Violent Intermediaries: Soldiers, Conquest, and Everyday Colonialism in German East Africa* (Athens: Ohio University Press, 2014); Carolyn A. Brown, "A 'Man' in the Village Is a 'Boy' in the Workplace: Colonial Racism, Worker Militance, and Igbo Notions of Masculinity in the Nigerian Coal Industry, 1930–1945," in *Men and Masculinities in Modern Africa*, ed. Lisa A. Lindsay and Stephan F. Miescher (Portsmouth, NH: Heinemann, 2003), 156–74; Patrick Harries, *Work, Culture, and Identity: Migrant Laborers in Mozambique and South Africa, c. 1860–1910* (Portsmouth, NH: Heinemann, 1994); Dunbar Moodie and Vivienne Ndatshe, *Going for Gold: Men, Mines, and Migration*

(Berkeley: University of California Press, 1994); and Jane L. Parpart, "The Household and the Mine Shift: Gender and Class Struggles on the Zambian Copperbelt, 1926–64," *Journal of Southern African Studies* 13 (1986): 36–56.

6. Dike sets up this continuum in his description of commercial middlemen in nineteenth-century Nigeria, but his argument can be extended to the twentieth century. See Kenneth Onwuka Dike, *Trade and Politics in the Niger Delta, 1830–1885: An Introduction to the Economic and Political History of Nigeria* (Oxford: Clarendon, 1956).

7. Lawrance, Osborn, and Roberts, "Introduction," 10–15.

8. Frederick Cooper, *Decolonization and African Society: The Labor Question in French and British Africa* (Cambridge: Cambridge University Press, 1996); Andreas Eckert, "Cultural Commuters: African Employees in Late Colonial Period Tanzania," in *Intermediaries, Interpreters, and Clerks: African Employees and the Making of Colonial Africa*, ed. Benjamin N. Lawrance, Emily Lynn Osborn, and Richard L. Roberts (Madison: University of Wisconsin Press, 2006), 248–69; Lisa A. Lindsay, *Working with Gender: Wage Labor and Social Change in Southwestern Nigeria* (Portsmouth, NH: Heinemann, 2003).

9. Stephan F. Miescher, *Making Men in Ghana* (Bloomington: Indiana University Press, 2005).

10. Brown, "A 'Man' in the Village," 157.

11. Jean Allman, Susan Geiger, and Nakanyike Musisi, eds., *Women in African Colonial Histories* (Bloomington: Indiana University Press, 2002), 1–15.

12. This literature mostly focuses on women in medicine. LaRay Denzer, *Women in Government Service in Colonial Nigeria, 1862–1945*, Working Papers in African Studies 136 (Boston: Boston University African Studies Center, 1989), argues that in both the French and British colonies, medicine was one of the first fields in which women had the opportunity for postprimary education. For important examples, see Nancy Rose Hunt, *A Colonial Lexicon of Birth Ritual, Medicalization, and Mobility in the Congo* (Durham, NC: Duke University Press, 1999); Shula Marks, *Divided Sisterhood: Race, Class, and Gender in the South African Nursing Profession* (New York: St. Martin's, 1994); Jane Turrittin, "Colonial Midwives and Modernizing Childbirth in French West Africa," in *Women in African Colonial Histories*, ed. Jean Allman, Susan Geiger, and Nakanyike Musisi (Bloomington: Indiana University Press, 2002), 71–91; and Anne Hugon, "Korle Bu and the Midwives Hostel as a Site of Memory for Ghanaian Pupil Midwives, 1930s–1950s," *Ghana Studies* 7 (2004): 43–58.

13. Claire Robertson, *Sharing the Same Bowl: A Socioeconomic History of Women and Class in Accra* (Bloomington: Indiana University Press, 1984), 15–16.

14. An exception was Gladys Edna Moore, a retail storekeeper celebrated as the first Gold Coast "lady employee" of the UAC, who was hired around 1934. Moore was the daughter of Nana Amonoo V, Omanhene of Anomabu, and the wife of G. N. Moore, a UAC produce manager in Agona Swedru, and she was educated at the elite Wesley Girls High School in Cape Coast. Swedru Correspondent, "Lady Storekeeper's Service Recognized," *Gold Coast UAC News* 3, no. 12 (1952): 1.

15. "Storekeeper's Agreements," 1927–1956, Sales and Marketing Records, UAC 2/20/6/2, UARM; George Darkwa Kwakye, interview with the author, Suhum, April 20, 2007; Edward Akurang Dankwa, interview with the author, Accra, November 8, 2007; Jutus Nii Kpakpo Allotey, interview with the author, Accra, June 13, 2007.

16. Edward Akurang Dankwa, the son of a UAC storekeeper, received a UAC scholarship in 1954 to attend Mfantsipim, one of the first secondary institutions located in Cape Coast; his younger brother also received one. Edward Akurang Dankwa, interview with the author, Accra, March 5, 2007; Dankwa interview, November 8, 2007. Also see, "Company Awards Scholarships for 1953," *UAC News* 4, no. 2 (1953).

17. This observation was in response to UAC directors in London who proposed closing their African-run retail stores and operating business solely from central or wholesale depots. Storekeepers were to be converted to credit customers, and all credit customers were to be supplied directly from wholesales stores. This policy would not occur until after World War II, as many prewar district managers vehemently opposed it. "Report of Mr. D. D. Pitcher's Visit, Gold Coast Business," December 1936, Visit Reports, UAC/2/20/5/1/2, UARM, p. 10.

18. Gareth Austin, *Labour, Land, and Capital in Ghana: From Slavery to Free Labour in Asante, 1807–1956* (Rochester, NY: University of Rochester Press, 2005); Gwendolyn Mikell, *Cocoa and Chaos in Ghana* (New York: Paragon House, 1989). See also Jan-Georg Deutsch, *Educating the Middlemen: A Political and Economic History of Statutory Cocoa Marketing in Nigeria, 1936–1946* (Berlin: Das Arabische Buch, 1995).

19. One UAC storekeeper in Suhum mentioned traveling often to a friend's store in Kumasi to check stocks; this was a way to confirm if his Suhum store had received fair allocations and to measure whether or not managers in his district were "acting corrupt." He described himself as an "energetic" storekeeper. George Darkwa Kwakye, interview with the author, Suhum, June 7, 2007.

20. E. K. Addo diaries (1932–34), July 1, 1932; July 6, 1932; and July 19, 1932; I am grateful to Stephan Miescher for providing me access to the diaries, which serve as a written record of Addo's work as a storekeeper in Nsawam. Addo's life history (1904–1998) is featured in Miescher, *Making Men in Ghana*.

21. G. Hoffman, Nsawam agent to head office, Basel, July 20, 1934, UTC 4485: Dunkwa, Abangoase, Tamale u.a. Correspondence, BMA; *Merchandise Clients from Up-Country Buying at Ports*, September 30, 1953, G. B. Ollivant Division: Circulars, file 32 (10), UAC/2/10/3/4, UARM.

22. E. K. Addo diaries (1932–34), August 19, 1932; March 10, 1933; March 11, 1933. Until the 1950s, before import restrictions, African storekeepers regularly used the medium of parcel post to order specialty items that firms did not offer. Gold Coast Government, *The Gold Coast Handbook* (London: Baylis, 1937), 77.

23. "Report of Enquiry into the Company's Distributive Organization and Proposals for the Future Distribution of General Goods Merchandise in Ghana," 1961–1962, UAC of Ghana: Sales and Marketing Records, UAC/2/20/6/4, UARM, p. 5.

24. Kwakye interview, June 7, 2007; S. G. Oduroh, interview with the author, July 19, 2007.

25. Dankwa interview, November 8, 2007.

26. Contract between the UAC and Benjamin Heywood Okine, April 5, 1933, UAC/2/20/6/2, UARM.

27. Dankwa interview, November 8, 2007.

28. Peter C. Garlick, *The Ghanaian Entrepreneur: Studies in Trading in Ghana* (Accra: Legon, 1962), 110–11.

29. Ibid., 109.

30. Ibid., 110–11.

31. S. G. Oduroh, interview with the author, Sunyani, October 11, 2007.

32. *Instructions for European Storekeepers (Private and Confidential)*, 1939, UTC 4198, BMA.

33. Jane Guyer, "Wealth in People, Wealth in Things—Introduction," *Journal of African History* 36, no. 1 (1995): 83–90.

34. African Staff Report Form: Igoe and corresponding letters, September 30, 1935, Ghana (Accra) Manager's Private Files, box 80, UAC/6, UAC/2/20/3/2, UARM. See also "I. A. Ogoe Presented with Silver Tray: Impressive Ceremony at Sekondi," *Gold Coast UAC News* 2, no. 7 (1951): 1.

35. By 1919 the Gold Coast possessed a completed railway from Sekondi (on the coast) to Kumasi. Dunkwa was a middle point on this line.

36. P. H. Fitz-Gerald to Gold Coast agents, December 9, 1954, UAC of Ghana Ltd. General Manager's Circulars, file 48, UAC/2/20/3/3, UARM.

37. In later years this was not the case. Garlick, *The Ghanaian Entrepreneur*, 110, illustrates that some independent traders preferred to open stores far away from hometowns and relatives. When asked, "Why don't you open a store in your home town?" one of Garlick's bigger storekeepers answered that "there is no one—no relative who is sufficiently reliable to be left in charge, and the family would chop [devour] it [the store's goods and the profits]."

38. African Staff Report Form: Igoe, September 30, 1935, Ghana (Accra) Manager's Private Files, box 80 UAC/6, UAC/2/20/3/2, UARM.

39. African Staff Report Form: Igoe, March 31, 1936, Ghana (Accra) Manager's Private Files, box 80 UAC/6, UAC/2/20/3/2, UARM.

40. African Staff Report Form: Igoe, March 31, 1938, Ghana (Accra) Manager's Private Files, box 80 UAC/6, UAC/2/20/3/2, UARM.

41. Storekeepers and agents provided general managers and company directors with price lists and other information on competing firms. Nkawkaw agent to board of directors, Basel, October 12, 1931, and April 15, 1933, UTC 4435: Nkoko Correspondence, BMA.

42. I. A. Ogoe to general manager, Accra, December 9, 1938, Ghana (Accra) Manager's Private Files, box 80 UAC/6, UAC/2/20/3/2, UARM.

43. I. A. Ogoe to district manager, Sekondi, February 24, 1949, Ghana (Accra) Manager's Private Files, box 80 UAC/6, UAC/2/20/3/2, UARM.

44. Miescher, *Making Men in Ghana*, 178.

45. General manager's remarks, African Staff Report Form: Igoe, March 31, 1944, Ghana (Accra) Manager's Private Files, box 80 UAC/6, UAC/2/20/3/2, UARM. Although Ogoe's documented age in 1944 was fifty-four, he may have been much older. Ex-managers who were interviewed claimed that others lied about their age to delay compulsory retirement policies.

46. Hockley, district manager, Sekondi, to general manager, Accra, ca. 1945, Ghana (Accra) Manager's Private Files, box 80 UAC/6, UAC/2/20/3/2, UARM.

47. Ibid. Ogoe's relatives remembered him in a similar way. He was an active member of Sekondi's Freemasons and held meetings in his attic. Edwin Obiri, personal correspondence with the author, July 3, 2016.

48. African Staff Report Form: Igoe, September 1948, Ghana (Accra) Manager's Private Files, box 80 UAC/6, UAC/2/20/3/2, UARM.

49. Ibid.

50. "I. A. Ogoe Presented with Silver Tray," 1.

51. P. H. Fitz-Gerald, general manager, Accra, to the UAC Gold Coast Department, London, March 2, 1951, Ghana (Accra) Manager's Private Files, box 80 UAC/6, UAC/2/20/3/2, UARM.

52. P. H. Fitz-Gerald, general manager, to district manager, Sekondi, ca. 1951, UAC/2/20/3/2, UARM.

53. Sarah Stockwell, *The Business of Decolonization: British Business Strategies in the Gold Coast* (Oxford: Clarendon, 2000), 140–46; Dmitri van den Bersselaar, "'Doorway to Success?': Reconstructing African Careers in European Business from Company House Magazines and Oral History Interviews," *History in Africa* 38 (2011): 257–94.

54. United Africa Company, "African Managers in the Gold Coast," *Statistical and Economic Review* 3 (1948): table 2.

55. A 1953 survey reported that the UAC employed 160 African managers in its merchandise departments throughout British West Africa; European managers numbered 521. Africans, however, were relegated to lower managerial staff positions only. *Africanisation of the UAC Groups' Managerial Staff in British West Africa*, October 23, 1953, UAC of Ghana Ltd. General Manager's Circulars, UAC/2/20/3/3, UARM.

56. Frederick Pedler, *The Lion and the Unicorn in Africa: United Africa Company, 1787–1931* (London: Heinemann, 1974), 107.

57. Credit customers could also receive commissions on certain types of items like textiles, haberdashery, and hardware. Commission was calculated monthly and added to a credit customer's deposit so that it formed the basis for further purchases. See Gloria Addae, "The Retailing of Imported Textiles in the Accra Market," in *Proceedings of the West African Institute of Social and Economic Research Conference, March 1954* (Ibadan, Nigeria: Ibadan University Press, 1956), 51–56.

58. Credit customer security form belonging to Rosina Ocansey, trinket record book, UAC of Ghana Ltd. Financial Records, UAC/2/20/2/10, UARM.

59. UAC Credit Customer Passbooks belonging to Helena Quansah, Mrs. Annah Manful, and Madam Amba Otwiwa, Financial Records, UAC/2/20/2/11, UARM.

60. Scholars have, however, questioned to what extent passbook trading was really a credit system, since credit customers were only able to take goods in the amount of their original deposit. See Addae, "The Retailing of Imported Textiles in the Accra Market"; and Gareth Austin, "Indigenous Credit Institutions in West Africa, c. 1750–c. 1960," in *Local Suppliers of Credit in the Third World, 1750–1960*, ed. Gareth Austin and Kaoru Sugihara (Basingstoke, England: Palgrave Macmillan, 1993), 132.

61. Paula Jones, "The U.A.C. in the Gold Coast/Ghana, 1920–1965," PhD diss., School of Oriental and African Studies, University of London, 1983, 65–71; P. T. Bauer, *A Study of Competition, Oligopoly and Monopoly in a Changing Economy* (Cambridge: Cambridge University Press, 1954), 61–62; Austin, "Indigenous Credit Institutions," 132.

62. Robertson, *Sharing the Same Bowl*; Beverly Grier, "Pawns, Porters, and Petty Traders: Women in the Transition to Cash Crop Agriculture," *Signs* 17, no. 2 (1992): 304–28; Gracia Clark, *Onions Are My Husband: Survival and Accumulation by West African Market Women* (Chicago: University of Chicago Press, 1994).

63. "Youngest Credit Customer," *Gold Coast UAC News* 4, no. 1 (1952): 3.

64. A. C. C. Baxter, "The Evolution of Merchandising in Africa," talk at City of London College, February 9, 1960, UAC Corporate Planning Department: Reports, UAC/1/9/1/6/2, UARM.

65. Addae, "The Retailing of Imported Textiles"; Ione Acquah, *Accra Survey: A Social Survey of the Capital of Ghana, Formerly Called the Gold Coast, Undertaken for the West African Institute of Social and Economic Research*, 1953–1956 (London: University of London Press, 1958), 68–71; Mansa Apeadu, "She Is an Important Factor in our Distributive Trade," *Ghana Trade Journal*, February 1961, 14–15.

66. Agatha Blewor Borti Tamakloe, "Keta Credit Customer Tells Her Own Story," *Gold Coast UAC News* 4, no. 4 (1953): 3.

67. "Kumasi Tobacco Queen: Mary Baiden—Thirty Years a Credit Customer," *Gold Coast UAC News* 3, no. 10 (1952): 3.

68. "Madam Esther Mensah: A Story of Rapid Success," *Gold Coast UAC News* 3, no. 8 (1952): 3.

69. "Obuasi Credit Customer for Coronation," *Gold Coast UAC News* 4, no. 5 (1953): 3. Others did the same; see "Mrs. Agatha Blewor Borti, Keta Credit Customer Tells Her Own Story," *Gold Coast UAC News* 4, no. 4 (1953): 3; and "Korforidua Credit Customer Started Young," *Gold Coast UAC News* 3, no. 6 (1952): 3.

70. Agnes Kwa Kwa, interview with the author, Cape Coast, June 1, 2010.

71. Gloria Ifeoma Chuku, "From Petty Traders to International Merchants: A Historical Account of Three Igbo Women of Nigeria in Trade and Commerce, 1886 to 1970" *African Economic History* 27 (1999): 1–22; Gloria Ifeoma Chuku, "Nzimiro, Mary (1898–1993)," in *Women in World History*, vol. 7, ed. Deborah Klezmer (Waterford, CT: Yorkin, 2000), 916–19. Other West African examples include Felicia I. Ekejiuba, "Omu Okwei, the Merchant Queen of Ossamari: A Biographical Sketch," *Journal of the Historical Society of Nigeria* 3, no. 4 (1967): 633–46; and Catherine Coquery-Vidrovitch, *African Women: A Modern History*, trans. Beth Gillian Raps (Boulder, CO: Westview, 1997).

72. J. F. Enninful, interview with the author, Cape Coast, June 2, 2010.

73. Addae, "The Retailing of Imported Textiles."

74. Isaac Kofi Annan, interview with the author, Cape Coast, June 3, 2010.

75. "Kumasi Tobacco Queen," 3; "Oda Credit Customer Establishes Family Business," *Gold Coast UAC News* 4, no. 3 (1953): 3; J. Etson-Ansah, "Sekondi's Ace Credit Customer," *Gold Coast UAC News* 3, no. 5 (1952): 3; Tamakloe, "Keta Credit Customer."

76. Etson-Ansah, "Sekondi's Ace Credit Customer"; "Oda Credit Customer."

77. "Korforidua Credit Customer Started Young," *Gold Coast UAC News* 3, no. 6 (1952): 3.

78. "Madam Esther Mensah: A Story of Rapid Success," 3.

79. Chuku, "From Petty Traders to International Merchants," 10.

80. Kwesi Akumenya Cato, interview with the author, Accra, September 13, 2007; the background on Mary Idun Cato comes from Pedler, *The Lion and the Unicorn*, 106–7.

81. Robertson, *Sharing the Same Bowl*, 99–101.

82. Addae, "The Retailing of Imported Textiles;" Chuku, "From Petty Traders," 9–10.

83. Beauty Boye, interview with the author, Accra, November 21, 2007.

84. For historical debates on marriage, financial autonomy, and domestic labor in Ghana, see Jean Allman and Victoria Tashjian, *"I Will Not Eat Stone": A Women's History of Colonial Asante* (Portsmouth, NH: Heinemann, 2000).

85. These terms were found in a survey of official company publications housed at UARM. For a specific example, see the *Statistical and Economic Review*, September 1950. See also "Consumer Survey: Replies concerning the *Statistical and Economic*

Review," April 27, 1950, UAC Public Relations Department: *Statistical and Economic Review*, UAC/1/11/19/89, UARM.

86. Kimberly Wallace-Sanders, *Mammy: A Century of Race, Gender, and Southern Memory* (Ann Arbor: University of Michigan Press, 2009); Micki McElya, *Clinging to Mammy: The Faithful Slave in Twentieth-Century America* (Cambridge, MA: Harvard University Press, 2007).

87. Leslie Craigan, "Craigan Takes Up in Nigeria," *BAT News*, 1984, UAC Public Relations Department, UAC/1/11/14/3/9, UARM.

88. Ann Laura Stoler, *Carnal Knowledge and Imperial Power: Race and the Intimate in Colonial Rule* (Berkeley: University of California Press, 2002), 42.

89. *Old Coasters Tales*, vols. 1–2, collected, typed and collated by the UAC Public Relations Department, September 1985, UAC/1/11/14/3/8, UARM.

90. Ochonu, *Colonialism by Proxy*, 11, argues that academic literature has also presented African intermediaries as "rebels or cunning tricksters out to circumvent the colonial process." Here I am interested in the concept of trickery not as a form of African resistance but as an ideology founded on a belief of European commercial superiority.

91. General manager H. Schiess (Accra) to all stations, December 15, 1954, G. B. Ollivant Division: Circulars, UAC/2/10/3/4, UARM.

92. Hans Rudolf Roth, *Because of Kwadua: Autobiography of Hans Rudolf Roth* (Accra: Afram, 2008), 89.

93. Stoler, *Carnal Knowledge and Imperial Power*, 24–25.

94. A. G. Hopkins, *An Economic History of West Africa* (London: Longman, 1973), 267.

95. A. G. Hopkins, "Economic Aspects of Political Movements in Nigeria and the Gold Coast, 1918–1939," *Journal of African History* 7, no. 1 (1966): 133–52; Cooper, *Decolonization and African Society*; Stockwell, *The Business of Decolonization*.

96. Re: Credit Trade, March 25, 1950, UAC of Ghana Ltd. General Manager's Circulars, UAC/2/20/3/3/4, UARM.

97. *African and Syrian Merchandise Trading Accounts*, May 19, 1953, G. B. Ollivant Division: Circulars, file 32 (9), UAC/2/10/3/4, UARM.

98. *General Goods Trade*, February 4, 1953, G. B. Ollivant Division: Circulars, file 32 (7), UAC/2/10/3/4, UARM.

99. *Principle Merchandise Clients*, September 24, 1954, G. B. Ollivant Division: Circulars, file 32 (16), UAC/2/10/3/4, UARM; *Circular Letter Ref. Merchandise No. 483: Merchandise Sales*, October 27, 1954, G. B. Ollivant Division: Circulars, file 32 (17), UAC/2/10/3/4, UARM.

100. *Principle Merchandise Clients*.

101. *Aged Stocks*, January 15, 1954, G. B. Ollivant Division: Circulars, file 32 (11), UAC/2/10/3/4, UARM; *Merchandise Sales*, February 26, 1954, G. B. Ollivant Division: Circulars, file 32 (12), UAC/2/10/3/4, UARM; *Sales and Selling Policy*, October 27, 1954, G. B. Ollivant Division: Circulars, file 32 (17), UAC/2/10/3/4, UARM.

102. *Merchandise Clients from Up-Country Buying at Ports*.

103. In an interesting twist, Bauer, *A Study of Competition*, 62–64, has found that credit customers also depended on their own definitions of "reliability" when dealing with firms. He cites as the main reason the fact that they had little to no redress for defective merchandise from the overseas producers.

104. Re: Credit Customers Account, January 25, 1955, UAC of Ghana Ltd. General Manager's Circulars, file 57, UAC/2/20/3/3, UARM.

105. Some of the credit customers began to import directly from manufacturers. P. H. Fitz-Gerald to Gold Coast agents, December 9, 1954, UAC of Ghana Ltd. General Manager's Circulars, UAC/2/20/3/3, UARM.

106. A. C. C. Baxter, London, to general manager, Accra, "UAC London Conference—Merchandise," Ghana (Accra) General Manager's Private Files, file 30, September 13, 1955, UAC/2/20/3/2, UARM.

107. Akuse agent to UTC headquarters, April 1, 1938, UTC 4481: Akuse Correspondence, BMA.

108. Baxter to general manager, September 13, 1955.

109. P. H. Fitz-Gerald to Gold Coast agents, file 116, October 22, 1958, UAC of Ghana Ltd. General Manager's Circulars, UAC/2/20/3/3, UARM.

110. Baxter to general manager, September 13, 1955.

111. Ibid.

112. Baxter, "The Evolution of Merchandising in Africa."

113. W. E. Conway, *Report of the Commission of Enquiry into the Distribution and Prices of Essential Imported Goods* (Accra: Government Printing Department, 1943), 2.

CHAPTER 3: "IN TIME FOR INDEPENDENCE"

1. "Housewife Sentenced for Stealing—Appeals Granted Bail," *Daily Graphic*, December 23, 1957. The amount cited in the article, "£2 2s. 1d.," is two British West African pounds, two shillings, and one pence.

2. "She Is Granted Leave to Appeal," *Daily Graphic*, February 12, 1958.

3. [missing title], *Daily Graphic*, January 13, 1958.

4. "Sentence on Housewife Reduced," *Daily Graphic*, September 17, 1958.

5. Gloria Lamptey, "It's Shocking," *Ghana Times*, July 8, 1958.

6. UTC directors advised its department store employees to frequently visit Kingsway in order to improve business. While there was competition between the two companies, the directors considered Kingsway's organization and relationship with African consumers superior to their own. Dr. Watcher (UTC vice director), "Department Stores," ca. 1958, UTC 4928, BMA.

7. Fitz-Gerald recognized that "the indicated return on the capital employed in the [department store trade in Ghana] is below that obtainable on general trade," P. H. Fitz-Gerald to Frederick Pedler, January 11, 1955, Ghana (Accra) General Manager's Private Files, file 4, UAC 2/20/3/2, UARM. See also Frederick Pedler, "How Nkrumah Gave to the United Africa Company the Site for Building Kingsway Stores, Accra," ca. 1960, Mss. Afr. S.1814, Box 8, FP 50/8, RHL.

8. See, for example, Brian Larkin, *Media, Infrastructure, and Urban Culture in Nigeria* (Durham, NC: Duke University Press, 2008).

9. For an excellent early history of Accra, see John Parker, *Making the Town: Ga State and Society in Early Colonial Accra* (Portsmouth, NH: Heinemann, 2000).

10. Stephan F. Miescher and Dzodzi Tsikata, "Hydro-Power and the Promise of Modernity and Development in Ghana: Comparing the Akosombo and Bui Dam Projects," *Ghana Studies* 12, no. 13 (2009–10): 16.

11. James Ferguson, *The Anti-Politics Machine: "Development," Depoliticization, and Bureaucratic Power in Lesotho* (London: Oxford University Press, 1994).

12. Charles Piot, *Remotely Global: Village Modernity in West Africa* (Chicago: University of Chicago Press, 1999), 173.

13. Andrew Ivaska, *Cultured States: Youth, Gender, and Modern Style in 1960s Dar es Salaam* (Durham, NC: Duke University Press, 2011).

14. Most of this scholarship focuses on the United States, Britain, and Western Europe. Important works include Susan Porter Benson, *Counter Cultures: Saleswomen, Managers, and Customers in American Department Stores, 1890–1940* (Champaign: University of Illinois Press, 1986); Erika Rappaport, *Shopping for Pleasure: Women in the Making of London's West End* (Princeton, NJ: Princeton University Press, 2000); Lizabeth Cohen, *A Consumer's Republic: The Politics of Mass Consumption in Postwar America* (New York: Vintage, 2004); and Victoria de Grazia, *Irresistible Empire: America's Advance through Twentieth-Century Europe* (Cambridge, MA: Belknap, 2005). For an important exception, see Nancy Reynolds, *A City Consumed: Urban Commerce, the Cairo Fire, and the Politics of Decolonization in Egypt* (Stanford, CA: Stanford University Press, 2012).

15. Deborah Quartey, interview with the author, Tema, June 19, 2007.

16. G. A. Attoh, interview with the author, Accra, June 8, 2010.

17. Abdoumaliq Simone, *City Life from Jakarta to Dakar: Movements at the Crossroads* (New York: Routledge, 2013), 3.

18. Benson, *Counter Cultures*, 6.

19. My thanks go to Professor Esi Sutherland-Addy for pointing out the phenomenon of "Kingsway babies."

20. "A Walk Down Regent Street" (Kingsway advertisement), *Sunday Mirror*, July 22, 1956, 17.

21. Formed in 1902, Miller-Swanzy (later a part of the African and Eastern Trade Corporation) comprised the firms F. & A. Swanzy and Miller Brothers. The Swanzys were Irish merchants who had traded in West Africa since the late eighteenth century; the Millers were Glasgow merchants who traded with the West Indies, but in 1868, turned their attention to West Africa. Frederick Pedler, *The Lion and the Unicorn in Africa: United Africa Company, 1787–1931* (London: Heinemann, 1974); Geoffrey Jones, *Merchants to Multinationals: British Trading Companies in the Nineteenth and Twentieth Centuries* (Oxford: Oxford University Press, 2000), 77.

22. Allister Macmillan, *The Red Book of West Africa: Historical and Descriptive, Commercial and Industrial Facts, Figures and Resources* (London: Cass, 1969), 173.

23. Larkin, *Media, Infrastructure, and Urban Culture*, 35–43.

24. Re: ED stores, September 21, 1954, UAC of Ghana Ltd. General Manager's Circulars, file 36, UARM, UAC/2/20/3/3.

25. Sarah Stockwell, *The Business of Decolonization: British Business Strategies in the Gold Coast* (Oxford: Clarendon, 2000); Stephanie Decker, "Corporate Legitimacy and Advertising: British Companies and the Rhetoric of Development in West Africa, 1950–1970," *Business History Review* 81 (2007); Bianca Murillo, "'The Devil We Know': Gold Coast Consumers, Local Employees, and the United Africa Company, 1940–60," *Enterprise and Society* 12, no. 2 (2011): 317–55.

26. UAC presentation to Unilever board, November 8, 1968, UAC/1/11/4/1/4, UARM; emphasis added.

27. Re: Proposal for new site at Adjabeng Lodge in Station Rd., January 11, 1955, Ghana (Accra) General Manager's Private Files, file 4, UARM UAC/2/20/3/2.

28. This £500,000 was the UAC's initial investment in Kingsway; the project most likely cost a lot more upon completion. Geoffrey Jones, *Renewing Unilever: Transformation and Tradition* (Oxford: Oxford University Press, 2005), 194.

29. Lagos, Nigeria, became the site of the UAC's first large-scale Kingsway project. Completed in 1948, the Lagos store often acted as a testing ground for new products to be sold in West Africa.

30. UAC records indicate that Pedler sent photographs and publicized information about Kingsway to directors and managers at British department stores, including the stores where he did his initial research. Instructions to "send copy of S & E Review, no. 12" to Jessups, John Lewis, Harrods, Marks & Spencer, October 2, 1953, UAC/2/10/B1/6, UARM. See also Re: Proposal for new site at Adjabeng Lodge in Station Rd., January 11, 1955, Ghana (Accra) General Managers' Private Files, file 4, UARM UAC/2/20/3/2; and "Cool Efficiency," *Unicorn* 4, no. 8 (1958): 10–11.

31. Review of Visit and Inspection Records, 1950–64, Kingsway Stores Ltd. UAC/2/10/B1/6, UARM.

32. Frederick Pedler to J. Benthall, Kingsway, Lagos, December 20, 1955, UAC/2/10/B1/6, UARM.

33. Interview with John Lewis, managing director and staff trainer, February 10, 1948, UAC/2/10/B1/6, UARM.

34. Ibid.

35. "Department Stores—United States, Notes of Visits Carried Out between 6–17 November 1952," November 27, 1952, Visit & Inspection Records, Kingsway Stores Ltd., UAC/2/10/B1/6, UARM.

36. For an excellent collection on the intersection of racism and retailing, see *Race and Retail Consumption Across the Color Line*, ed. Mia Bay and Anne Fabian (New Brunswick, NJ: Rutgers University Press, 2015).

37. For scholarship on African American consumers, see Robert Weems, *Desegregating the Dollar: African American Consumerism in the Twentieth Century* (New York: New York University Press, 1988); and Cohen, *A Consumer's Republic*.

38. Stockwell, *The Business of Decolonization*, 3.

39. The *Statistical and Economic Review*'s intended audience included African government officials, the press, business associates and competitors, and UAC staff.

40. According to the UAC, specialty trading included the distribution of luxury consumer items, gasoline, cars, drugs, building materials, and machinery. See United Africa Company, "Merchandise Trading in British West Africa," *Statistical and Economic Review* 6 (1950): 1–41; and "What Is the Company's Retail Trade Policy?," *Unicorn* 2, no. 8 (1956).

41. United Africa Company, "Kingsway Stores, Lagos," *Statistical and Economic Review* 12 (1953); 1–30, esp. 4, 5.

42. "How Nkrumah Gave to the UAC," Mss. Afr. S.1814, FP 50/7–11, RHL.

43. United Africa Company, "Merchandise Trading in British West Africa," *Statistical and Economic Review* 5 (1950): 14. Shortly after independence, the company also saw a rise in the sale of more specialized items such as photographic materials and office equipment. See Paula Jones, "The U.A.C. in the Gold Coast/Ghana, 1920–1965," PhD diss., School of Oriental and African Studies, University of London, 1983.

44. Ghana Central Bureau of Statistics, 1960 *Population Census of Ghana*, vol. 2, *Demographic Characteristics* (Accra: Ghana Central Bureau of Statistics, 1964).

45. The *Daily Graphic* claimed to have had a total distribution of 22,800,000 copies in 1958—more than twice that of its closest competitor. Nate Plageman, "'Accra Is Changing, Isn't It?': Urban Infrastructure, Independence, and the Nation in the Gold Coast's *Daily Graphic*, 1954–57," *International Journal of African Historical Studies* 43, no. 1 (2010): 146, 152.

46. Pedler, "How Nkrumah Gave to the UAC," 50/9.

47. Ibid.

48. Ibid., 50/8.

49. Ibid.

50. Advertisement for the opening of Kingsway, Accra, *Daily Graphic*, January 28, 1957.

51. "The Kingsway Story," *Daily Graphic*, January 31, 1967, 10; emphasis in the original.

52. "New Kingsway Stores Opened: Extracts from the Prime Minister's Speech," *Unicorn* 3, no. 2 (1957): 2.

53. Pedler, "How Nkrumah Gave to the UAC," 50/10.

54. "Personal: Watches, Suits, Clothing, etc.," Kwame Nkrumah Papers, December 29, 1956–January 21, 1962, SC/BAA/184 (RG/17/1/6), PRAAD-A.

55. Stephan Miescher, *A Dam for Africa: The Volta River Project and Modernization in Ghana* (Bloomington: Indiana University Press, forthcoming).

56. Homi K. Bhabha, "Of Mimicry and Man: The Ambivalence of Colonial Discourse," in *The Location of Culture* (New York: Routledge, 1994), 85–92; James Ferguson, *Global Shadows: Africa in the Neoliberal World Order* (Durham, NC: Duke University Press, 2006); Jeremy Prestholdt, *Domesticating the World: African Consumerism and the Genealogies of Globalization* (Berkeley: University of California Press, 2008).

57. The Kingsway store in Accra had 60,000 square feet of selling space; the store in Kumasi had about 11,000, and the store in Takoradi had 3,570. "Premises," 1959, GLD 1/1/144, UGL.

58. Esther Addai, interview with the author, Accra, June 21, 2007.

59. Alice van der Staaij-Ghartey, interview with the author, Accra, November 5, 2007.

60. Emmanuel Idun, interview with the author, Accra, June 6, 2007.

61. Kwesi Akumenya Cato, interview with the author, Accra, September 13, 2007.

62. Nana Anwasi Agyemang (aka Joseph Kwasi Onwonah), interview with the author, Sunyani, October 12, 2007.

63. Pedler, "How Nkrumah Gave to the UAC," 50/10.

64. Stephan F. Miescher and Dzodzi Tsikata, "Hydro-Power and the Promise of Modernity and Development in Ghana: Comparing the Akosombo and Bui Dam Projects," *Ghana Studies* 12–13 (2009–10): 15–53.

65. Janet Hess, "Imagining Architecture: The Structure of Nationalism in Accra, Ghana," *Africa Today* 47, no. 2 (2000): 45; background document on Kingsway, GLD 1/1/144, UGL.

66. "Princess Aida at Kingsway on State Visit," photo, *Unicorn* 6, no. 12 (1960):

67. Merchandise meetings/conferences, minutes, September 26–27, 1957, UTC 4928, BMA.

68. Van der Staaij-Ghartey interview.

69. Ibid.

70. Sadiku Musah, interview with the author, Accra, April 7, 2007.

71. Emmanuel Akyeampong, *Drink, Power, and Cultural Change: A Social History of Alcohol in Ghana, c. 1800 to Recent Times* (Portsmouth, NH: Heinemann, 1996), 145–48.

72. "Kingsway Stores Ltd: Photograph Album—Opening of Kingsway Stores, Accra," January 31, 1957, UAC/2/10/B3/6/1/1, UARM.

73. United Africa Company, "Kingsway Stores, Lagos," 28–29.

74. George Darkwa Kwakye, interview with the author, Suhum, April 20, 2007.

75. "Braindt Goes to Germany," *Guinea Times*, March 12, 1958.

76. "New Manageress," *Ghanaian Times*, January 7, 1961; "Commissioner's Daughter Promoted," *Ashanti Pioneer*, January 7, 1961; "Big Job for Her," *Daily Graphic*, January 7, 1961.

77. "She Is Miss Kingsway 1960," *Ghana Times*, May 30, 1960; information on staff dance to take place in Kingsway parking lot, GLD1/1/144, UGL; "Minutes of the Joint Consultative Committee of Kingsway Stores," November 11, 1971, Kingsway Stores of Ghana Ltd. UAC/2/10/B3/3/3, UARM.

78. "Training for Salesmen," *Gold Coast UAC News* 4, no. 7 (1953): 1–2.

79. "Kingsway Manager's Course," *Unicorn* 6, no. 10 (1960). Other department stores, including those of the UTC and Compagnie Française de l'Afrique Occidentale, also ran similar staff training and sales courses. "Minutes of the Joint Consultative Committee of Kingsway Stores," May 4, 1972, Kingsway Stores of Ghana Ltd., UAC /2/10/B3/3/3, UARM.

80. Walter A. Friedman, *Birth of a Salesman: The Transformation of Selling in America* (Cambridge, MA: Harvard University Press, 2004).

81. Quartey interview, June 19, 2007.

82. "Kingsway Sales Manual," 1964, Kingsway Stores Ltd., UAC/2/10/B1/8/1, UARM.

83. Ibid., 9.

84. Van der Staaij-Ghartey interview.

85. The UAC hired Eleanor MacDonald in 1959 to work in the Public Relations Department of the Kingsway division as the "Advisor on African women's needs." "Organization of the Public Relations Department," ca. 1960, UAC/1/3/3/6/1, UARM; "Beauty Expert Joins U.A.C," *Ghana Times*, April 4, 1959. See also Eleanor MacDonald, *Nothing by Chance! An Autobiography of a Pioneer Business Woman* (Alton, England: Nimrod, 1987).

86. "Beauty Expert Joins U.A.C."; "Fashion Expert Back," *Daily Graphic*, March 26, 1960.

87. "Shop and Office Managers," *Ghana Evening News*, April 2, 1958.

88. Response from Mr. H. J. Somuah, in "Mirror Forum: Are Ghana's Salesgirl's Courteous?," *Sunday Mirror*, March 12, 1961.

89. Response from Miss Ruby Van Derjuije, in "Mirror Forum."

90. "Mirror Forum."

91. Discussion on rapid saleswoman turnover initiated debates on whether Kingsway should begin employing less-educated women. One Kingsway committee member argued that many saleswomen joined Kingsway as an interim measure before undertaking other work, like nursing; he proposed that the store consider hiring women with only an elementary education, justifying that these less-educated women would stay longer. "Minutes of the Joint Consultative Committee," November 11, 1971.

91. UAC Personnel Department, *Training of African Managers*, August 9, 1954, UAC/1/10/3/3/10, UARM.

93. "B. J. Dale's notes on visit to Ghana 19th November–18th December 1967," p. 4, Correspondence of F. J. Pedler, Kingsway Division-Visits to West African Stores (1964–1968), UAC/1/3/4/7/5, UARM.

94. Quartey interview, June 19, 2007.

95. Ibid.

96. Carmel Dinan, "Sugar Daddies and Gold-Diggers: The White Collar Single Women in Accra," in *Female and Male in West Africa* ed. Christine Oppong (London: Allen and Unwin, 1983).

97. Quartey interview, June 19, 2007.

98. The advertisement reads: "Shopping is such a pleasure at Kingsway, they have everything. Arrange to see your friends there too, it's the most popular meeting place in town." "Your Way," advertisement for Kingsway, *Daily Graphic*, ca. 1955, UARM.

99. Christine Oppong, *Middle Class African Marriage: A Family Study of Ghanaian Senior Servants* (London: Allen and Unwin, 1981), 110.

100. "Smart Man Competition," photo, *Daily Graphic*, June 22, 1961.

101. "Kwame in an Accra Store: Just a Few Minutes: But What a Crowd!" *Evening News*, September 4, 1959.

102. Gerardo Serra, "An Uneven Statistical Topography: The Political Economy of Household Budget Surveys in Late Colonial Ghana, 1951–1957," *Canadian Journal of Development Studies* 35, no. 1 (2014): 14, notes that "all household budget surveys in the 1950s took place in the southern and central regions, to the exclusion of the northern ones, which included some of the poorest areas. Additionally four out of the five produced dealt with urban areas."

103. Jordanna Bailkin, *The Afterlife of Empire* (Berkeley: University of California Press, 2012), argues that this data was also used to develop welfare and immigration policy in Britain.

104. See Serra, "An Uneven Statistical Topography," table 2.

105. Ibid.

106. Diana Gladys Azu, *The Ga Family and Social Change* (Leiden: Africa-Studiecentrum, 1974); Oppong, *Middle Class African Marriage*; Roger Sanjek, "Female and Male Domestic Cycles in Urban Africa: The Adabraka Case," in *Female and Male in West Africa*, ed. Christine Oppong (London: Allen and Unwin, 1983), 57–103. For studies on nonelite women, see Gracia Clark, *Onions Are My Husband: Survival and Accumulation by West African Market Women* (Chicago: University of Chicago Press, 1994); and Claire Robertson, *Sharing the Same Bowl: A Socioeconomic History of Women and Class in Accra* (Bloomington: Indiana University Press, 1984).

107. Zakariah Ali, *Walk with the Devil: My Endless Struggle against the Cunning and Tarps with the Devil* (Bloomington, IN: Xlibris, 2012).

108. Sanjek, "Female and Male Domestic Cycles," 88.

109. Ione Acquah, *Accra Survey: A Social Survey of the Capital of Ghana, Formerly Called the Gold Coast, Undertaken for the West African Institute of Social and Economic Research*, 1953–1956 (London: University of London Press, 1958).

110. I. Neustadt and E. N. Omaboe, *Social and Economic Survey of Tema* (Accra: Office of the Government Statistician in conjunction with the Tema Development Corporation, 1959), 27–29.

111. Eleanor MacDonald, outline of presentation to the Public Relations Conference, December 10, 1964, UAC Public Relations Department, UAC/1/11/4/1/3, UARM; "Progress Sheet," July 22, 1963, UAC Public Relations Department, UAC/1/11/4/1/3,

UARM, pp. 2–3; D. H. Buckle, UAC public relations director, to Head of Units, London, July 16, 1963, UAC Public Relations Department, UAC/1/11/4/1/3, UARM.

112. Attoh interview. Shoes were an important class marker; great attention was paid to style, brand, and material (canvas versus leather). Among Ghanaians there is still today a running joke that before you are quoted a price in the market, a seller will first look down at your shoes; higher-quality shoes mean higher prices. Shoes were required in many places, including mission and government schools, but some people—and especially children—preferred the comfort of going without them.

113. Van der Staaij-Ghartey interview.

114. Nate Plageman, *Highlife Saturday Night: Popular Music and Social Change in Urban Ghana* (Bloomington: Indiana University Press, 2008). See also the copyright infringement cases on UAC textiles, UAC Ltd. v. R. JoJo, April 30, 1957, and UAC Ltd. v. Irani, April 30, 1957, SCT 2/6/25, PRAAD-A.

115. Van der Staaij-Ghartey interview.

116. Acquah, *Accra Survey*, 69.

117. Michael N. Ankumah, interview with the author, Accra, September 4, 2007.

118. United Africa Company, "Kingsway Stores, Lagos," 28–29.

119. "B. J. Dale's notes on visit to Ghana 19th November–18th December 1967," January 11, 1968, p. 1, Correspondence of F. J. Pedler, Kingsway Division-Visits to West African Stores (1964–1968), UAC/1/3/4/7/5, UARM; B.J. Dale, "Kingsway Accra." Tour no. 33, December 21, 1967, UAC/1/3/4/7/6, UARM.

120. Jeffrey Ahlman, *Living with Nkrumahism: Nation, State, and Pan-Africanism in Ghana* (Athens: Ohio University Press, 2017).

121. K. B. Asante, "Nkrumah and State Enterprises," in *The Life and Works of Kwame Nkrumah: Papers of a Symposium Organised by the Institute of African Studies University of Ghana*, ed. Kwame Arhin (Trenton, NJ: Africa World Press, 1993), 259–60.

122. The founder, A. G. Leventis, was formally general manager of G. B. Ollivant. P. T. Bauer, *A Study of Competition, Oligopoly and Monopoly in a Changing Economy* (Cambridge: Cambridge University Press, 1954), 79–86.

123. Carl D. Reindorf, "Focus on GNTC State Shopping Project," *The Ghanaian*, June 1964, 14–15, 23.

124. By 1970 the government established other GNTC department store branches at Roraima Lodge ("The People's Shop"), Accra Tesano, Accra Ringway Estate, Accra Kanda Estate, Accra Labone, Tema, Korforidua, Akosombo, Kumasi, Takoradi, Sunyani, Ho, and Cape Coast. The number of wholesale and retail stores also rose to 355. "Ghana National Trading Corporation," *Ghana Business Guide*, 1972.

125. Willie A. Abraham, *Report of the Commission of Enquiry into Trade Malpractices in Ghana* (Accra: State Publishing Corporation, 1965), 25–30.

CHAPTER 4: "SHOP WINDOW ON THE WORLD"

1. "Welcome to the Fair," *Business Weekly*, January 30, 1967.

2. In 1966 the Ghana Army consisted of about six hundred officers and fourteen thousand rank-and-file members. It was then the largest in West Africa, and the cost of maintaining it was the fifth highest of any army on the continent. The police force, which at the time of independence had numbered about six thousand men, had grown to fourteen thousand by the time of the coup. See Robert Dowse, "Military and Police

Rule," in *Politicians and Soldiers in Ghana, 1966–1972*, ed. Dennis Austin and Robin Luckham (London: Cass, 1975), 16–36, esp. 16.

3. E. N. Omaboe and the Economic Committee of the NLC, *Ghana's Economy and Aid Requirements in 1967* (Accra: State Publishing Corporation, 1967). See also Dennis Austin and Robin Luckham, eds., *Politicians and Soldiers in Ghana, 1966–1972* (London: Cass, 1975); and Eboe Hutchful, *The IMF and Ghana: The Confidential Record* (London: Zed, 1987).

4. "Ankrah: Fair Will Improve Economic Ties" (full text of opening speech by J. A. Ankrah), *Daily Graphic*, February 2, 1967.

5. Dennis Austin, "Introduction," in *Politicians and Soldiers in Ghana, 1966–1972*, ed. Dennis Austin and Robin Luckham (London: Cass, 1975), 2.

6. I am inspired here by feminist critiques of globalization literature that seek to challenge the local-global articulations approach that "analytically defines the global, as political-economic and the local as cultural." For a brilliant overview of literature that breaks down this structural binary, see Carla Freeman, "Is Local: Global as Feminine: Masculine? Rethinking the Gender of Globalization," *Signs* 26, no. 4 (2001): 1007–37, esp.1017.

7. See, for example, Emmanuel Akyeampong, *Drink, Power, and Cultural Change: A Social History of Alcohol in Ghana, c. 1800 to Recent Times* (Portsmouth, NH: Heinemann, 1996); Dmitri van den Bersselaar, *The King of Drinks: Schnapps Gin from Modernity to Tradition* (Boston: Brill, 2007); and Jeremy Prestholdt, *Domesticating the World: African Consumerism and the Genealogies of Globalization* (Berkeley: University of California Press, 2008).

8. Walter Birmingham, I. Neustadt, and E. N. Omaboe, eds., *A Study of Contemporary Ghana*, vol. I, *The Economy of Ghana* (London: Allen and Unwin, 1966).

9. Willie A. Abraham, *Report of the Commission of Enquiry into Trade Malpractices in Ghana* (Accra: State Publishing Corporation, 1965), 28–29.

10. Republic of Ghana, *White Paper on the Report of the Commission of Enquiry into Alleged Irregularities and Malpractices in the Connection with the Grant of Import Licenses* (Accra-Tema: State Publishing Corporation, 1967).

11. Hans Buser, *In Ghana at Independence: Stories of a Swiss Salesman* (Basel: Basler Afrika Bibliographien, 2010), 67–76.

12. Abraham, *Report of the Commission of Enquiry*, 6.

13. By 1965, the GNTC held a near monopoly over the importation of essential goods. Ibid., 6–7.

14. Notes taken at meeting held between the World Bank Mission and the National Planning Commission, September 22–24, 1965, SC/BAA/505, PRAAD-A.

15. It is important to note that opposition existed prior to Nkrumah's election. Both the (Ashanti) National Liberation Movement and the Northern People's Party were part of the political opposition that opposed the CPP, and to some extent the NLC should be considered as a continuation of this opposition. See Jean Marie Allman, *Quills of the Porcupine: Asante Nationalism in an Emergent Ghana* (Madison: University of Wisconsin Press, 1993); and Dennis Austin, *Politics in Ghana 1946–60* (Oxford: Oxford University Press, 1964).

16. Akyeampong, *Drink, Power, and Cultural Change*, 145.

17. Takyiwaa Manuh, "Women and Their Organisations during the Convention People's Party Period," in *The Life and Work of Kwame* Nkrumah, ed. Kwame Arhin (Trenton, NJ: Africa World Press, 1983), 113.

18. United Kingdom High Commission in Ghana to the Secretary of State for Commonwealth Relations (confidential), May 17, 1961, Prime Minister's Office: Correspondence and Papers, PREM 11/3369, NAUK.

19. Kojo Bentsil, "Girls Give Up Those Luxuries," *Daily Graphic*, February 7, 1966.

20. Mabel Dove, "The Coup Was a Healing Tonic: Examine Your Conscience," *Ghanaian Times*, April 15, 1966, reprinted in Mabel Dove, *Selected Writings of a Pioneer West African Feminist*, ed. Stephanie Newell and Audrey Gadzekpo (Nottingham, England: Trent, 2004), 118.

21. See, for example, Mike Anane, "I Maintained 3 Houses in 1962—Boateng," *Evening News*, May 15, 1968; and Mike Anane, "I Never Gave Pocket Money to My Wife—Atta Mensah," *Evening News*, June 4, 1968. See also T. C. McCaskie, "Accumulation, Wealth and Belief in Asante History II: The Twentieth Century," *Africa: Journal of the International African Institute* 56, no. 1 (1986): 18; and Buser, *In Ghana at Independence*, 70–71.

22. "Africa: On the Beach," *Time*, January 6, 1967, 37.

23. Full text of a broadcast speech by the chairman of the NLC, March 2, 1966, UAC Corporate Planning Department: Ghana, UAC/1/9/4/2/1, UARM.

24. Andrew Apter, *The Pan-African Nation: Oil and the Spectacle of Culture in Nigeria* (Chicago: University of Chicago Press, 2005), 119.

25. After independence, the *Daily Graphic* was owned and managed by the Graphic Corporation, a commercial organization controlled by the Nkrumah government. Following the coup, the NLC appointed a group of officials to act as a caretaker board and appointed their own minister of information. By 1966, daily sales were at about 170,000, yet actual readership was probably much higher. "Ghana Press Dismissal of Editors by NLC—Confidential Correspondence," letter to D. K. Middleton, Commonwealth Relations Office, West Africa Political Department, 1966, DO 153/56, NAUK.

26. Special correspondent, "Ghana Plans for a Trade Fair," *Daily Graphic*, December 14, 1964.

27. Special correspondent, "Ghana's Trade Fair Gets Off the Ground," *Financial Times*, January 31, 1967; "30 Countries Expected to Take Part in Ghana Fair," *New York Times*, January 27, 1967.

28. British high commissioner H. Smedley to secretary of state for commonwealth affairs, April 25, 1967, Ghana: Internal: Fairs and Exhibitions, FCO 38/56, NAUK.

29. Industrial correspondent, "Developing Africa: Ghana's First International Trade Fair," *Business Weekly*, January 30, 1962, 2.

30. Thirty governments took part in the fair. Nine were from Africa (Dahomey, Ivory Coast, Liberia, Morocco, Niger, Nigeria, Senegal, Togo, and Upper Volta); thirteen were from Europe (Austria, Britain, Czechoslovakia, the German Democratic Republic, the German Federal Republic, Hungary, Italy, the Netherlands, Norway, Poland, Spain, Switzerland, and Yugoslavia); five were from Asia (India, Israel, Japan, Lebanon, and Taiwan, Republic of China); and three were from the Americas (Brazil, Canada, and the United States).

31. Restricted report from Trade Fair adviser R. H. C. Hammond to UK Ministry of Overseas Development, February 22, 1967, Ghana: Internal: Fairs and Exhibitions, FCO 38/56, NAUK.

32. Although each participant's motivations varied, decisions were also influenced by the Ghana government's undertaking to give twenty-two old cedis' (about ten pounds') worth of import licenses for every square foot of space rented; for example,

the British pavilion measured 36,750 square feet, equaling a total of £367,500 in import licenses. Industrial correspondent, "Developing Africa."

33. Ghana International Trade Fair brochure and official application form, ca. 1966, DO 221/128, NAUK.

34. Hammond Report.

35. Ibid.

36. "6,000,000 in U.S. Goods Sold at the Ghana Trade Exhibit," *New York Times*, February 20, 1967.

37. "Exhibitors Claim Success at Ghana Trade Fair," *Financial Times*, February 13, 1967.

38. Mike Adjei, "Trade Fair Opens Today," *Daily Graphic*, February 1, 1967.

39. Elaine Tyler May, *Homeward Bound: American Families in the Cold War Era*, rev. and updated edition (New York: Basic Books, 1999); Lizabeth Cohen, *A Consumer's Republic: The Politics of Mass Consumption in Postwar America* (New York: Vintage, 2004); Victoria de Grazia, *Irresistible Empire: America's Advance through Twentieth-Century Europe* (Cambridge, MA: Belknap, 2005).

40. Katherine Pence, "Showcasing Cold War Germany in Cairo: 1954 and 1957 Industrial Exhibitions and the Competition for Arab Partners," *Journal of Contemporary History* 47, no. 1 (2012): 69–95.

41. Special correspondent, "Ghana's Trade Fair Gets off the Ground."

42. Felix Akom Nyarku, "Ghana-China Bilateral Relations: A Treasured Fifty Years of Diplomatic, Cultural, Economic, and Trade Relations," *GhanaWeb* (2012), http://www.ghanaweb.com/GhanaHomePage/blogs/blog.article.php?blog=70375&ID=1000145821.

43. Smedley to Secretary of State for Commonwealth Affairs, April 25, 1967.

44. Lloyd Garrison, "Exit Nkrumah, an Old Dreamer; Enter Ankrah, a New Realist," *New York Times*, April 3, 1966.

45. Hammond Report.

46. British high commissioner to V. E. Davies, Commonwealth Relations Office, West Africa Economic Department, June 2, 1966, 1967 Ghana Trade Fair, DO 221/128, NAUK.

47. De Grazia, *Irresistible Empire*, esp. chap. 4.

48. "U.S. Jewellery for Fair," *Daily Graphic*, January 4, 1967.

49. Smedley to Secretary of State for Commonwealth Affairs, April 25, 1967.

50. John D. Esseks, "Government and Indigenous Private Enterprise in Ghana," *Journal of Modern African Studies* 9 (1971): 11–29. This commitment to local businessmen was further institutionalized through the passing of the Ghanaian Enterprises Decree in December 1968.

51. Smedley to Secretary of State for Commonwealth Affairs, April 25, 1967.

52. Similar expectations of political authority and leadership exist among other groups in Ghana. See McCaskie, "Accumulation, Wealth and Belief in Asante History II," 6.

53. Ibid., 27.

54. Ibid., 13.

55. See also the discussion in McCaskie, "Accumulation, Wealth and Belief in Asante History II," 13, about the conflict between the Asantehene and *akonkofoo* (what McCaskie identifies as the first manifestation of business class interests that emerged in serious opposition to the authority of the Asante state between 1910 and the 1930s).

56. Smedley to Secretary of State for Commonwealth Affairs, April 25, 1967.

57. Through native court reforms, Nkrumah dismantled chiefly jurisdiction and replaced chiefs with "nontraditional" figures. See Richard Rathbone, *Nkrumah and the Chiefs: The Politics of Chieftaincy in Ghana* (Athens: Ohio University Press, 2000), 1–7, 52–58.

58. Dowse, "Military and Police Rule," 21–22.

59. McCaskie, "Accumulation, Wealth and Belief in Asante History II," 13.

60. Jennifer Hart, "'One Man, No Chop': Licit Wealth, Good Citizens, and the Criminalization of Drivers in Postcolonial Ghana," *International Journal of African Historical Studies* 46, no. 3 (2013): 373–96.

61. Ghana International Trade Fair brochure and official application. For a similar public opinion view, see Togbi Yao, "Social Reforms and Economic Planning: They Must Begin and End in the Kitchen," *Sunday Mirror*, August 26, 1967.

62. Colonel A. A. Afrifa, *The Ghana Coup: 24th February 1966* (London: Cass, 1967), 77. See also A. K. Ocran, *Politics of the Sword: A Personal Memoir on Military Involvement in Ghana and of Problems with Military Government* (London: Collings, 1977).

63. Nate Plageman, *Highlife Saturday Night: Popular Music and Social Change in Urban Ghana* (Bloomington: Indiana University Press, 2012).

64. Jeffrey S. Ahlman, "A New Type of Citizen: Youth, Gender, and Generation in the Ghanaian Builder's Brigade," *Journal of African History* 53, no. 1 (2012): 87–105.

65. For examples from the colonial period, see Akyeampong, "'Wope tam won pe ba' ('You like cloth but you don't want children'): Urbanization, Individualism and Gender Relations in Colonial Ghana, c. 1900–39," in *Africa's Urban Past*, ed. David M. Anderson and Richard Rathbone (Oxford: Currey, 1999), 222–34; and Jean Marie Allman, "Rounding Up Spinsters: Gender Chaos and Unmarried Women in Colonial Asante," *Journal of African History* 37, no. 2 (1996): 195–214.

66. Manuh, "Women and Their Organisations."

67. "Maintaining Authority in the Home," *Evening News*, May 13, 1968.

68. Ofori-Atta strongly opposed Nkrumah's economic policies and was active during the period of the NLC and the term of Prime Minister Kofi Abrefa Busia; he was also deputy minister of economic affairs under Busia. Jones Ofori-Atta, "To Achieve Social Solidarity Which Is Essential for Stable Society Base Values Must be Eschewed" (third address at Nkonya Secondary School), *Evening News*, June 12, 1968, 3.

69. "Youth Need Sound Moral Education—Chief," *Daily Graphic*, June 13, 1968.

70. "Centre Plans Education in Three Stages," *Daily Graphic*, August 1, 1967.

71. "Jiagge—Let's Have Women's Organisation in the Country," *Evening News*, May 24, 1968.

72. Yaw Boakye Ghanatta, *Kofi Brokeman* comic strip, *Evening News*, December 5, 1968; Yaw Boakye Ghanatta, *Kofi Brokeman* comic strip, *Evening News*, December 20, 1968. The comic strip character's name most likely came from the popular dish of roasted, semi-sweet plantain and roasted groundnuts (peanuts) called "Kofi Broke Man"; historically the dish was associated with low wage laborers and the poor because of its low cost.

73. Yaw Boakye Ghanatta, *Kofi Brokeman* comic strip, *Evening News*, December 20, 1968.

74. Yaw Boakye Ghanatta, *Kofi Brokeman* comic strip, *Evening News*, December 19, 1968; Yaw Boakye Ghanatta, *Kofi Brokeman* comic strip, *Evening News*, December 28, 1968.

75. Ahlman, "A New Type of Citizen," 104, notes that the NLC would, however, later celebrate the brigade's contributions to Ghana's material welfare.

76. Rathbone, *Nkrumah and the Chiefs*, 24.

77. Photograph of female pavilion guides, *Daily Graphic*, February 4, 1967.

78. The *Daily Graphic* reported that Ohene was "competing actively in both quality and quantity with her men counterparts in the manufacturing of handkerchiefs, waistslips, children's dresses, ladies blouses, bedsheets, and men's shirts." "Our Women are Helping to Build Ghana," "Made-In-Ghana" supplement, *Daily Graphic*, February 22, 1967.

79. Ghana Ministry of Commerce and Industry, *Handbook of Commerce and Industry* (Accra: Ghana Ministry of Commerce and Industry, 1967).

80. I have written elsewhere about the 1967 Ideal Home Exhibition as part of the NLC's efforts to enforce social order. See Bianca Murillo, "Ideal Homes and the Gender Politics of Consumerism in Postcolonial Ghana, 1960–70," *Gender and History* 21, no. 3 (2009): 560–75.

81. See also "Aluminum Utensils Help Ideal Homes," *Daily Graphic*, December 2, 1967.

82. For an excellent study on this topic, see Carmel Dinan, "Sugar Daddies and Gold-Diggers: The White Collar Single Women in Accra," in *Female and Male in West Africa*, ed. Christine Oppong (London: Allen and Unwin, 1983), 344–66.

83. These issues were not specific to Ghana; Amina Mama, "Khaki in the Family: Gender Discourses and Militarism in Nigeria," *African Studies Review* 41, no. 2 (1998): 469–94, argues that in Nigeria military reforms often focused on reestablishing or reemphasizing conservative gender roles.

84. Claire Robertson, *Sharing the Same Bowl: A Socioeconomic History of Women and Class in Accra* (Bloomington: Indiana University Press, 1984); Gracia Clark, *Onions Are My Husband: Survival and Accumulation by West African Market Women* (Chicago: University of Chicago Press, 1994); Claire Robertson, "The Death of Makola and Other Tragedies," *Canadian Journal of African Studies* 17, no. 3 (1989): 469–94.

85. Freeman, "Is Local: Global as Feminine: Masculine?"; R. W. Connell, "Masculinities, Change, and Conflict in Global Society: Thinking about the Future of Men's Studies," *Journal of Men's Studies* 11, no. 3 (2003): 249–66.

86. Dove, "The Coup Was a Healing Tonic."

CHAPTER 5: "POWER TO THE PEOPLE"

1. While this process began in September 1966 with the establishment of a constitutional commission, it was not until April 1969 that the NLC permitted the formation of political parties and announced plans to hold a general election. See Robin Luckham, "The Constitutional Commission 1966–69," in *Politicians and Soldiers in Ghana, 1966–1972*, ed. Dennis Austin and Robin Luckham (London: Cass, 1975), 62; and Robert Dowse, "Military and Police Rule," in *Politicians and Soldiers in Ghana, 1966–1972*, ed. Dennis Austin and Robin Luckham (London: Cass, 1975), 32.

2. Cutting allowances included putting an end to subsidies for water, electricity, and telephone bills and increasing rent payments. Valerie Plave Bennett, "Epilogue: Malcontents in Uniform—The 1972 Coup d'Etat," in *Politicians and Soldiers in Ghana, 1966–1972*, ed. Dennis Austin and Robin Luckham (London: Cass, 1975), 302;

Youry Petchenkine, *Ghana: In Search of Stability, 1957–1992* (Westport, CT: Praeger, 1993), 52–53.

3. Bennett, "Malcontents in Uniform," 309.

4. E. Gyimah-Boadi and Richard Jefferies, "The Political Economy of Reform," in *Economic Reforms in Ghana: The Miracle and The Mirage*, ed. Ernest Aryeetey, Jane Harrigan, and Machiko Nissanke (Trenton, NJ: Africa World Press, 2000), 35.

5. Naomi Chazan, *An Anatomy of Ghanaian Politics: Managing Political Recession, 1969–1982* (Boulder, CO: Westview, 1983), 163–64.

6. Acheampong's time in office can thus be divided into two parts: 1972–74 (NRC) and 1975–78 (SMC).

7. Chazan, *An Anatomy of Ghanaian Politics*, 194–96.

8. J. F. Enninful, interview with the author, Cape Coast, June 2, 2010.

9. One of the major challenges of writing the history of Ghana in the 1970s is a lack of archival sources. Many records from this period have disappeared or were destroyed by the military government. Recent scholarship has begun to fill in these gaps through oral histories and research in archival collections outside Ghana. See Alice Wiemers, "A 'Time of Agric': Rethinking the 'Failure' of Agricultural Programs in 1970s Ghana," *World Development* 66 (2015): 104–17; Jennifer Hart, "*Nife Nifa:* Technopolitics, Regionalism, and Authoritarianism in Acheampong's Ghana," paper presented at the Annual Meeting of the African Studies Association, Indianapolis, November 20–23, 2014.

10. This literature is authored mostly by political scientists, economists, and development scholars. Important works include Deborah Pellow and Naomi Chazan, *Ghana: Coping with Uncertainty* (Boulder, CO: Westview, 1986); Chazan, *An Anatomy of Ghanaian Politics*; Mike Oquaye, *Politics in Ghana, 1972–1979* (Accra: Tornado, 1980); Jonathan Frimpong-Ansah, *The Vampire State in Africa: The Politics of Decline in Ghana* (Trenton, NJ: Africa World Press, 1992); and Petchenkine, *Ghana: In Search of Stability*.

11. Dennis Austin, "Introduction," in *Politicians and Soldiers in Ghana, 1966–1972*, ed. Dennis Austin and Robin Luckham (London: Cass, 1975), 13.

12. Brenda Chalfin, *Neoliberal Frontiers: An Ethnography of Sovereignty in West Africa* (Chicago: University of Chicago Press, 2010), 11.

13. These regions were: Ashanti, Brong-Ahafo, the Central Region, the Eastern Region, Greater Accra, the Northern Region, the Upper Region (later divided into Upper East and Upper West), Volta, and the Western Region. Ghana Central Bureau of Statistics, *Ghana Statistical Yearbook* (Accra: Central Bureau of Statistics, 1973).

14. Not all Brong and Ahafo chiefs sought independent statehood, however. Some chiefs remained loyal to the Kumasi state and the Asantehene. See Dennis Austin, *Politics in Ghana, 1946–1960* (Oxford: Oxford University Press, 1964); John Dunn and A. F. Robertson, *Dependence and Opportunity: Political Change in Ahafo* (Cambridge: Cambridge University Press, 1973); and A. F. Robertson, "Histories and Political Opposition in Ahafo, Ghana," *Africa: Journal of the International African Institute* 43, no. 1 (1973): 41–58, esp. 43–47.

15. The utilization of resources in Brong-Ahafo came relatively late, with the cocoa and logging industries in the area being among the youngest in Ghana. Timber companies opened up new sites for cocoa farming and Mim Timbers, the largest firm, was not established until 1948. Walter Birmingham, I. Neustadt, and E. N. Omaboe, eds., *A Study of Contemporary Ghana*, vol. 1, *The Economy of Ghana* (London: Allen and

Unwin, 1966), 95; C. Okali, *Dominase: A Mobile Cocoa Farming Community in Brong-Ahafo*, Technical Publication Series 35 (Legon: Institute of Statistical, Social, and Economic Research, University of Ghana, 1975).

16. Regional commissioner, Brong-Ahafo, "Monthly Report on Activities in Brong-Ahafo Region for Period Ended 31st March 1962," April 12, 1962, BRG 1/9/15, PRAAD-S; "The Face of Brong-Ahafo," *Daily Graphic*, August 21, 1965.

17. Brong-Ahafo Regional Administration, *This Is Brong-Ahafo: Rural Development in Action* (Sunyani: Brong-Ahafo Regional Administration, 1971).

18. Gwendolyn Mikell, *Cocoa and Chaos in Ghana* (New York: Paragon House, 1989), 194–95, notes that Busia's plans benefitted established and prosperous male food farmers, rather than poor men and women who were most in need of assistance.

19. To compare population density per square mile, here were the statistics for the more populated regions in 1970: Ashanti, 157,000; Brong-Ahafo, 50,000; Central Region, 233,000; Eastern Region, 164,000; Greater Accra, 233,000; Volta 119,000. Ghana Central Bureau of Statistics, *Ghana Statistical Yearbook* (Accra: Central Bureau of Statistics, 1973), table 7.

20. Ghana Central Bureau of Statistics, *Statistical Handbook of the Republic of Ghana* (Accra: Central Bureau of Statistics, 1970), 15–16.

21. The roots of the Customs Service can be traced to 1839, when a group of British merchants were mandated to collect duties on all goods and merchandise coming into Gold Coast settlements. Chalfin, *Neoliberal Frontiers*, 62.

22. For some examples, see C of C v. Adojoa Meboa and Kwame Nhroma, Magistrate Court, Sunyani, March 12, 1942, and C of C v. Karafa Wangara, Magistrate Court, Sunyani, January 8, 1943, ADM 54/4/1, PRAAD-A. Many of these problems stemmed from the artificial borders created by the colonial state. For instance, the Brong people originally occupied a territory that stretched from the Comoé River in Ivory Coast (in the west) to the Volta River (in the east). The same issues continued into the 1970s; as one border guard pointed out, the Brong-Ahafo-Ivory Coast border was difficult to control as "border lines [ran] through villages, farmsteads, and large cocoa farms." See Ghana/Ivory Coast Incidents, report, February 23, 1970, BRG 1/4/6, PRAAD-S.

23. Paul Nugent, *Smugglers, Secessionists, and Loyal Citizens on the Ghana-Togo Frontier* (Athens: Ohio University Press, 2002), 249.

24. J. B. Danquah, commanding officer, "Arrest of Smugglers," January 15, 1973, BRG 1/4/7, PRAAD-S.

25. Stories that circulated in Sunyani at the time of my fieldwork in 2007 characterized the Third Battalion in these terms.

26. Danquah, "Arrest of Smugglers."

27. S. G. Oduroh, interview with the author, Sunyani, July 19, 2007. See also Sunyani District Court Criminal and Civil Record Books, 1972–74, which contain records on civil and criminal cases held at the district headquarters of the Brong-Ahafo region, as well as at Atebubu, Berekum, Dormaa-Ahenkro, Duaya-Nkwanta, Goaso, Nkoranza, Techiman, and Wenchi. For examples of "illegally importing restricted goods," see The Republic v Timite Almany, October 17, 1972, and The Republic v Joyce Senkyire and Kwasi Barimah, September 3, 1973, SCC 3/9, 3/10, PRAAD-S.

28. Ghana National Redemption Council, "Price Control Decree 17" in *National Redemption Council Decrees* (Accra: Ghana Publishing Corporation, 1972).

29. The colonial government was the first to implement price control legislation in 1949. This legislation remained in place until Nkrumah's CPP government passed the

much more comprehensive Control of Prices Act in 1962. See K. Ansa-Asare, "Legislative History of the Legal Regime of Price Control in Ghana," *Journal of African Law* 29 (1985): 103–4; Kodwo Ewusi, *The Determinants of Price Fluctuations in Ghana*, Discussion Papers 2 (Legon: Institute of Statistical, Social, and Economic Research, University of Ghana, 1977).

30. "Price Control Decree 17," section 6.

31. A. I. C. Joshua, Bechem, to regional commissioner, Sunyani, September 18, 1975, BRG 1/1/52, PRAAD-S.

32. Frimpong-Ansah, *The Vampire State in Africa*, 111.

33. E. B. Mensah, interview with the author, Accra, July 7, 2007.

34. Military regimes followed the legacy of information control left by Nkrumah and tended to exercise outright control over the press through repressive decrees and other institutional arrangements. Jennifer Hasty, *The Press and Political Culture in Ghana* (Bloomington: Indiana University Press, 2005), 34–35.

35. "Trader Jailed," *Daily Graphic*, January 21, 1975. A note on currency: following the coup d'état, the external value of the Ghanaian cedi was revalued on February 7, 1972, to stand at GH₵1.00=US$0.78, or US$1.00=GH₵1.28.

36. P. Ernest Amoo Acheampong, "Kintampo Butchers," *Daily Graphic*, January 20, 1975; Ghana News Agency, "Size of Bread Still the Same in B.A.," *Ghanaian Times*, September 20, 1976; Emmanuel K. Addae-Duah, "Newspapers," *Ghanaian Times*, September 22, 1976; Alex I. Yamba, Amatin, to regional commissioner, October 24, 1977, BRG 1/1/52, PRAAD-S.

37. Tro-tros were trucks customized locally for carrying either passengers or goods. "2 Drivers, Overseers 'Hot,'" *Daily Graphic*, March 3, 1977.

38. "Profiteering, Trader Gets 6 Months," *Daily Graphic*, May 13, 1975.

39. "Patriotic Citizen," Wenchi, to regional commissioner, "The Main Source of Profiteering at Wenchi," January 26, 1976, BRG 1/1/52, PRAAD-S.

40. Joseph Brown, Atebubu, to regional commissioner, "The Enemies of the Revolution," February 3, 1976, BRG 1/1/52, PRAAD-S.

41. Docas Boateng, Japekrom, to regional commissioner, "Smuggling: Ghana and Ivory Coast Border," ca. 1972, BRG 1/4/7, PRAAD-S.

42. Nana Anwasi Agyemang (aka Joseph Kwasi Onwonah), interview with the author, Sunyani, July 14, 2007.

43. Salamatu Idrisu Samu, interview with the author, Wenchi, July 1, 2010.

44. Nana Opare Ameyaw, interview with the author, Kyeraa, July 20, 2007.

45. Oduroh interview, July 19, 2007.

46. Nugent, *Smugglers, Secessionists, and Loyal Citizens*, 246.

47. Alhaji Abdul Momin Musah, interview with the author, Wenchi, June 27, 2010.

48. Samu interview.

49. Ameyaw interview.

50. J. K. Davies, commanding officer, Third Battalion, to Brong-Ahafo Regional Administration Office, Sunyani, "Operation Bring Out," January 9, 1973, BRG 1/1/52, PRAAD-S.

51. Ameyaw interview.

52. Mikell, *Cocoa and Chaos*, 202.

53. Agyemang interview, July 14, 2007.

54. Ameyaw interview.

55. Agyemang interview, July 14, 2007.

56. Ibid.

57. Samu interview.

58. Musah interview.

59. S. Frafra, Adjaponkrom, to regional commissioner, Sunyani, March 15, 1973, BRG 1/1/52, PRAAD-S.

60. Peter K. Opuku, Wenchi, to regional commissioner, Sunyani, September 23, 1975, BRG 1/1/52, PRAAD-S.

61. Yao Sarfo, Nkoranza, to regional commissioner, Sunyani, BRG 1/1/52, PRAAD-S.

62. Kwame Armah to regional commissioner, Sunyani, and district administrative office, Wenchi, July 29, 1973, BRG 1/1/52, PRAAD-S.

63. District office, Wenchi, to regional office, Sunyani, September 14, 1973, BRG 1/1/52, PRAAD-S.

64. George Yaw Twi, Kyeraa, to regional office, Sunyani, September 5, 1975, BRG 1/1/52, PRAAD-S.

65. Stephanie Newell, *The Power to Name: A History of Anonymity in Colonial West Africa* (Athens: Ohio University Press, 2013).

66. Mallam Alhassan Siddi, Yeji, to regional commissioner, Sunyani, February 23, 1973, BRG 1/1/52, PRAAD-S.

67. Mikell, *Cocoa and Chaos*, 202.

68. Agyemang interview, July 14, 2007.

69. Nana Anwasi Agyemang (aka Joseph Kwasi Onwonah), interview with the author, Sunyani, October 12, 2007.

70. Oduroh interview.

71. Ameyaw interview.

72. Agyemang interview, July 14, 2007.

73. During the 1950s, price inspectors were government civil servants attached to the Ministry of Commerce and Industry in Accra who made regularly scheduled visits; the inspectors were assisted by local police once they arrived in a city. Controller of prices, Department of Commerce, Accra, to commanding police officer, Sunyani, November 28, 1952, and June 1, 1953, BRG 1/1/52, PRAAD-S.

74. Regional commissioner's notes on receiving and processing price inspector applications, January 6, 1968, BRG 1/1/52, PRAAD-S.

75. "Power to the People—War against Profiteers," *Daily Graphic*, October 29, 1977.

76. Application from Charles Owusu Boateng, Wenchi, November 1, 1977, BRG 1/1/52, PRAAD-S.

77. Application from E. M. Kuma-Amoako, Kwame-Danso, October 12, 1977, BRG 1/1/52, PRAAD-S.

78. Application from Kwaku Agyare, E. K. Asante, K. A. Acheampong, and A. Owusu Tabiri, Kintampo, December 24, 1977, BRG 1/1/52, PRAAD-S.

79. Application from Addai Ampoma Cosmos, September 7, 1977, BRG 1/1/52, PRAAD-S.

80. Application from Joseph Domoah, Yeji, November 16, 1977, BRG 1/1/52, PRAAD-S.

81. Application from Kwabena Marmo, Yeji, December 23, 1977, BRG 1/1/52, PRAAD-S.

82. Application from P&T Employees Credit Union, Sunyani, November 9, 1977, BRG 1/1/52, PRAAD-S.

83. Yaw Barimah to regional commissioner, Sunyani, "We Are Suffering," January 28, 1976, BRG 1/1/52, PRAAD-S.

84. Joseph Brown, Atebubu, to regional commissioner, "The Enemies of the Revolution," February 3, 1976, BRG 1/1/52, PRAAD-S.

85. Application from Wilson Owusu Badu, Bomaa, September 7, 1977, BRG 1/1/52, PRAAD-S; application from Y. S. Nkrumah, Nsoatre, September 22, 1977, BRG 1/1/52, PRAAD-S.

86. Application from W. A. Kusi, Ayomso, via Goaso, October 31, 1977, BRG 1/1/52, PRAAD-S.

87. Regional commissioner's summary, Sunyani, January 6, 1978, BRG 1/1/52, PRAAD-S.

AFTERWORD: FROM STRUCTURAL ADJUSTMENT TO SHOPPING MALLS

1. Kevin Shillington, *Ghana and the Rawlings Factor* (New York: St. Martin's, 1992), 48.

2. Claire Robertson, "The Death of Makola and Other Tragedies," *Canadian Journal of African Studies* 17, no. 3 (1989): 469. See also Gracia Clark, *"Onions Are My Husband": Survival and Accumulation by West African Market Women* (Chicago: University of Chicago Press, 1994), 390–95; Takyiwaa Manuh, "Women, the State and Society under the PNDC," in *Ghana under PNDC Rule*, ed. E. Gyimah-Boadi (Dakar, Senegal: CODESRIA, 1993): 176–94.

3. Events took place as follows: first Rawlings coup (Armed Forces Revolutionary Council), June 4, 1979; return to civilian government under Hilla Limann, September 24, 1979; second Rawlings coup (PNDC), December 31, 1981.

4. Jeffrey Herbst, The Politics of Reform in Ghana, 1981–1991 (Berkeley: University of California Press, 1993), 26.

5. Deborah Pellow and Naomi Chazan, *Ghana: Coping with Uncertainty* (Boulder, CO: Westview, 1986), 168.

6. Shillington, *Ghana and the Rawlings Factor*, 112.

7. Kwamina Panford, *IMF–World Bank and Labor's Burdens in Africa: Ghana's Experience* (Westport, CT: Praeger, 2001), 10.

8. George J. S. Dei, "Coping with the Effects of the 1982–83 Drought in Ghana: The View from the Village," *Africa Development* 13, no. 1 (1988): 107–22.

9. Lynne Brydon, "Ghanaian Responses to the Nigerian Expulsions of 1983," *African Affairs* 84 (1985): 561–86.

10. Shillington, *Ghana and the Rawlings Factor*, 110–111.

11. In November 1983, the PNDC convened a donors' conference in Paris and received pledges of some US$750 million to support its plan to revamp the country's shattered infrastructure and to pay for the importation of raw materials necessary to revitalize the industry. Pellow and Chazan, *Ghana: Coping with Uncertainty*, 83.

12. Yakubu Azindow, "Beyond Promises: Politics, Institutions and Neoliberal Reforms in Four African Countries," PhD diss., University of Massachusetts–Amherst, 2011.

13. Some important works in the literature are Lynne Brydon and Karen Legge, *Adjusting Society: The World Bank, the IMF and Ghana* (London: Tauris, 1996);

Gracia Clark and Takyiwaa Manuh, "Women Traders in Ghana and the Structural Adjustment Program," in *Structural Adjustment and African Women Farmers*, ed. Christina H. Gladwin (Gainesville: University of Florida Press, 1991), 217–36; Ernest Aryeetey, Jane Harrigan, and Machiko Nissanke, eds., *Economic Reforms in Ghana: The Miracle and the Mirage* (Trenton, NJ: Africa World Press, 2000); and Kwadwo Konadu-Agyemang, ed. *IMF and World Bank Sponsored Structural Adjustment Programs in Africa: Ghana's Experience, 1983–1999* (Aldershot, England: Ashgate, 2001).

14. Eboe Hutchful, *The IMF and Ghana: The Confidential Record* (London: Zed, 1987); John Williamson, ed. *IMF Conditionality* (Washington, DC: Institute for International Economics, 1983).

15. Lynne Brydon, "'With a Little Bit of Luck . . .': Coping with Adjustment in Urban Ghana, 1975–90," *Africa* 69, no. 3 (1999): 366–85.

16. Even Nkrumah and the CPP entered into negotiations in their last years. From 1983 to the late 1990s, Ghana was acknowledged in the donor community as one of the "successfully adjusted" nations. Panford, *IMF–World Bank and Labor's Burdens*, 52.

17. I am inspired here by Brenda Chalfin's brilliant work on neoliberalism in Ghana. Brenda Chalfin, *Neoliberal Frontiers: An Ethnography of Sovereignty in West Africa* (Chicago: University of Chicago Press, 2010), 48.

18. Pellow and Chazan, *Ghana: Coping with Uncertainty*, 174.

19. Although Accra Mall's official inauguration was not until July 2008, some mall businesses opened as early as May 2007. The mall houses two large South African chain stores (Shoprite and Game), restaurants, a nightclub, a movie theater, and sixty-five retail shops.

20. Accra Mall website, "About the Mall: History of the Mall," accessed October 15, 2008, http://www.accramall.com/about_mall.htm.

21. Deborah Hobden, "'A Man, a Plan, a Mall': The Role of Globalizing Elites in the Development of Accra, Ghana," *global-e: A Global Studies Journal* 8, no. 7 (2014), http://globalstudiesconsortium.org/global-e/4c10b5197315 86d5bfd6365bbb528dff.

22. Inauguration speech by Joseph Owusu-Akyaw, initiating partner of Accra Mall Development, July 8, 2008, accessed November 18, 2008, http://www.accramall.com/latestnews.php?id=6.

23. Akosua Keseboa Darkwah, "Going Global: Ghanaian Female Transnational Traders in an Era of Globalization," PhD diss., University of Wisconsin, 2002, 22.

24. "Shoprite Opens in Accra Mall! Tetteh Quarshie Roundabout, Grand Opening November 1, 2007" (Shoprite weekly sales circular), November 2007, author's personal collection.

25. Current research on the Accra Mall is engaging some of these exact questions. See, for example, Deborah Hobden, "'Your Mall with It All': Luxury Development in a Globalizing African City," *Perspectives on Global Development and Technology* 13, nos. 1–2 (2014): 129–47.

Bibliography

ARCHIVES CONSULTED

Basel Mission Archives, Basel
Institute of Statistical, Social, and Economic Research, University of Ghana, Legon
Public Records and Archives Administration Department, Accra
Public Records and Archives Administration Department, Cape Coast
Public Records and Archives Administration Department, Sunyani
Rhodes House Library, Oxford
National Archives, Kew
UAC Ghana Ltd., Accra
Unilever Archives and Records Management, Port Sunlight

NEWSPAPERS AND MAGAZINES

African Mail
Ashanti Pioneer
Business Weekly
Daily Graphic
Evening News
Financial Times
Ghana Business Guide
Ghana Evening News
Ghana Times
Ghana Trade Journal
The Ghanaian
Ghanaian Times
Gold Coast Independent
Gold Coast Leader
Gold Coast UAC News
Guinea Times
Men's Wear Organiser
New Commonwealth
New York Times
Old Coasters Magazine
Progress

Star
Sunday Mirror
Time
Unicorn
West African Review

INTERVIEWS

All interviews were digitally recorded, except those that are marked with an asterisk, and were conducted in English, Twi, or Hausa. During interviews in Twi and Hausa, I was supported by a research assistant who helped in translating and later in transcribing interview texts.

Addai, Esther. Accra, June 21, 2007.
Agyemang, Nana Anwasi (aka Joseph Kwasi Onwonah). Sunyani, July 14, 2007.
———. Sunyani, October 12, 2007.
Allotey, Jutus Nii Kpakpo. Accra, June 8, 2007.
———. Accra, June 13, 2007
Ameyaw, Nana Opare. Kyeraa, July 20, 2007. With the assistance of Benjamin Buadu Codjoe.
Ankumah, Michael N. Accra, September 4, 2007.
Annan, Isaac Kofi. Cape Coast, June 3, 2010.
Asare, Akosua. Accra, May 25, 2007.*
Atiemo, Samuel O., Jr. Accra, June 28, 2007.
Attoh, G. A. Accra, June 8, 2010.
Boye, Beauty. Accra, November 21, 2007.*
Brown, Anthony. Tema, July 4, 2007.
Butler, Janet. Accra, May 22, 2007.
Cato, Kwesi Akumenya. Accra, September 13, 2007.
———. Accra, November 7, 2007.
Dankwa, Edward Akurang. Accra, March 5, 2007.*
———. Accra, March 13, 2007.*
———. Accra, November 8, 2007.
Enninful, J. F. Cape Coast, June 2, 2010.
Gyamfi. Sunyani, July 14, 2007.
Hammond, Kojo Sakyi. Cape Coast, June 1, 2010.
Idun, Emmanuel. Accra, June 6, 2007.*
———. Accra, June 26, 2007.
Krofah, W. A. Accra, March 26, 2007.
———. Accra, July 9, 2007.
Kwa Kwa, Agnes. Cape Coast, June 1, 2010. With the assistance of Kobina Dodoo.
Kwakye, George Darkwa. Suhum, April 20, 2007.*
———. Suhum, June 7, 2007.*
Mensah, E. B. Accra, July 7, 2007.
Mensah, Rebecca. Kumasi, July 3, 2010.
Musah, Alhaji Abdul Momin. Wenchi, June 27, 2010.
Musah, Sadiku. Accra, March 20, 2007.

———. Accra, April 7, 2007.*
Oduroh, S. G. Sunyani, July 19, 2007.*
———. Sunyani, October 11, 2007.*
Osbourne, Kofi. Sunyani. May 30, 2007.*
Osei, A. K. Sunyani, July 16, 2007.
Oworae, Nana. Kyeraa, July 20, 2007. With the assistance of Benjamin Buadu Codjoe.
Quansah, William. Cape Coast, June 1, 2010.
Quartey, Deborah. Tema, June 19, 2007.
———. Tema, July 5, 2007.
Samu, Salamatu Idrisu. Wenchi, July 1, 2010. With the assistance of Mustapha Gbande.
Van der Staaij-Ghartey, Alice. Accra, November 5, 2007.

PUBLISHED SOURCES

Abraham, Willie A. *Report of the Commission of Enquiry into Trade Malpractices in Ghana*. Accra: State Publishing Corporation, 1965.

Acquah, Ione. *Accra Survey: A Social Survey of the Capital of Ghana, Formerly Called the Gold Coast, Undertaken for the West African Institute of Social and Economic Research, 1953–1956*. London: University of London Press, 1958.

Addae, Gloria. "The Retailing of Imported Textiles in the Accra Market." In *Proceedings of the West African Institute of Social and Economic Research Conference, March 1954*, 51–56. Ibadan: Ibadan University Press, 1956.

Adshead, P. W. *Report of the Commission of Enquiry into Conditional Sales*. Lagos: Government Printer, 1948.

Afrifa, Colonel A. A. *The Ghana Coup: 24th February 1966*. London: Cass, 1967.

Ahlman, Jeffrey S. *Living with Nkrumahism: Nation, State, and Pan-Africanism in Ghana*. Athens: Ohio University Press, 2017.

———. "A New Type of Citizen: Youth, Gender, and Generation in the Ghanaian Builder's Brigade." *Journal of African History* 53, no. 1 (2012): 87–105.

Ali, Zakariah. *Walk with the Devil: My Endless Struggle against the Cunning and Traps of the Devil*. Bloomington, IN: Xlibris, 2012.

Akonor, Kwame. *Africa and IMF Conditionality: The Unevenness of Compliance, 1983–2000*. New York: Routledge, 2006.

Akyeampong, Emmanuel. *Drink, Power, and Cultural Change: A Social History of Alcohol in Ghana, c. 1800 to Recent Times*. Portsmouth, NH: Heinemann, 1996.

———. "Memories of Place and Belonging: Identity, Citizenship, and the Lebanese in Ghana." *Ghana Studies* 7 (2004): 25–42.

———. "Race, Identity, and Citizenship in Black Africa: The Case of the Lebanese in Ghana." *Africa* 76, no. 3 (2006): 297–323.

———. "Sexuality and Prostitution among the Akan of the Gold Coast c. 1650–1950." *Past and Present* 156 (1997): 144–73.

———. "'Wope tam won pe ba' ('You like cloth but you don't want children'): Urbanization, Individualism and Gender Relations in Colonial Ghana, c. 1900–39." In *Africa's Urban Past*, edited by David M. Anderson and Richard Rathbone, 222–34. Oxford: Currey, 1999.

Allman, Jean, and Victoria Tashjian. *"I Will Not Eat Stone": A Women's History of Colonial Asante*. Portsmouth, NH: Heinemann, 2000.

Allman, Jean, Susan Geiger, and Nakanyike Musisi, eds. *Women in African Colonial Histories*. Bloomington: Indiana University Press, 2002.

Allman, Jean Marie. *Quills of the Porcupine: Asante Nationalism in an Emergent Ghana*. Madison: University of Wisconsin Press, 1993.

———. "Rounding Up Spinsters: Gender Chaos and Unmarried Women in Colonial Asante." *Journal of African History* 37, no. 2 (1996): 195–214.

Alpern, Stanley B. "What Africans Got for Their Slaves: A Master List of European Trade Goods." *History in Africa* 22 (1995): 5–43.

Amoah-Boampong, Cyrelene. "Defying Merchant Capital in the Gold Coast." *History in Action* 4, no. 1 (2014): 1–9.

Ansa-Asare, K. "Legislative History of the Legal Regime of Price Control in Ghana." *Journal of African Law* 29 (1985): 103–17.

Apter, Andrew. *The Pan-African Nation: Oil and the Spectacle of Culture in Nigeria*. Chicago: University of Chicago Press, 2005.

Arhin, Kwame. *West African Traders in Ghana in the Nineteenth and Twentieth Centuries*. London: Longman, 1979.

Arson, Andrew. *Interlopers of Empire: The Lebanese Diaspora in Colonial French West Africa*. Oxford: Oxford University Press, 2014.

Aryeetey, Ernest, Jane Harrigan, and Machiko Nissanke, eds. *Economic Reforms in Ghana: The Miracle and the Mirage*. Trenton, NJ: Africa World Press, 2000.

Asante, K. B. "Nkrumah and State Enterprises." In *The Life and Works of Kwame Nkrumah: Papers of a Symposium Organised by the Institute of African Studies University of Ghana*, edited by Kwame Arhin, 251–71. Trenton, NJ: Africa World Press, 1993.

Asante, Kofi Takyi. "Collusion, Collaboration (Cooperation) and Conflict: How African Merchants Shaped the Formation of the Colonial State in the Gold Coast, 1850–1950." Paper presented at the *3rd Annual Symposium of Graduate Students in African Studies*, Bloomington, Indiana University, March 2013.

———. "Purchased Allies or 'Thorns in the Side of the Government'? African Merchants and Colonial State Formation in the Nineteenth Century Gold Coast." PhD diss., Northwestern University, 2016.

Austin, Dennis. *Politics in Ghana, 1946–1960*. Oxford: Oxford University Press, 1964.

Austin, Dennis, and Robin Luckham. *Politics and Soldiers in Ghana, 1966–1975*. London: Cass, 1964.

Austin, Gareth. "Capitalists and Chiefs in the Cocoa Hold-Ups in South Asante, 1927–1939." *International Journal of African Historical Studies* 21, no. 1 (1988): 63–95.

———. "Indigenous Credit Institutions in West Africa, c. 1750–c. 1960." In *Local Suppliers of Credit in the Third World, 1750–1960*, edited by Gareth Austin and Kaoru Sugihara, 117–30. Basingstoke, England: Palgrave Macmillan, 1993.

———. *Labour, Land, and Capital in Ghana: From Slavery to Free Labour in Asante, 1807–1956*. Rochester, NY: University of Rochester Press, 2005.

Azindow, Yakubu. "Beyond Promises: Politics, Institutions and Neoliberal Reforms in Four African Countries." PhD diss., University of Massachusetts–Amherst, 2011.

Azu, Diana Gladys. *The Ga Family and Social Change*. Leiden: Africa-Studiecentrum, 1974.

Bailkin, Jordanna. *The Afterlife of Empire*. Berkeley: University of California Press, 2012.

Ballantyne, Tony, and Antoinette Burton. *Moving Subjects: Gender, Mobility, and Intimacy in the Age of Global Empire*. Champaign: University of Illinois Press, 2009.

Bauer, P. T. A *Study of Competition, Oligopoly and Monopoly in a Changing Economy*. Cambridge: Cambridge University Press, 1954.
Bay, Mia, and Anne Fabian, eds. *Race and Retail Consumption across the Color Line*. New Brunswick, NJ: Rutgers University Press, 2015.
Beckman, Ericka. *Capital Fictions: The Literature of Latin America's Export Age*. Minneapolis: University of Minnesota Press, 2012.
Bennett, Valerie Plave. "Epilogue: Malcontents in Uniform—The 1972 Coup d'Etat." In *Politicians and Soldiers in Ghana, 1966–1972*, edited by Dennis Austin and Robin Luckham, 300–313. London: Cass, 1975.
Benson, Susan Porter. *Counter Cultures: Saleswomen, Managers, and Customers in American Department Stores, 1890–1940*. Champaign: University of Illinois Press, 1986.
Berry, Sara S. *No Condition Is Permanent: The Social Dynamics of Agrarianism Change in Sub-Saharan Africa*. Madison: University of Wisconsin Press, 1993.
Bhabha, Homi K. "Of Mimicry and Man: The Ambivalence of Colonial Discourse." In *The Location of Culture*, 85–92. New York: Routledge, 1994.
Birmingham, Walter, I. Neustadt, and E. N. Omaboe, eds. *A Study of Contemporary Ghana*. Vol. 1, *The Economy of Ghana*. London: Allen and Unwin, 1966.
Boahen, A. Adu. *African Perspectives on Colonialism*. Baltimore: Johns Hopkins University Press, 1987.
Bose, Purnima. *Organizing Empire: Individualism, Collective Agency, and India*. Durham, NC: Duke University Press, 2003.
Bose, Purnima, and Laura E. Lyons, eds. *Cultural Critique and the Global Corporation*. Bloomington: Indiana University Press, 2010
Breen, T. H. *The Marketplace of Revolution: How Consumer Politics Shaped American Independence*. Oxford: Oxford University Press, 2004.
Brong-Ahafo Regional Administration. *This Is Brong-Ahafo: Rural Development in Action*. Sunyani: Brong-Ahafo Regional Administration, 1971.
Brown, Carolyn A. "A 'Man' in the Village Is a 'Boy' in the Workplace: Colonial Racism, Worker Militance, and Igbo Notions of Masculinity in the Nigerian Coal Industry, 1930–1945." In *Men and Masculinities in Modern Africa*, edited by Lisa Lindsay and Stephan F. Miescher, 156–74. Portsmouth, NH: Heinemann, 2003.
Brydon, Lynne. "Ghanaian Responses to the Nigerian Expulsions of 1983." *African Affairs* 84 (1985): 561–86.
———. "'With a Little Bit of Luck . . .': Coping with Adjustment in Urban Ghana, 1975–90." *Africa* 69, no. 3 (1999): 366–85.
Brydon, Lynne, and Karen Legge. *Adjusting Society: The World Bank, the IMF and Ghana*. London: Tauris, 1996.
Burke, Timothy. "Fork Up a Smile: Marketing, Colonial Knowledge and the Female Subject in Zimbabwe." *Gender and History* 8, no. 3 (1996): 440–56.
———. *Lifebuoy Men, Lux Women: Commodification, Consumption, and Cleanliness in Modern Zimbabwe*. Durham, NC: Duke University Press, 1996.
Burton, Antoinette. "Introduction: Archive Fever, Archive Stories." In *Archive Stories: Facts, Fiction, and the Writing of History*, edited by Antoinette Burton, 1–24. Durham, NC: Duke University Press, 2006.
Buser, Hans. *In Ghana at Independence: Stories of a Swiss Salesman*. Basel: Basler Afrika Bibliographien, 2010.
Chalfin, Brenda. "Cars, the Customs Service, and Sumptuary Rule in Neoliberal Ghana." *Society for Comparative Studies in Society and History* 50 (2008): 424–53.

——. *Neoliberal Frontiers: An Ethnography of Sovereignty in West Africa*. Chicago: University of Chicago Press, 2010.
——. *Shea Butter Republic: State Power, Global Markets, and the Making of an Indigenous Commodity*. New York: Routledge, 2004.
Chazan, Naomi. *An Anatomy of Ghanaian Politics: Managing Political Recession, 1969–1982*. Boulder, CO: Westview, 1983.
Chuku, Gloria Ifeoma. "From Petty Traders to International Merchants: A Historical Account of Three Igbo Women of Nigeria in Trade and Commerce, 1886 to 1970." *African Economic History* 27 (1999): 1–22.
——. "Nzimiro, Mary (1898–1993)." In *Women in World History*, vol. 7, edited by Deborah Klezmer, 916–19. Waterford, CT: Yorkin, 2000.
Clark, Gracia. *Onions Are My Husband: Survival and Accumulation by West African Market Women*. Chicago: University of Chicago Press, 1994.
Clark, Gracia, and Takyiwaa Manuh. "Women Traders in Ghana and the Structural Adjustment Program." In *Structural Adjustment and African Women Farmers*, edited by Christina H. Gladwin, 217–36. Gainesville: University Press of Florida, 1991.
Cohen, Lizabeth. *A Consumer's Republic: The Politics of Mass Consumption in Postwar America*. New York: Vintage, 2004.
Cole, Catherine. *Ghana's Concert Party Theatre*. Bloomington: Indiana University Press, 2001.
Comaroff, Jean, and John Comaroff, eds. *Modernity and Its Malcontents: Ritual and Power in Postcolonial Africa*. Chicago: University of Chicago Press, 1993.
——. *Of Revelation and Revolution: Christianity, Colonialism and Consciousness in South Africa*, vol. 1. Chicago: University of Chicago Press, 1991.
——. *Theory from the South: Or How Euro-America Is Evolving toward Africa*. Boulder, CO: Paradigm, 2012.
Connell, R. W. "Masculinities, Change, and Conflict in Global Society: Thinking about the Future of Men's Studies." *Journal of Men's Studies* 11, no. 3 (2003): 249–66.
Constantine, Stephan. "'Bringing the Empire Alive': The Empire Marketing Board and Imperial Propaganda, 1926–1933." In *Imperialism and Popular Culture*, edited by John M. Mackenzie, 192–231. Manchester, England: Manchester University Press, 1986.
Conway, W. E. *Report of the Commission of Enquiry into the Distribution and Prices of Essential Imported Goods*. Accra: Government Printing Department, 1943.
Cooper, Frederick. "Africa and the World Economy." *African Studies Review* 24, no 2/3 (1981): 1–86.
——. *Africa in the World: Capitalism, Empire, Nation-State*. Cambridge, MA: Harvard University Press, 2014.
——. *Decolonization and African Society: The Labor Question in French and British Africa*. Cambridge: Cambridge University Press, 1996.
——. "What Is the Concept of Globalization Good For? An African Historian's Perspective." *African Affairs* 100, no. 399 (2001): 189–213.
Coquery-Vidrovitch, Catherine. *African Women: A Modern History*. Translated by Beth Gillian Raps. Boulder, CO: Westview, 1997.
——. "L'Impact des Interests Coloniaux: S. C. O. A. et C. F. A. O. dans l'Ouest Africain, 1910–1965." *Journal of African History* 16, no. 4 (1975): 595–621.
Crisp, Jeff. *The Story of an African Working Class: Ghanaian Miners' Struggles, 1870–1980*. London: Zed, 1984.

Curtin, P. D. "'The White Man's Grave': Image and Reality, 1780–1850." *Journal of British Studies* 1, no. 1 (1961): 94–110.
Daaku, Kwame. *Trade and Politics on the Gold Coast, 1600–1720: A Study of the African Reaction to European Trade.* London: Clarendon, 1970.
Darkwah, Akosua Keseboa. "Going Global: Ghanaian Female Transnational Traders in an Era of Globalization." PhD diss., University of Wisconsin, 2002.
Date-Bah, Eugenia. "Male and Female Factory Workers in Accra." In *Female and Male in West Africa*, edited by Christine Oppong, 266–74. London: Allen and Unwin, 1983.
Decker, Stephanie. "Building Up Goodwill: British Business, Development, and Economic Nationalism." PhD diss., University of Liverpool, 2006.
———. "Corporate Legitimacy and Advertising: British Companies and the Rhetoric of Development in West Africa, 1950–1970." *Business History Review* 81 (2007): 59–86.
———. "Postcolonial Transitions in Africa: Decolonization in West Africa and Present Day South Africa." *Journal of Management Studies* 47, no. 5 (2010): 791–813.
De Grazia, Victoria. *Irresistible Empire: America's Advance through Twentieth-Century Europe.* Cambridge, MA: Belknap, 2005.
Dei, George J. S. "Coping with the Effects of the 1982–83 Drought in Ghana: The View from the Village." *Africa Development* 13, no. 1 (1988): 107–22.
Denzer, LaRay. *Women in Government Service in Colonial Nigeria, 1862–1945.* Working Papers in African Studies 136. Boston: Boston University African Studies Center, 1989.
Deutsch, Jan-Georg. *Educating the Middlemen: A Political and Economic History of Statutory Cocoa Marketing in Nigeria, 1936–1946.* Berlin: Das Arabische Buch, 1995.
Dickson, Kwamina B. *A Historical Geography of Ghana.* Cambridge: Cambridge University Press, 1971.
Dike, Kenneth Onwuka. "The Liverpool "Sect' and British West African Policy." *African Affairs* 70, no. 281 (1971): 349–64.
———. *Trade and Politics in the Niger Delta, 1830–1885: An Introduction to the Economic and Political History of Nigeria.* Oxford: Clarendon, 1956.
Dinan, Carmel. "Sugar Daddies and Gold-Diggers: The White Collar Single Women in Accra." In *Female and Male in West Africa*, edited by Christine Oppong, 344–66. London: Allen and Unwin, 1983.
Donkor, David Afriyie. *Spiders of the Market: Ghanaian Trickster Performance in a Web of Neoliberalism.* Bloomington: Indiana University Press, 2016.
Dove, Mabel. *Selected Writings of a Pioneer West African Feminist.* Edited by Stephanie Newell and Audrey Gadzekpo. Nottingham, England: Trent, 2004.
Dowse, Robert. "Military and Police Rule." In *Politicians and Soldiers in Ghana, 1966–1972*, edited by Dennis Austin and Robin Luckham, 16–36. London: Cass, 1975.
Dumett, Raymond E. "African Merchants of the Gold Coast, 1860–1905: Dynamics of Indigenous Entrepreneurship." *Comparative Studies in Society and History* 25, no. 4 (1983): 661–93.
———. *El Dorado in West Africa: The Gold-Mining Frontier, African Labor, and Colonial Capitalism, 1875–1900.* Athens: Ohio University Press, 1998.
———. "John Sarbah, the Elder, and African Entrepreneurship in the Gold Coast in the Late Nineteenth Century." *Journal of African History* 14, no. 4 (1973): 653–79.

Dunn, John, and A. F. Robertson. *Dependence and Opportunity: Political Change in Ahafo*. Cambridge: Cambridge University Press, 1973.

Eckert, Andreas. "Cultural Commuters: African Employees in Late Colonial Period Tanzania." In *Intermediaries, Interpreters, and Clerks: African Employees and the Making of Colonial Africa*, edited by Benjamin N. Lawrance, Emily Lynn Osborn, and Richard L. Roberts, 248–69. Madison: University of Wisconsin Press, 2006.

Ekejiuba, Felicia I. "Omu Okwei, the Merchant Queen of Ossamari: A Biographical Sketch." *Journal of the Historical Society of Nigeria* 3, no. 4 (1967): 633–46.

Esseks, John D. "Government and Indigenous Private Enterprise in Ghana." *Journal of Modern African Studies* 9 (1971): 11–29.

Ewusi, Kodwo. *The Determinants of Price Fluctuations in Ghana*. Discussion Papers 2. Legon: Institute of Statistical, Social, and Economic Research, University of Ghana, 1977.

Ferguson, James. *The Anti-Politics Machine: "Development," Depoliticization, and Bureaucratic Power in Lesotho*. London: Oxford University Press, 1994.

——. *Global Shadows: Africa in the Neoliberal World Order*. Durham, NC: Duke University Press, 2006.

Fieldhouse, D. K. *Merchant Capital and Economic Decolonization: The United Africa Company 1929–1994*. Oxford: Clarendon, 1994.

Foster, Phillip. *Education and Social Change in Ghana*. Chicago: University of Chicago Press, 1965.

Fox, Richard Wightman, and T. J. Jackson Lears, eds., *The Culture of Consumption: Critical Essays in American History 1880–1980*. New York: Pantheon, 1983.

Freeman, Carla. "Is Local: Global as Feminine: Masculine? Rethinking the Gender of Globalization." *Signs* 26, no. 4 (2001): 1007–37.

Friedman, Walter A. *Birth of a Salesman: The Transformation of Selling in America*. Cambridge, MA: Harvard University Press, 2004.

Frimpong-Ansah, Jonathan. *The Vampire State in Africa: The Political Economy of Decline*. Trenton, NJ: Africa World Press, 1992.

Gannon, Margaret. "The Basle Mission Trading Company and British Colonial Policy in the Gold Coast, 1918–1928." *Journal of African History* 24, no. 4 (1983): 503–15.

Garlick, Peter C. "The Development of Kwahu Business Enterprise in Ghana since 1874—An Essay in Recent Oral Tradition." *Journal of African History* 8, no. 3 (1967): 463–80.

——. *The Ghanaian Entrepreneur: Studies in Trading in Ghana*. Accra: University of Ghana, 1962.

Geschiere, Peter. *The Modernity of Witchcraft: Politics and the Occult in Postcolonial Africa*. Charlottesville: University of Virginia Press, 1997.

Ghana Central Bureau of Statistics. *Ghana Statistical Yearbook*. Accra: Central Bureau of Statistics, 1973.

——. 1960 *Population Census of Ghana*. Vol. 2, *Demographic Characteristics*. Accra: Central Bureau of Statistics, 1964.

——. *Statistical Handbook of the Republic of Ghana*. Accra: Central Bureau of Statistics, 1970.

Ghana Ministry of Commerce and Industry. *Handbook of Commerce and Industry*. Accra: Ghana Ministry of Commerce and Industry, 1967.

Ghana National Redemption Council. *National Redemption Council Decrees*. Accra: State Publishing Corporation, 1972.

Gold Coast Government. *Blue Book for 1914*. Accra: Government Printer, 1915.
———. *The Gold Coast Handbook*. London: Baylis, 1937.
Grier, Beverly. "Pawns, Porters, and Petty Traders: Women in the Transition to Cash Crop Agriculture." *Signs* 17, no. 2 (1992): 304–28.
Guyer, Jane. *Money Matters: Instability, Values, and Social Payments in the Modern History of West African Communities*. Portsmouth, NH: Heinemann, 1995.
———. "Wealth in People, Wealth in Things—Introduction." *Journal of African History* 36, no. 1 (1995): 83–90.
Gyimah-Boadi, E., and Richard Jefferies. "The Political Economy of Reform." In *Economic Reforms in Ghana: The Miracle and The Mirage*, edited by Ernest Aryeetey, Jane Harrigan, and Machiko Nissanke. Trenton, NJ: Africa World Press, 2000.
Hansen, Karen Tranberg, ed. *African Encounters with Domesticity: Women in African Colonial Histories*. New Brunswick, NJ: Rutgers University Press, 1992.
Harneit-Sievers, Axel. "African Business, 'Economic Nationalism,' and British Colonial Policy: Southern Nigeria, 1935–1954." *African Economic History* 23 (1995): 70–128.
Harries, Patrick. *Work, Culture, and Identity: Migrant Laborers in Mozambique and South Africa, c. 1860–1910*. Portsmouth, NH: Heinemann, 1994.
Hart, Jennifer A. *Ghana on the Go: African Mobility in the Age of Motor Transportation*. Bloomington: Indiana University Press, 2015.
———. "*Nife Nifa*: Technopolitics, Regionalism, and Authoritarianism in Acheampong's Ghana." Paper presented at the Annual Meeting of the African Studies Association, Indianapolis, November 20–23, 2014.
———. "'One Man, No Chop': Licit Wealth, Good Citizens, and the Criminalization of Drivers in Postcolonial Ghana." *International Journal of African Historical Studies* 46, no. 3 (2013): 373–96.
———. "'Suffer to Gain': Citizenship, Accumulation, and Motor Transportation in Late-Colonial and Postcolonial Ghana." PhD diss., Indiana University, 2011.
Hasty, Jennifer. *The Press and Political Culture in Ghana*. Bloomington: Indiana University Press, 2005.
Heaton, Matthew. *Black Skin, White Coats: Nigerian Psychiatrists, Decolonization, and the Globalization of Psychiatry*. Athens: Ohio University Press, 2013.
Herbst, Jeffrey. *The Politics of Reform in Ghana, 1981–1991*. Berkeley: University of California Press, 1993.
Hess, Janet. "Imagining Architecture: The Structure of Nationalism in Accra, Ghana." *Africa Today* 47, no. 2 (2000): 35–58.
Hill, Polly. *The Migrant Cocoa-Farmers of Southern Ghana: A Study in Rural Capitalism*. Cambridge: Cambridge University Press, 1963.
Hobden, Deborah. "'A Man, A Plan, A Mall': The Role of Globalizing Elites in the Development of Accra, Ghana." *global-e: A Global Studies Journal* 8, no. 7 (2014).
———. "'Your Mall with It All': Luxury Development in a Globalizing African City." *Perspectives on Global Development and Technology* 13, nos. 1–2 (2014): 129–47.
Hodgson, Dorothy L., and Sheryl A. McCurdy, eds. *"Wicked" Women and the Reconfiguration of Gender in Africa*. Portsmouth, NH: Heinemann, 2001.
Hopkins, A. G. "African Economic History: The First Twenty-Five Years." *Journal of African History* 30, no. 1 (1989): 157–63.
———. "Economic Aspects of Political Movements in Nigeria and the Gold Coast, 1918–1939." *Journal of African History* 7, no. 1 (1966): 133–52.
———. *An Economic History of West Africa*. London: Longman, 1973.

Howard, Rhoda. *Colonialism and Underdevelopment in Ghana.* New York: Africana, 1978.

Hugon, Anne. "Korle Bu and the Midwives Hostel as a Site of Memory for Ghanaian Pupil Midwives, 1930s–1950s." *Ghana Studies* 7 (2004): 43–58.

Hunt, Nancy Rose. *A Colonial Lexicon of Birth Ritual, Medicalization, and Mobility in the Congo.* Durham, NC: Duke University Press, 1999.

Hutchful, Eboe. *The IMF and Ghana: The Confidential Record.* London: Zed, 1987.

Israel, Adrienne M. "Ex-Servicemen at the Crossroads: Protest and Politics in Post-War Ghana." *Journal of Modern African Studies* 30, no. 2 (1992): 359–68.

Ivaska, Andrew. *Cultured States: Youth, Gender, and Modern Style in 1960s Dar es Salaam.* Durham, NC: Duke University Press, 2011.

"*JAH* Forum: Africa and Global History." *Journal of African History* 54, no. 3 (2013): 317–49.

Jalloh, Alusine. *African Entrepreneurship: Muslim Fula Merchants in Sierra Leone.* Athens: Ohio University Press, 1999.

——. "Reconstructing Modern African Business History." In *Africanizing Knowledge: African Studies across Disciplines,* edited by Toyin Falola and Christian Jennings, 149–61. New Brunswick, NJ: Transaction, 2002.

Jefferies, Richard. *Class, Power and Ideology in Ghana: The Railwaymen of Sekondi.* Cambridge: Cambridge University Press, 1978.

Jones, Geoffrey. *Merchants to Multinationals: British Trading Companies in the Nineteenth and Twentieth Centuries.* Oxford: Oxford University Press, 2000.

——. *Renewing Unilever: Transformation and Tradition.* Oxford: Oxford University Press, 2005.

Jones, Paula. "The U.A.C. in the Gold Coast/Ghana, 1920–1965." PhD diss., School of Oriental and African Studies, University of London, 1983.

Kea, Ray. *Settlements, Trade, and Politics in the Seventeenth-Century Gold Coast.* Baltimore: Johns Hopkins University Press, 1982.

Konadu-Agyemang, Kwadwo, ed. *IMF and World Bank Sponsored Structural Adjustment Programs in Africa: Ghana's Experience, 1983–1999.* Aldershot, England: Ashgate, 2001.

Kyei, Thomas E. *Our Days Dwindle: Memories of My Childhood Days in Asante,* edited by Jean Allman. Portsmouth, NH: Heinemann, 2001.

Larkin, Brian. *Media, Infrastructure, and Urban Culture in Nigeria.* Durham, NC: Duke University Press, 2008.

Law, Robin, ed. *From Slave Trade to "Legitimate" Commerce: The Commercial Transition in Nineteenth-Century West Africa.* Cambridge: Cambridge University Press, 1995.

Lawrance, Benjamin N., Emily Lynn Osborn, and Richard L. Roberts, eds. *Intermediaries, Interpreters, and Clerks: African Employees in the Making of Colonial Africa.* Madison: University of Wisconsin Press, 2006.

Lears, Jackson. *Fables of Abundance: A Cultural History of Advertising in America.* New York: Basic Books, 1995.

Likaka, Osumaka. *Naming Colonialism: History and Collective Memory in the Congo, 1870–1960.* Madison: University of Wisconsin Press, 2009.

Lindsay, Lisa A. *Working with Gender: Wage Labor and Social Change in Southwestern Nigeria.* Portsmouth, NH: Heinemann, 2003.

Lindsay, Lisa A., and Stephan E. Miescher, eds. *Men and Masculinities in Modern Africa.* Portsmouth, NH: Heinemann, 2003.

Lionnet, Françoise, and Shu-mei Shih, eds. *Minor Transnationalism*. Durham, NC: Duke University Press, 2005.

Luckham, Robin. "The Constitutional Commission 1966–69." In *Politicians and Soldiers in Ghana, 1966–1972*, edited by Dennis Austin and Robin Luckham, 62–88. London: Cass, 1975.

Lydon, Ghislaine. *On Trans-Saharan Trails: Islamic Law, Trade Networks, and Cross Cultural Exchange in Nineteenth-Century Western Africa*. Cambridge: Cambridge University Press, 2012.

MacDonald, Eleanor. *Nothing by Chance! An Autobiography of a Pioneer Business Woman*. Alton, England: Nimrod, 1987.

MacGaffey, Janet. *Entrepreneurs and Parasites: The Struggle for Indigenous Capitalism in Zaire*. Cambridge: Cambridge University Press, 1987.

MacGaffey, Janet, and Rémy Bazenguissa-Ganga. *Congo-Paris: Transnational Traders on the Margins of the Law*. Bloomington: Indiana University Press, 2000.

Macmillan, Allister. *The Red Book of West Africa: Historical and Descriptive, Commercial and Industrial Facts, Figures and Resources*. London: Cass, 1969.

Mager, Anne Kelk. *Beer, Sociability, and Masculinity in South Africa*. Bloomington: Indiana University Press, 2010.

Malki, Isaac Xerxes. "Productive Aliens: Economic Planning and the Lebanese in Ghana, c. 1930–1972." *Mashriq and Mahjar* 1, no. 1 (2013): 85–114.

Mama, Amina. "Khaki in the Family: Gender Discourses and Militarism in Nigeria." *African Studies Review* 41, no. 2 (1998): 469–94.

Manuh, Takyiwaa. "Women and Their Organisations during the Convention People's Party Period." In *The Life and Work of Kwame Nkrumah*, edited by Kwame Arhin, 101–27. Trenton, NJ: Africa World Press, 1993.

———. "Women, the State and Society under the PNDC." In *Ghana under PNDC Rule*, edited by E. Gyimah-Boadi, 176–94. Dakar, Senegal: CODESRIA, 1993.

Marchand, Roland. *Advertising the American Dream: Making Way for Modernity, 1920–1940*. Berkeley: University of California Press, 1986.

Marks, Shula. *Divided Sisterhood: Race, Class, and Gender in the South African Nursing Profession*. New York: St. Martin's, 1994.

Marx, Karl. *Capital: A Critique of Political Economy*, vol. 1. Trans. B. Fowkes. Harmondsworth: Penguin, 1977.

May, Elaine Tyler. *Homeward Bound: American Families in the Cold War Era*. Rev. and updated ed. New York: Basic Books, 1999.

Mbembe, Achille. *On the Postcolony*. Berkeley: University of California Press, 2001.

———. "The Power of the Archive and Its Limits." In *Reconfiguring the Archive*, edited by Carolyn Hamilton, Verne Harris, Jane Taylor, Michele Pickover, Graeme Reid, and Razia Saleh. Dordrecht: Kluwer Academic, 2002.

McCaskie, T. C. "Accumulation, Wealth and Belief in Asante History II: The Twentieth Century." *Africa: Journal of the International African Institute* 56, no. 1 (1986): 3–23.

McCulloch, Jock. *Colonial Psychiatry and "The African Mind."* Cambridge: Cambridge University Press, 1995.

McElya, Micki. *Clinging to Mammy: The Faithful Slave in Twentieth-Century America*. Cambridge, MA: Harvard University Press, 2007.

McKendrick, Neil, John Brewer, and J. H. Plumb, *The Birth of a Consumer Society: The Commercialization of Eighteenth-Century England.* London: HarperCollins, 1984.

Meyer, Birgit. "Christian Mind and Worldly Matters: Religion, Materiality in the Nineteenth-Century Gold Coast." In *Modernization on a Shoestring: Dimensions of Globalization, Consumption, and Development in Africa and Beyond,* edited by Richard Fardon, W. M. J. van Binsbergen, and R. A. van Dijk. Leiden: EIDOS, 1999.

———. "Commodities and the Power of Prayer: Pentecostalist Attitudes towards Consumption in Contemporary Ghana." In *Globalization and Identity: Dialectics of Flow and Closure,* edited by Birgit Meyer and Peter Geschiere, 151–76. Oxford: Wiley-Blackwell, 1999

Miescher, Stephan F. *A Dam for Africa: The Volta River Project and Modernization in Ghana.* Bloomington: Indiana University Press, forthcoming.

———. *Making Men in Ghana.* Bloomington: Indiana University Press, 2005.

Miescher, Stephan F., and Dzodzi Tsikata. "Hydro-Power and the Promise of Modernity and Development in Ghana: Comparing the Akosombo and Bui Dam Projects." *Ghana Studies* 12–13 (2009–10): 15–53.

Mikell, Gwendolyn. *Cocoa and Chaos in Ghana.* New York: Paragon House, 1989.

The Modern Girl around the World Research Group: Alys Eve Weinbaum, Lynn M. Thomas, Priti Ramamurthy, Uta G. Poiger, Madeleine Yue Dong, and Tani E. Barlow, eds. *The Modern Girl around the World: Consumption, Modernity, and Globalization.* Durham, NC: Duke University Press, 2008.

Moodie, Dunbar, and Vivienne Ndatshe. *Going for Gold: Men, Mines, and Migration.* Berkeley: University of California Press, 1994.

Moore, Henrietta L., and Todd Sanders, eds. *Magical Interpretations: Material Realities: Modernity, Witchcraft and the Occult in Postcolonial Africa.* London: Routledge, 2001.

Moyd, Michelle. *Violent Intermediaries: Soldiers, Conquest, and Everyday Colonialism in German East Africa.* Athens: Ohio University Press, 2014.

Mudimbe, V. Y. *The Invention of Africa.* Bloomington: Indiana University Press, 1988.

Murillo, Bianca. "'The Devil We Know': Gold Coast Consumers, Local Employees, and the United Africa Company, 1940–60." *Enterprise and Society* 12, no. 2 (2011): 317–55.

———. "Ideal Homes and the Gender Politics of Consumerism in Postcolonial Ghana, 1960–70." *Gender and History* 21, no. 3 (2009): 560–75.

Neustadt, I., and E. N. Omaboe. *Social and Economic Survey of Tema.* Accra: Office of the Government Statistician in conjunction with the Tema Development Corporation, 1959.

Newell, Stephanie. *Ghanaian Popular Fiction: "Thrilling Discoveries in Conjugal Life" and Other Tales.* Athens: Ohio University Press, 2000.

———. "An Introduction to the Writings of J. G. Mullen, an African Clerk, in the *Gold Coast Leader,* 1916–19." *Africa* 70, no. 3 (2008): 384–400.

———. *The Power to Name: A History of Anonymity in Colonial West Africa.* Athens: Ohio University Press, 2013.

Nugent, Paul. *Big Men, Small Boys and Politics in Ghana: Power, Ideology and the Burden of History, 1982–1994.* London: Pinter, 1995.

———. *Smugglers, Secessionists, and Loyal Citizens on the Ghana-Togo Frontier.* Athens: Ohio University Press, 2002.

Nworah, Kenneth Dike. "The Liverpool 'Sect' and British West African Policy." *African Affairs* 70, no. 281 (1971): 349–64.

Nyarku, Felix Akom. "Ghana-China Bilateral Relations: A Treasured Fifty Years of Diplomatic, Cultural, Economic, and Trade Relations." *GhanaWeb* (2012). http://www.ghanaweb.com/GhanaHomePage/blogs/blog.article.php?blog=70375&ID=1000145821.

Obbo, Christine. *African Women: Their Struggle for Economic Independence.* London: Zed, 1980.

Ocansey, John Emanuel. *African Trading, or, The Trials of William Narh Ocansey of Addah, West Coast of Africa, River Volta.* 3rd ed. Accra: Ghana Academy of Arts and Sciences, 1989.

Ochonu, Moses. *Colonialism by Proxy: Hausa Imperial Agents and Middle Belt Consciousness in Nigeria.* Bloomington: Indiana University Press, 2014.

Ocran, A. K. *Politics of the Sword: A Personal Memoir on Military Involvement in Ghana and of Problems with Military Government.* London: Collings, 1977.

Okali, C. *Dominase: A Mobile Cocoa Farming Community in Brong-Ahafo.* Technical Publication Series 35. Legon: Institute of Statistical, Social, and Economic Research, University of Ghana, 1975.

Omaboe, E. N., and the Economic Committee of the NLC. *Ghana's Economy and Aid Requirements in 1967.* Accra: State Publishing Corporation, 1967.

Oppong, Christine, ed. *Female and Male in West Africa.* London: Allen and Unwin, 1983.

———. *Middle Class African Marriage: A Family Study of Ghanaian Senior Servants.* London: Allen and Unwin, 1981.

Oppong-Boateng, Juliet. "Economic Enterprises of the Basel Mission Society in the Gold Coast: A Study of the Basel Mission Trading Company from 1959–1917." M.Phil thesis, Institute of African Studies, University of Ghana, 2014.

Oquaye, Mike. *Politics in Ghana, 1972–1979.* Accra: Tornado, 1980.

Owusu, Maxwell. *Uses and Abuses of Political Power: A Case Study of Continuity and Change in the Politics of Ghana.* Chicago: University of Chicago Press, 1970.

Panford, Kwamina. *IMF–World Bank and Labor's Burdens in Africa: Ghana's Experience.* Westport, CT: Praeger, 2001.

Parker, John. *Making the Town: Ga State and Society in Early Colonial Accra.* Portsmouth, NH: Heinemann, 2000.

Parpart, Jane L. "The Household and the Mine Shift: Gender and Class Struggles on the Zambian Copperbelt, 1926–64." *Journal of Southern African Studies* 13 (1986): 36–56.

Pedler, Frederick. *The Lion and the Unicorn in Africa: United Africa Company, 1787–1931.* London: Heinemann, 1974.

Pellow, Deborah. *Women in Accra: Options for Autonomy.* Algonac, MI: Reference Publications, 1977.

Pellow, Deborah, and Naomi Chazen. *Ghana: Coping with Uncertainty.* Boulder, CO: Westview, 1986.

Pence, Katherine. "Showcasing Cold War Germany in Cairo: 1954 and 1957 Industrial Exhibitions and the Competition for Arab Partners." *Journal of Contemporary History* 47, no. 1 (2012): 69–95.

Petchenkine, Youry. *Ghana: In Search of Stability, 1957–1992*. Westport, CT: Praeger, 1993.

Pierre, Jemima. *The Predicament of Blackness: Postcolonial Ghana and the Politics of Race*. Chicago: University of Chicago Press, 2013.

Piot, Charles. *Remotely Global: Village Modernity in West Africa*. Chicago: University of Chicago Press, 1999.

Plageman, Nate. "'Accra Is Changing, Isn't It?': Urban Infrastructure, Independence, and the Nation in the Gold Coast's *Daily Graphic*, 1954–57." *International Journal of African Historical Studies* 43, no. 1 (2010): 137–59.

———. *Highlife Saturday Night: Popular Music and Social Change in Urban Ghana*. Bloomington: Indiana University Press, 2012.

Powell, M. C. "A Study of the Behavior and Personality of Clerks and Other Literate Employees in the Office of a European Firm Trading in Ghana, 1954–58." Unpublished manuscript, Mss. Afr. S.1433, Rhodes House Library, Oxford University.

Prestholdt, Jeremy. *Domesticating the World: African Consumerism and the Genealogies of Globalization*. Berkeley: University of California Press, 2008.

Priestley, Margaret. *West Africa Trade and Coast Society: A Family Study*. London: Oxford University Press, 1969.

Quayson, Ato. *Oxford Street, Accra: City Life and the Itineraries of Transnationalism*. Durham, NC: Duke University Press, 2014.

Ramamurthy, Anandi. *Imperial Persuaders: Images of Africa and Asia in British Advertising*. Manchester, England: Manchester University Press, 2003.

Rappaport, Erika. *Shopping for Pleasure: Women in the Making of London's West End*. Princeton, NJ: Princeton University Press, 2000.

Rappaport, Erika, Sandra Trudgen Dawson, and Mark J. Crowley, eds. *Consuming Behaviours: Identity, Politics, and Pleasure in Twentieth-Century Britain*. London: Bloomsbury, 2015.

Rathbone, Richard. "Businessmen in Politics: Party Struggle, 1945–57." *Journal of Development Studies* 9, no. 3 (1973): 391–401.

———. *Nkrumah and the Chiefs: The Politics of Chieftaincy in Ghana*. Athens: Ohio University Press, 2000.

———. "World War I and Africa: Introduction." *Journal of African History* 19, no. 1 (1978): 1–9.

Ray, Carina E. *Crossing the Color Line: Race, Sex, and the Contested Politics of Colonialism in Ghana*. Athens: Ohio University Press, 2015.

Republic of Ghana. *White Paper on the Report of the Commission of Enquiry into Alleged Irregularities and Malpractices in the Connection with the Grant of Import Licenses*. Accra: State Publishing Corporation, 1967.

Reynolds, Edward. *Trade and Economic Change on the Gold Coast, 1807–1874*. London: Longman, 1974.

Reynolds, Nancy. *A City Consumed: Urban Commerce, the Cairo Fire, and the Politics of Decolonization in Egypt*. Stanford, CA: Stanford University Press, 2012.

Robertson, A. F. "Histories and Political Opposition in Ahafo, Ghana." *Africa: Journal of the International African Institute* 43, no. 1 (1973): 41–58.

Robertson, Claire. "The Death of Makola and Other Tragedies." *Canadian Journal of African Studies* 17, no. 3 (1989): 469–94.

———. *Sharing the Same Bowl: A Socioeconomic History of Women and Class in Accra*. Bloomington: Indiana University Press, 1984.

Rodney, Walter. *How Europe Underdeveloped Africa.* Washington, DC: Howard University Press, 1974.

Roth, Hans Rudolf. *Because of Kwadua: Autobiography of Hans Rudolf Roth.* Accra: Afram, 2008.

Sachs, Eric. *Report of the Commission of Enquiry into the Representations made by W. E. Conway, A. D. W. Allen, A. G. Leventis, and A. G. Leventis and Co. Repudiating Allegations in the Report of the Commission of Enquiry into the Conduct and Management of the Supplies and Customs Departments.* Accra: Government Printing Department, 1948.

Sanjek, Roger. "Female and Male Domestic Cycles in Urban Africa: The Adabraka Case," in *Female and Male in West Africa*, edited by Christine Oppong, 57–103. London: Allen and Unwin, 1983.

Schweizer, Peter. *Survivors on the Gold Coast: The Basel Missionaries in Colonial Ghana.* 2nd ed. Accra: Smartline, 2000.

Seikaly, Sherene. *Men of Capital: Scarcity and Economy in Mandate Palestine.* Stanford, CA: Stanford University Press, 2016.

Serra, Gerardo. "An Uneven Statistical Topography: The Political Economy of Household Budget Surveys in Late Colonial Ghana, 1951–1957." *Canadian Journal of Development Studies* 35, no. 1 (2014): 9–27.

Shillington, Kevin. *Ghana and the Rawlings Factor.* New York: St. Martin's, 1992.

Simone, Abdoumaliq. *City Life from Jakarta to Dakar: Movements at the Crossroads.* New York: Routledge, 2013.

Smallwood, Stephanie E. *Saltwater Slavery: A Middle Passage from Africa to American Diaspora.* Cambridge, MA: Harvard University Press, 2007.

Southall, Roger. "Farmers, Traders and Brokers in the Gold Coast Economy." *Canadian Journal of African Studies* 12, no. 2 (1978): 185–211.

Stearns, Peter N. *Consumerism in World History: The Global Transformation of Desire.* London: Routledge, 2001.

Stein, Sarah Abrevaya. *Plumes: Ostrich Feathers, Jews, and the Lost World of Global Commerce.* New Haven, CT: Yale University Press, 2010.

Stephan, Daniel Mark. "'The White Man's Grave:' British West Africa and the British Exhibition of 1924–1925." *Journal of British Studies* 48, no. 1 (2009): 102–28.

Stockwell, Sarah. *The Business of Decolonization: British Business Strategies in the Gold Coast.* Oxford: Clarendon, 2000.

Stoler, Ann Laura. *Along the Archival Grain: Epistemic Anxieties and Colonial Common Sense.* Princeton, NJ: Princeton University Press, 2010.

———. *Carnal Knowledge and Imperial Power: Race and the Intimate in Colonial Rule.* Berkeley: University of California Press, 2002.

Stoller, Paul. *Money Has No Smell: The Africanization of New York City.* Chicago: University of Chicago Press, 2002.

Tignor, Robert. *Capitalism and Nationalism at the End of Empire: State and Business in Decolonizing Egypt, Nigeria, and Kenya, 1945–1963.* Princeton, NJ: Princeton University Press, 1998.

Tomlinson, B. R. "The British Economy and the Empire, 1900–1939." In *A Companion to Early Twentieth Century Britain*, edited by Chris Wrigley, 198–211. Oxford: Blackwell, 2003.

Trentmann, Frank. *Free Trade Nation: Commerce, Consumption, and Civil Society in Modern Britain.* Oxford: Oxford University Press, 2009.

——. "Introduction." In *The Making of the Consumer: Knowledge, Power and Identity in the Modern World*. Oxford: Berg, 2006.

——. "The Modern Genealogy of the Consumer: Meanings, Identities, and Political Synapses." In *Consuming Cultures, Global Perspectives: Historical Trajectories, Transnational Exchanges*, edited by John Brewer and Frank Trentmann, 19–70. Oxford: Berg, 2006.

Tsing, Anna L. *Friction: An Ethnography of Global Connection*. Princeton, NJ: Princeton University Press, 2005.

Turrittin, Jane. "Colonial Midwives and Modernizing Childbirth in French West Africa." In *Women in African Colonial Histories*, edited by Jean Allman, Susan Geiger, and Nakanyike Musisi, 71–91. Bloomington: Indiana University Press, 2002.

United Africa Company. "Kingsway Stores, Lagos." *Statistical and Economic Review* 12 (1953): 1–30.

——. "Merchandise Trading in British West Africa." *Statistical and Economic Review* 5 (1950): 1–36.

——. "Merchandise Trading in British West Africa." *Statistical and Economic Review* 6 (1950): 1–40.

Van den Bersselaar, Dmitri. "'Doorway to Success?': Reconstructing African Careers in European Business from Company House Magazines and Oral History Interviews." *History in Africa* 38 (2011): 257–94.

——. *The King of Drinks: Schnapps Gin from Modernity to Tradition*. Boston: Brill, 2007.

Van der Laan, H. Lauren. "Modern Inland Transport and the European Trading Firms in Colonial West Africa." *Cahiers d'Études Africaines* 21, no. 84 (1981): 547–75.

Vaughan, Megan. *Curing Their Ills: Colonial Power and African Illness*. Stanford, CA: Stanford University Press, 1991.

Wallace-Sanders, Kimberly. *Mammy: A Century of Race, Gender, and Southern Memory*. Ann Arbor: University of Michigan Press, 2009.

Watson, Aiken. *Report of the Commission of Enquiry into the Disturbances in the Gold Coast*. Accra: Government Printing Department, 1948.

Weems, Robert. *Desegregating the Dollar: African American Consumerism in the Twentieth Century*. New York: New York University Press, 1988.

White, Luise. *Speaking with Vampires: Rumor and History in Colonial Africa*. Berkeley: University of California Press, 2000.

White, Luise, Stephan F. Miescher, and David William Cohen, eds. *African Words, African Voices: Critical Practices in Oral History*. Bloomington: Indiana University Press, 2001.

Wiemers, Alice. "A 'Time of Agric': Rethinking the 'Failure' of Agricultural Programs in 1970s Ghana." *World Development* 66 (2015): 104–17.

Wilks, Ivor. *Forests of Gold: Essays: Essays on the Akan and the Kingdom of Asante*. Athens: Ohio University Press, 1993.

Williamson, John, ed. *IMF Conditionality*. Washington, DC: Institute for International Economics, 1983.

Wrangham, Elizabeth. "An African Road Revolution: The Gold Coast in the Period of the Great War." *Journal of Imperial and Commonwealth History* 32, no. 1 (2004): 1–18.

Index

Page numbers followed by f indicate figures; those followed by t indicate tables.

CPSIA information can be obtained
at www.ICGtesting.com
Printed in the USA
FFOW03n1610230218
45146196-45676FF

9 780821 422892